SOCIAL CHANGE IN WEST MAUI

SOCIAL CHANGE
IN
WEST MAUI

edited by

BIANCA K. ISAKI AND LANCE D. COLLINS

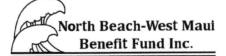

North Beach-West Maui
Benefit Fund Inc.

Lahaina, Maui, Hawai'i

24 23 22 21 20 19   6 5 4 3 2 1

ISBN 978-0-8248-8167-2 (pbk : alk. paper)

Published by the North Beach-West Maui Benefit Fund, Inc.
P O Box 11329
Lahaina, Hawai'i 96761

Distributed by University of Hawai'i Press
2840 Kolowalu Street
Honolulu, HI 96822-1888

Cover photo of Honokahua burial site during excavations,
by Ken Miller, *Honolulu Star-Bulletin,* Tues. Jan. 3, 1989.
Courtesy of the Hawai'i State Archives.

This book is printed on acid-free paper and
meets the guidelines for permanence and durability
of the Council on Library Resources.

Print-ready files provided by North Beach-West Maui Benefit Fund, Inc.

Dedicated to Sharyn Matin
He ʻaloʻalo kuāua no kuahiwi.

Contents

PREFACE
Dick Mayer

When the plantations mechanized in the 1950s, there were no jobs and Maui's workers had to leave to find employment elsewhere. Elected officials, government agencies and appointed commissioners facilitated tourist projects by minimally enforcing regulations. They entitled vacant plantation and ranch land for hotels, condominiums, golf courses and shopping centers.

Both unemployed agricultural workers, and recent graduates found on-island jobs. Construction companies benefited, while growing numbers of Realtors made money selling properties to tourists. The growing tourist industry saved Maui's economy. However, the biggest beneficiaries were off-island investors. They exported their profits, instead of providing promised affordable workforce housing and paying higher salaries. Investors loved Maui's low property tax assessments with Hawaii's lowest hotel property tax rate.

Economic prosperity disguised negative and often unwelcome impacts to the environment, local traditions and culture. Tourists, not Maui residents, selected Maui as the *"top tourist-destination island!"* Locals find that the quiet beaches that families previously enjoyed are congested with tourists, kayak rentals, scuba operations, weddings and beach chairs. Beaches lack parking and access. Tourist guidebooks and social media highlight our *"special secret places."* Tourist spots are overburdened. Twin Falls has hundreds of parked cars with visitors streaming to waterfalls. Helicopters fly over residential areas. Downhill bikers endanger local traffic. Hana residents cannot deal with the Hana Highway traffic. Haleakala National Park requires advance permits for sunrise viewing.

Overtourism results in long commutes, day and night shifts with unattended children, multiple jobs, overcrowded schools, a shortage of doctors, dangerous intersections, wastewater finding its way into the coral reefs, lost views, pesticides draining from golf courses, brown-water advisories, etc. Tourist industry salaries do not keep up with housing costs; families have to co-habit residences. Second home *"McMansions"* are built for part-time tourists, while needed affordable units are neglected. Infrastructure for a quality community is not built because tourist facilities do not have to pay needed impact fees.

State bureaucrats and tourism champions advocate shifting Oahu's tourism onto Maui by increasing Kahului Airport capacity, increasing short-term visitor rentals in residential neighborhoods, and constructing even more hotels. Local residents suffer as off-island investors convert potential housing into vacation rentals. Unfortunately, as Maui's quality of life deteriorates, political leaders do not acknowledge or even address the situation. Many politicians are stuck in the past thinking that they must promote a bigger tourist industry. Those days are over. Maui now has a mature tourist industry that needs to protect itself from overtourism. We need political leaders who will assist residents, not corporate investors, and who will enable affordable housing, not more hotels and gated communities. The Hawai'i Tourism Strategic Plan recognized the change from 50 years ago when it warned, *"The relationship between the number of residents and visitors on the island at any given time cannot be overlooked as an important public policy discussion point. Resort communities... have grappled with the "golden goose" debate, whereby the tourism experience may be compromised by the very nature of the area's popularity."*

Fortunately, Maui's legal tools can promote a tourist industry that will protect jobs, and not disappoint future tourists with a deteriorating visitor experience. Our County Council in 2012 passed the Maui Island Plan (part of the General Plan), a legally binding county ordinance. The plan makes tourist industry regulation an important requirement to preserve and protect Maui's quality of life. The Maui Island Plan (pages 4–14) states: *"Maximize residents' benefits from the visitor industry"* and *"Promote a desirable island population by striving to not exceed an islandwide visitor population of roughly 33 percent of the resident population."* That means that if Maui island has 156,000 residents, as we now have, then we should not have more than 52,000 tourists on an average day. However, in July 2018, we had an average of 75,000 tourists each day! Obviously, we already have too many tourist accommodations, most legal, but enough illegal, to reduce housing availability for residents.

The plan (pages 4–12) states: *"Increase the economic contribution of the visitor industry to the island's environmental well-being and for the island's residents' quality of life."*

INTRODUCTION
Social Change in West Maui
by Bianca Isaki

"Kāʻanapali wāwae ʻulaʻula."—*ʻŌlelo Noʻeau No. 1280*

(The red-footed people of Kāʻanapali.)

"Ka ulu lāʻau ma kai."—*ʻŌlelo Noʻeau No. 1625.*

(The growing forest of trees in the ocean.)

West Maui is a battleground. This was the sentiment relayed by Keʻeaumoku Kapu, manager of the Na Aikane o Maui Cultural Center. Na Aikane lies on one end of the heavily-touristed Front Street and in the heart of Lahaina's historic district. Kapu's observation is a canny one. In West Maui, capital from international and American tourism and real property development is arrayed against people holding steadfast to the lands for history, identity, and culture. Since the eighteenth century's incursions of settler trade ships populating Lahaina harbor with masts so thick they appeared to be trees—"ka ulu lāʻau ma kai." West Maui faced a plethora of political and economic forces that in large part contradicted the systems and infrastructure that grounded its society. Later, Western trade gave way to large scale plantations as the primary driver of capitalist society. Native Hawaiians variously resisted plantations in kīpuka of loʻi kalo, resisted plantation exploitation through labor organizing, worked for the plantation, and ignored the plantation. They were also some of the hardest hit by Lahaina's famine in the 1860s. Lahaina, once the fount of much of Maui's food—so much so that ships would carry food away to other islands—could no longer feed its own people. The analysis of the issue was straightforward. Too many had left their sweet potato and loʻi kalo fields in favor of waged labor under Pioneer Mill. The elderly were too old to plant and harvest. The young were uninterested in farming. Also, many had passed away from new diseases and a lack of medicine. Waged labor on the plantations became one of the few viable means to maintain one's self as an economic being.

During the 1946 sugar strike, Pioneer Mill strikers were amongst the longest hold outs. Labor strikers prevented, physically, other Mill employees and supervisors from watering the fields. The building that now houses Na Aikane, at that time, was a soup kitchen for plantation workers and their families during the strike against the Pioneer Mill.

Through the first half of the twentieth century, however, plantations increasingly mechanized their operations, labor unions strengthened, and former-workers returned from World War II to take advantage of GI Bill educational benefits. These factors, as well as Hawaii's increasing attraction as a tourism destination, led plantation owners, including American Factors (AmFac) would seek to develop large tracts of their lands in Kāʻanapali for a burgeoning tourism enterprise. West Maui was to harbor the second Waikīkī according to experts on Maui's developing economy. AmFac was able to trade both on widespread nostalgia and attachment to plantation communities to maintain its hold on West Maui water and lands, while also gaining advantages in new tourism development. AmFac's Kāʻanapali resort area has become one of the most profitable in the islands. The plantation did not die in West Maui in the 1999s. Instead, it hedged its bets well to survive in tourism and real property development.

There is a certain hubris in an attempt to chronicle West Maui's social history. The attempt would approach Umberto Eco's map of empire. Nor, on the other hand, does this collection seek only to postulate theories predictive or explanatory of social change. The essays in the book engage with events, projects, and developments in ways that describe a host of social relationships and, often, the problems that themselves maintain those social relations as inherently conflicted ones. By attending to particular historical events and structures these chapters unravel some of the dynamics that animate social changes in West Maui. The aim, however, is not only documentary.

Writing about social change is also a way of comprehending problems posed at this particular moment for West Maui's singular situation. One purpose in doing so is to mark transformations in social, political economic, and ecological relationships that herald new possibilities for those relations. "In considering such transformations a distinction should always be made between the material transformation of the economic conditions of production, which can be determined with the precision of natural science, and the legal, political, religious, aesthetic, or philosophic—in short, ideological forms in which men become conscious of this conflict and fight it out."[1] This is a Marxist conception of social awareness rooted in a material relationships. The point is to discern the forms in which conflicts and crises that drive social change are realized in the material space and historical moments of West Maui. Each chapter, in varying ways, inventories the realized forms of conflict and engages in an analysis of ways such forms drive ongoing social transformations in West Maui.

Social change is not only the documentation of historical happenings, but the singular, material confluence of historical factors that drives futurity. This is where the authors assembled here have focused. The post-plantation era has also mobilized a sense of belonging amongst those who have seen so much change over the past decades. How that sense of belonging coalesces amidst change is what is manifest in the various social movements, phenomena, and events discussed in this volume.

Bon dance culture has taken singular, diverse forms in Hawai'i and throughout the islands. Diane K. Letoto's chapter, "Lahaina Bon Dances and Japanese Plantation Memories" examines West Maui's social change from plantation agriculture to tourism through the communities, institutions, and materials that comprise bon dance in West Maui. Japanese bon dances in West Maui are annually held at the Lahaina Shingon, Lahaina Jodo, Lahaina Hongwanji, and Lāna'i Hongwanji missions. Letoto is herself a dancer and the founder of the Phoenix Dance Chamber Chinese Dance School of Honolulu. She earned her Ph.D. from the University of Hawai'i at Mānoa and holds a Master's Degree in both American Studies and Dance. Her dissertation was entitled "Silenced Practices: A Politics of Dancescapes."

For many years, sugar and pineapple agribusiness dominated the economy and social life of West Maui. Immigrants from a number of countries came to work on the sugar plantations—and subsequently for the pineapple industry. Most plantation laborers and their families had lives structured by plantation camps. In the 1950s, with the decline of sugar and the rise of tourism, lives lived in plantation camps came to an end and the last of the first generation to be born in plantation camps—the nisei (or second-generation) Japanese—are disappearing due to old age.

One of the methods of the plantations to maintain labor and ethnic

---

1　Karl Marx, "The Material Basis of Society," in *Karl Marx on Society and Social Change: With Selections by Friedrich Engels*, Neil J. Smelser ed. (Chicago & London: U. Chicago Press 1973), 5.

peace was supporting Japanese Buddhist churches and, in particular, bon dances. While Japan has "bon dances" once a year, the Hawai'i bon dance tradition is unique. West Maui's bon dance have their own identity separate from other Maui dances. While bon dances today are a shadow of their previous position within West Maui society, they have persisted. The changes however are connected to economic changes within West Maui society more generally. For example, when Pāhala, a former sugar plantation area on the Big Island, held its last bon dance in 1999, many older Japanese residents publicly expressed pride in the end of bon dances—which they said represented economic development and progress from the poverty of sugar agricultural. Yet, there was an undercurrent of sadness that cultural forms were disappearing. What emerges from Letoto's depictions is particularly Japanese post-plantation community that is struggling to renew their institutions, with varying success, and a plethora of rich cultural memories from the first generation plantation camp born West Maui residents.

Brian Richardson's "Regional planning emerging from a plantation world: the case of West Maui" attends to context and textual cues of mid-twentieth century planning documents focused on West Maui. These planning documents were written by and for large landowners' designs for Lahaina, but were also intended to sell these ideas to the wider population, which had little say in the scope, purpose, or development of these documents. This inequitable relationship between landowners, their plans, and the community that was supposed to accept them, was conditioned by the imbrication of those landowners and the state. "The corporatist system offered little space for political discourse," Richardson writes, "Planning for the region, as a result, was closely tied to the needs of the landowners and the power structures of the plantation economy." These disrepairs in Lahaina's planning infrastructure persisted even as a new tourist-based planning horizon came into view.

Richardson tracks the ways that "residents" came into view for planners, even as actual people's roles in planning processes became highly circumscribed by their new role as consumers, users, and a local labor pool. Richardson's chapter describes one way local planning dispersed West Maui civic engagement by calling for "public input" as opposed to community-based decision making. Community members were put into a posture of the consulted, as opposed to active lobbyists for the public interest. Through his close readings of early planning documents, Richardson illuminates one of the ways that planning processes were set up to advance interests of large West Maui landowners.

The historical plantation home has taken a new significance in West

Maui's gentlemen's estates. Bianca Isaki's "Six theses on the problem of gentlemen's estates in West Maui" critically assesses social changes signaled by the proliferation of gentlemen's estates in West Maui from Makila Plantation in Kauaʻula to Kapalua Plantation Estates. The transformation of Pioneer Mill lands into tracts of gentlemen's estates tracks changes land use regulation, planning, and transactions between large landowners and developers (which are often subsidiaries of each other).

From its creation in the mid-1860s, Pioneer Mill obtained, sometimes questionable, title to vast tracts of land in West Maui. Pioneer Mill sought total control over lands it cultivated as well as adjoining lands, water sources, and infrastructure. With an exchange of land to move the highway island, American Factors (AmFac, the owner of Pioneer Mill) was able to develop Kāʻanapali as a self-contained resort community. As discussed in Brian Richardson's chapter, regulation of land use and planning at the state and county levels were minimal and largely conciliatory towards large landowners such as AmFac and Pioneer Mill.

As the Pioneer Mill plantation era drew to a close in 1999, AmFac lands were sold to land speculators and developers. The Kāʻanapali lands were not entirely transformed into resorts for various reasons, including local and state efforts towards diverse land use regulation and planning. In some instances, this meant developers or speculators were unable to obtain land use entitlements to develop luxury residential properties in these former agricultural areas. In other instances, the developers determined not to pursue large-scale resort development. "Gentleman's estate" subdivisions of luxury homes, which generally did not require land use redistricting and thus, fewer government approvals, appeared on former sugar lands. To conform with agriculturally zoned district requirements, gentlemen's estates are nominally considered "farm dwellings" and conduct some measure of activity characterized as agricultural. This multi-pronged effort between developers and those desirous of gentlemen's estates to flout the intention and purpose of laws governing agricultural land uses results in multimillion dollar mansions, replete with pools and "farm dwellings" sprawling across the hillsides of West Maui. Here, sod-farming is an "agricultural activity." Far from being units of a productive small scale farm economy, many of these gentlemen's estates are operated as vacation rentals by entities in North America and elsewhere and Honolulu. Isaki's chapter takes aim at six ways that gentlemen's estates in West Maui have been approached as a problem and indicates what this may mean for the shape of the society that suffers them.

Ikaika Hussey's "Modern History of West Maui's Wastewater" also examines the ways top-down planning processes failed West Maui. For decades, government officials have continued to approve developments without regard to the limited capacity of wastewater treatment systems. Today, the lack of capacity in wastewater facilities continues to beleaguer West Maui. This chapter examines societal changes in economic transitions between agriculture to tourism in West Maui by looking at the history of wastewater regulation and management.

During the long domination of sugar and pineapple agriculture in West Maui little or no thought was put into the disposal of waste and specifically wastewater. West Maui's pristine shoreline water quality was taken for granted. In the 1960s, West Maui began the transition from an industrial agriculture-driven economy to one focused on tourism and luxury second home destinations. This transition meant both an increased density in population and a population with a new set of expectations for environmental health and sanitation.

In 1972, Congress adopted the Clean Water Act and the Safe Drinking Water Act in 1974. West Maui's burgeoning population put significant pressures on agricultural infrastructure that was already insufficient to meet federal standards. Plantation wastewater systems already resulted in noticeable pollution. With the added tourism and resort population influx, wastewater management was a pressing need. The Department of Health ordered the closing of Maui Land & Pine's Honolua camp, which had been disposing wastewater directly into Oneloa Bay. The Department of Health's order also stopped Pioneer Mill's dumping of agricultural wastewater into the ocean at Launiupoko. These early examples signaled a shift in wastewater management for West Maui.

The County of Maui then took the step of using injection well technology to "dispose" of treated wastewater. Over the years, however, injection wells have proven to merely better camouflage pollution of nearshore coastal waters. More recently, environmental groups sued to stop the practice of injection wells and won in federal court. Hussey's chapter sets out this timeline of wastewater management struggles in West Maui.

Sydney Iaukea's "Saving Honolua Bay" describes several facets of the decades-long efforts to protect Honolua Bay and Lipoa Point from Maui Land and Pine's planned developments. The West Maui ahupua'a of Honolua was first incorporated into the expanding Baldwin agricultural empire after the overthrow of the Hawaiian Kingdom as part of the Baldwin's "Honolua

Ranch." From the 1920s until the 1970s, the Cameron branch of the Baldwin family grew pineapple in Honolua. By the 1970s, the Honolua Ranch lands were being re-envisioned for both resort and luxury home development. However, the lands at Honolua remained undeveloped or in pineapple cultivation until after 2000. Honolua Bay has been a long time diving, fishing and surfing spot for local residents.

As Honolua became an increasingly popular tourist destination, the landowner, Maui Land & Pine began to expand luxury home development north of Kapalua to Honolua. Tourism and land development activities came into conflict with native Hawaiian and other local resident uses of the area. These groups came together to form Save Honolua which sought to prevent the coastal areas of the Honolua ahupua'a from being developed into luxury homes, protecting both Honolua Bay and Lipoa Point. As described in other chapters, the changing shape of West Maui's society was intimately tied to agreements concerning its physical environs. Honolua Bay and Lipoa Point did not become an enclave for luxury development because the community and government partners brought an alternative that allowed Maui Land and Pine to meet at least some of its pension fund obligations without developing the area.

Central to Iaukea's chapter, however, are the Hōkūle'a voyagers and Save Honolua Coalition. The Hōkūle'a had its initial launch from Honolua Bay and recently returned to a huge homecoming celebration there. Iaukea interviewed kanaka maoli watermen who navigate and crew the Hōkūle'a, including Nainoa Thompson and Archie Kalepa who were each born and raised in Lahaina. The Save Honolua Coalition owned much to West Maui's Tamara Paltin and Elle Cochran, both of whom are surfers from West Maui and politically engaged. Here, the story of West Maui's social change emerges from kanaka maoli leadership and a commitment to a singularly Hawaiian identity for Honolua and Lipoa. Thompson directed the planting of koa seedlings in the area. West Maui fishers maintained their rights to bag akule. Conservation management tools, a vibrant surfing culture, government interests in tourism and constituencies, Lahaina community organizers, Hawaiian cultural practitioners, and Lahaina's longstanding corporate institution, Maui Land and Pine itself, participated in the shape and status of these places today.

Why is affordable housing not being built in West Maui? Lance Collins' "Fast-Tracking the Luxury Housing Crisis in West Maui" critically reviews the prevailing wisdom that land use regulation and land planning regulation is the primary cause of the lack of affordable housing in Hawai'i. The state has long had a so-called "fast track" exemption process whereby development projects that had at least half of its units within an "affordable" range could be exempted from most state and county laws "relating to planning, zoning, construction standards for subdivisions, development and improvement of land, and the construction of dwelling units". For this, amongst other reasons, land use regulation has not been the obstacle to affordable housing that it has been perceived to be.

Affordable housing is rarely built for the sake of affordable housing. It is more typically obtained as a condition of permitting or zoning for hotel or luxury home development. However, mandatory affordable housing requirements easily turn into thin air. While there are a whole series of requirements regarding qualifications for buyers and owners, in many instances, the requirements of affordability are not maintained. For example, Maui county has long imposed a buy back provision for affordable units that were sold before the affordability period expired. In many cases, the County declined to exercise its buy back rights and the unit disappeared from the inventory of affordable housing.

Collins' chapter investigates the legal regime of affordable housing in West Maui and catalogues specific information regarding the various planned, required, and built affordable housing projects in West Maui from 1959 to present and compare what was planned and/or required to what actually exists today. He contends that continued subsidizing of private developers to incentivize housing construction, low and no interest loans, tax credits, and other supports will not overcome failures of the market to produce affordable housing. "[B]ecause the problem is not a sufficiency of capital for affordable housing, but the commodification of housing, these significant interventions barely touch the problem."

As Collins' research shows, the false equation between affordable housing shortages and government regulation in Hawai'i has a history in the tacit alliance between tenement owners and sugar plantations. In the early 1920s, tenement owners and sugar planters commonly opposed ordinances establishing fire and building codes, zoning, and other land use controls. Tenement owners complained that the cost of compliance would be too high, while sugar plantations opposed infringements on their land ownership rights. Together, however, these forces combined to limit working class housing options.

The two final chapters both address the historic struggle to protect iwi at West Maui's Honokahua. Tomone K. T. Hanada and Halealoha Ayau write at different times and situations to document the threats and effort to protect

Hawaiian burials at Honokahua. The issue stemmed from the Kapalua resort project district, which was developed in part within the ahupuaʻa of Hono-kahua, West Maui. When Maui Land & Pine began to develop the coastal areas near Makapunalua in the late 1980s, construction workers began discov-ered massive Hawaiian burials within the coastal sand dunes and surround-ing areas. Word began to spread within the local Hawaiian community and throughout the state that massive burials had been uncovered and disturbed and that neither the landowner nor the contractors were taking any action to avoid further disturbances or were planning to protect or re-inter disturbed burials. This led to massive protests and occupation of the construction sites. Eventually the resort was built with modified plans and Chapter 6E, Hawaii Revised Statutes, relating to historic preservation was amended by Act 306 of 1989 which provided an entire regulatory regime for the protection of Hawai-ian burials statewide.

Tomone K. T. Hanada's chapter examines the initial conflict, the dispute resolution negotiations, the role of intervenors and agents, and the solution arrived at between Maui Land and Pine, Native Hawaiian activist groups, and the State of Hawaiʻi. This examination provides an overview of the stake-holders and decisionmakers, including the Maui Planning Commission, the Office of Hawaiian Affairs, the State Historic Preservation Division, Maui Land and Pineapple Company, and various other government and private entities involved in the Honokahua controversy. Her documentation of the interactions between these government decisionmaking bodies, commercial resorts, and Hui o Alanui o Mākena, amongst other Hawaiian groups and actors, sets up a solid background for Ayau's more pointed discussion and perspective.

Halealoha Ayau writes of the ways that his experiences first with Hui Alanui o Mākena and their collective decision to become active at Honoka-hua. Their efforts not only led to the protection of iwi at Honokahua, but also led him into other efforts towards repatriation and iwi protection under Hui Mālama i Nā Kupuna o Hawaiʻi Nei. His chapter examples social change regarding development in West Maui by looking at the struggles over the burials at Honokahua, the subsequent enactment of the Hawaiian burials protection law, how the law has been implemented and its impact since then. Ayau is a licensed attorney in the State of Hawaiʻi and resident of Molokaʻi. He has lectured around the United States regarding native burials and indige-nous cultural patrimony. He is presently the Acting District Supervisor of the Molokaʻi District Office of the Department of Hawaiian Home Lands and was the cultural protocol adviser for the restoration of the Hāpaialiʻi Heiau, Keʻekū Heiau and Makoleʻa Heiau.

The hope for this collection is to offer discussion of several concrete changes that have contributed to the shape of West Mauiʻs social institutions and communities.

LAHAINA BON DANCES AND JAPANESE PLANTATION MEMORIES

Diane Letoto

INTRODUCTION

On the evening of June 3, 2017, I climbed the temple stairs of Lahaina, Maui's Shingon Mission, where an O-bon[1] service was taking place. My gaze moved from the priests, who were chanting at the altar, to the window next to me. Below, the crowd dressed in yukata[2] and happi[3] coats, some of them sitting while others stood in small groups scattered throughout the grounds, chatting and laughing, or just observing others.

At the center of the grounds stood a yagura[4] decorated with a skirt made of blue cloth and patterned with large, white plumeria flowers. There were strings of small international flags that ran from the top frame of the yagura to the perimeter of the grounds. Interspersed with the flags were lanterns and light bulbs. It was odd to see various countries' flags, since it was more common to see just the strings of lanterns.[5]

Reverend George Kitagawa, a visiting minister from Wailuku, stood at the podium and gave a sermon on the history of bon dance. In Japan, he explained, the O-bon[6] service is held from around August 13 through 15.[7] On Maui, O-bon is celebrated as early as June and continues almost every weekend until August. This was in large part because during plantation days, the minister would have to ride on horseback from one church to another to perform the O-bon service.

Bon dance provided a venue for plantation workers to get together after months of hard work. During the plantation era, most of the dances were about work and harvest. Kitagawa chuckled, adding that when he was a young, bon dance was a place, "where boys could meet girls." In addition, there are yet others who observed and participated in the bon dance as a remembrance for ancestors who have passed.

Shingon Mission. Courtesy of Diane Letoto.

After a few church announcements, Kitagawa and the other priests slowly walked down the aisle toward the door. The congregation filed out, row by row, behind them. As the priests neared the bon dance grounds, they walked over to a small altar at the mauka[8] side of the grounds. After performing short rites, they walked to the yagura. This signaled the start of the bon dance.

The first song and dance of the night was Daishi Ondo, the Shingon Church song.[9][10] Participants danced in a circle around the yagura, two to three circles of dancers. It appeared that most of the dancers knew, or were at least familiar with, the dances. Those who did not know the dance followed the lead dancers in the innermost circle,[11] or others who knew the dance. The dances that followed were done to recorded music, which lasted about thirty minutes. This set of music brought a close to the first half of the bon dance.

After a short intermission, dancing resumed to a variety of music. Toward the end of the bon dance, live music by Maui Taiko picked up the pace with Fukushima Ondo, a traditional bon dance with an accompaniment of drums, flutes, and singers.[12] Fukushima Ondo appeared to be a crowd favorite, as the ring of dancers thickened and younger participants in street clothes joined in. After Fukushima Ondo, Maui Taiko played a second taiko song, Ei Ja Nai Ka, which is not usually performed at Hawai'i bon dances. It is a contemporary dance, arranged and choreographed by San Jose Taiko Artistic Director PJ Hirabayashi, and introduced to the bon dance by Kay Fukumoto, founder of Maui Taiko.[13] The evening's last dance was performed to a recording of "Beautiful Sunday," which was accompanied by a drummer who added an enthusiastic accompaniment to the music. The smiles and high energy, with occasional prancing from one set of movements to the next, created an exuberant atmosphere of fun and enjoyment as Lahaina's first bon dance of the season came to an end.

The experience described above was the first bon dance I attended as part of field research on West Maui during the summer of 2017. For this project, I attended the bon dance at Shingon Mission, Lahaina Jodo Mission, Lāna'i Hongwanji, and Lahaina Hongwanji. The ethnological method that I used was a *talk story* format, consisting of in-person interviews and telephone calls with individuals affiliated with the church, longtime participants of bon dance, and individuals who are instrumental in the perpetuation and/ or revival of bon dance on West Maui. I began with open-ended questions regarding bon dance and plantation memories, and from there, their stories began. Whenever possible, I sent the individuals copies of sections that referenced them. When requested, I refrained from citing their names.

In this chapter, I interweave the participants' stories with written works on bon dance, such as Christine Yano's, "Japanese Bon Dance Music In Hawai'i: Continuity, Change, and Variability," Judy Van Zile's *The Japanese Bon Dance in Hawai'i*, and Hatsumi Onishi's "Bon and Bon-odori in Hawai'i." Some of the material regarding plantation days were drawn from written works such as, Gary Okihiro's *Cane Fire*, Ronald Takaki's *Raising Cane: The World of Plantation Hawai'i*, and *Strangers from a Different Shore: a History of Asian Americans*, to name a few.

The descriptive scene of the bon dance at the beginning of this chapter attempts to recreate its ephemerality and then pause in order to read and analyze some of the underlying forces that affect the bon dance on Maui. Through this narrative, I posit that the practice of politics underlies cultural practices such as bon dance. Moreover, the power of politics, driven by capitalists' interests, is silent yet a major contributor to the existence, production, and transformation of the bon dance on West Maui.

HISTORICAL BACKGROUND

The rise of sugar plantations in Hawai'i was an orchestrated movement of politics and capitalist interests that changed the landscape, ethnoscape, and culturescape. This orchestration of politics and capitalism began in 1848 with the Great Māhele (Division of Lands). The Māhele made Hawaii's lands available for purchase. Though the lands were available to both Native Hawaiians and foreigners, the majority of land ownership was by foreigners. The notion of land tenure was a foreign concept to Native Hawaiians since the land was part of their cultural and spiritual existence—something that could not be purchased and sold.[14]

Later, the Kuleana Act of 1850 provided means for access to lands for all people. However, the debt, diseases, and deaths of Native Hawaiians made the bureaucratic process incomplete. Roughly 10 percent of the people who had claims to land died by 1854.[15] In addition, there were those who lacked a desire for individual ownership preferring the traditional system. Some simply did not understand the permanent nature of the land division.[16] The usurpation of Hawaiian lands allowed for exploitation by foreigners. Subsequently on Maui, Lahaina's agricultural lands were transformed into sugar plantations.[17]

Arrival of Japanese Immigrants

The rise in sugar plantations and their need for workers led to recruitment of laborers from different Asian countries. The first group of laborers, primarily Chinese men, arrived in 1852. After their contracts expired, some became freelance laborers and ventured into other businesses, or returned to China. Japan was already a site for possible cheap labor, however, Japan was not open to Western recruitment until 1868.[18] Through an agreement with Eugene Van Reed, the Hawaiian consul general stationed in Yokohama, 148 Japanese immigrants (140 men, six women, and two children) were sent to Hawai'i. The workers of this first group of Japanese immigrants, claiming poor treatment on the job, accused the Hawaiian government of violating contracts.[19] Approximately forty Japanese laborers were returned to their homeland by the Hawaiian government.[20]

In 1881, King Kalākaua met with Emperor Meiji to improve relations between Hawai'i and Japan. According to Nordyke and Matsumoto, relations between the Kingdom of Hawai'i and Japan improved, resulting in better contracts for laborers. Contrarily, historian Lawrence H. Fuchs indicates that the meeting failed and Kalākaua later sent Curtis Iʻaukea to try to improve relations, which also failed. Instead, starvation caused by two years of bad seasons in Japan was the impetus for thousands of Japanese peasants to emigrate to Hawaiʻi.[21]

When the Japanese immigrants arrived, they were placed in camps that were separate from the Chinese who came before them. This segregation practice continued with subsequent national immigrant groups. Ronald Takaki highlights the segregated camps with camp names. On Maui, for example,

> "Puʻunēnē Plantation…had sixteen camps, including many Japanese as well as Filipino camps and also "Young Hee Camp," "Ah Fong Camp," "Spanish A Camp," "Spanish B Camp," and "Alabama Camp."[22]

In addition to having camp names indicating their segregated nature, Jane Imai[23] recalled that in Lahaina there was:

> Keawe Camp and Mill Camp…[it] was near the mill. PuʻukoliʻiCamp was isolated from Lahaina. Waineʻe Village was called Pump Camp because it was near the pump. Kīlauea Crater Village had two big camps— Honokahua and Puʻukoliʻi. There were many.

However, the ethnically segregated camps allowed Japanese immigrants to speak their own language.[24]

Eventually, a common language developed, as workers of different ethnicities and languages intermingled and communicated with each other and their lunas.[25] This fusion of languages resonates with Reverend Takayuki Meguro's experience in 2003, when he became minister of Shingon Mission. He explained that most of the Japanese were from Kyushu or Oshima and since he did not speak English, they spoke to him in Japanese. Yet, he could not understand what they were saying because to him it was:

> A mix up of Japanese, Hawaiian, and Pidgin, [with] Japanese grammar. It is like Japanese but not Japanese. For example, "little more pau ke chozu no hen harapa shi nai" means "almost pau so have to lock the doors around the bathroom.[26]

Meguro added that he felt the Japanese spoken in Lahaina was much more reflective of what he called Hogen or old language. The notion of hanging onto a national language is important for "generating imagined communities [and] building in effect *particular solidarities.*"[27] As Benedict Anderson explains, the power of language is that it allows for inclusiveness rather than exclusion. Thus, although it was important to speak Japanese, which is evidenced by the numerous Japanese schools that were established in Hawai'i, speaking pidgin allowed for inclusivity in what was yet another imagined community of diverse people within the colonized space of Hawai'i.

Japanese immigration ended when the Immigration Act of 1907 prevented Japanese contract laborers from entering the United States and its territories. In 1908, the Gentlemen's Agreement imposed further restrictions, limiting Japanese immigration to "former residents...parents, wives, and children of residents."[28] This gave rise to a period called *Yobiyose Jidai* (the period of summoning) from 1908–1920.[29] During the *Yobiyose Jidai*, brides and families entered Hawai'i. Many brides, called picture brides, were part of an arrangement in which they would marry men they had never met until their arrival. By 1920, the population in Hawai'i was approximately 256,000 of which about 109,000 or 43 percent were Japanese. Of the 109,000 Japanese, around 47,000 or 43 percent of the Japanese population were women. [30]

The Japanese immigration experience differed from that of the Chinese, who came before them. Chinese immigrants were primarily men and they did not bring staged or publicly performed dance practices. The Japanese immigration experience included men, women, and children. In addition, when the Japanese arrived on Maui, they brought their religion with them. One of the religions that the Japanese immigrants brought with them was the Shingon sect of Buddhism. According to Meguro, these immigrants formed prayer groups, or Odaishiko. In 1902, the Odaishiko were instrumental in building the Shingon Mission.[31] In other camps, planters either donated lands or subsidized Buddhist temples as a stabilizing influence on the workers.[32] One of the important Buddhist traditions that Japanese immigrants brought with them was the Obon observance. Reverend Gensho Hara[33], resident minister of the Lahaina Jodo Mission, provided the following historical account of how the practice of bon dance became affiliated with the Buddhist Obon festival.

Hara's Origin of Bon Dance[34]

Buddhism has over 2,500 years of history. Since there was no written language at the time of Shakyamuni Buddha, his teachings were passed on through an oral tradition. After Buddha's passing, monks would gather annually. The elder monk recited the Buddha's teachings, which the gathered monks would repeat, in unison.[35] Eventually, written scriptures were created. Hara added that the Buddhist teachings were introduced through the Silk Road, from India to Central Asian countries, China, Tibet, Korea, and Japan. Dunhuang, in China, is known for the thousands of caves that are along the Silk Road that contain Buddhist carvings and murals.[36]

The Obon originates from the *Ullambana sutra*, which tells about one of Buddha's ten great disciples, Maudgalyāyana (Mokuren in Japanese).[37]

> Mokuren, a great disciple of the Buddha, understood the true nature of existence and could see into the afterlife. After he gained power, Maudga-lyāyana went searching for his beloved mother, who was suffering in hell. He offered food to her [that] would turn into flames each time she tried to touch it. Saddened by this, he asked the Buddha how he could save his mother. The Buddha answered that the prayers of many would be needed so Maudgalyāyana asked his fellow monks to pray for his mother after their summer retreat, and through their collective prayers, their departed loved ones were saved. Seeing this, Maudgalyāyana danced with joy. This dance is said to be the origin of the colorful Bon Dance." (Excerpt from the Lahaina Jodo Mission Obon festival pamphlet.)

Bon dance and a lantern floating ceremony are part of the Obon. The Floating Lanterns Ceremony, called Toro Nagashi, is held after the Obon and symbolizes sending the spirit back.[38]

LAHAINA JODO MISSION: TORO NAGASHI

At Lahaina Jodo Mission, the lantern floating is held after the service and before the bon dance. Approximately 200 people carry candle-lit lantern boats to the ocean and set them afloat. According to one individual, the Toro Nagashi at Jodo Mission did not always have a large turnout.[39] The increase in people participating in the Jodo Mission lantern floating began after the popularization of the Shinnyo-en Lantern Floating at Magic Island on Oahu.[40] The popularization through media raised awareness to a broader community of people about the significance of the Toro Nagashi. This significance and connection to family is portrayed in the film *Picture Bride*, written by Kayo Hatta, Mari Hatta, and Diane Mei Lin Mark.

In the film *Picture Bride*, Riyo (Youki Kudoh) is sent to Hawai'i in 1918 to marry a man in an arranged marriage. Matsuji (Akira Takayama), Riyo's husband-to-be, sent a photo that was taken when he was a young man to the go-between in Japan. Expecting to meet a young man, Riyo is in disbelief when she arrives in Hawai'i and discovers that he is more than twice her age. Upon arrival they are married, however, Riyo refuses to accept Matsuji as her husband and the marriage is not consummated. Eventually, Riyo resigned herself to a life of hard work on the plantation with the intent to save enough money to return to Japan. Recognizing Riyo's despair, Kana (Tamlyn Tomita) befriends Riyo.

During a sugar cane burning scene, a shift in wind moves the fire towards the children of the workers. When Kana discovers her child, Kei, is missing, she runs into the field to search for her and both disappear. Riyo is stricken with grief.

In the meantime, Matsuji builds a shrine to honor Riyo's parents. This shrine brings a turning point to their relationship as husband and wife. Matsuji takes Riyo to participate in the Toro Nagashi that begins with the floating lanterns in a stream. Riyo floats a lantern for her parents and a second one for Kana and Kei. Following the lantern floating, Riyo and Matsuji participate in a bon dance. The yukata worn by the entire cast provides a sense of Japaneseness as they danced around a yagura in the middle of a sugar cane field. This scene ends with Riyo, Matsuji, and the other workers smiling and dancing to taiko rhythms and the song Fukushima Ondo.

The portrayals of the Toro Nagashi and the Obon in *Picture Bride* signify the importance of family in Japanese culture. The significance is an important one for the writers of the film, illustrating how that connection managed to be a turning point for a relationship built on deceit. In addition, the shrine that was built signified a permanent connection to family in a foreign country that traversed time and space. While the representation in *Picture Bride* and Hara's origin of bon dance discussed a connection to the spirits of those that have passed, Lahaina Hongwanji has yet another perspective.

Lahaina Hongwanji: A Departure from the Departed

According to Reverend Ai Hironaka, resident minister of Lahaina Hongwanji, the Hongwanji sect does not believe that the spirits return to the earth. Instead, once a person passes, their spirit moves on to the Pureland.[41] Hironaka explained that August 15 begins the bon yasumi (vacation or break)[42] rather than a return of the spirits. In Japan, there are two times in the year that workers have the

Yagura at Lahaina Jodo Mission. Courtesy of Diane Letoto.

Crowd waiting during the Toro Nagashi at Lahaina Jodo Mission. Courtesy of Diane Letoto.

opportunity to either return home or to a home village—bon yasumi and summer yasumi. According to those of the Hongwanji sect of Buddhism, the bon yasumi is a time to reconnect with family. Participation in the bon dance brings the community together in celebration of peace and joy.[43]

The belief in the return of spirits differs among sects. However, the kinesthetic energy that occurs through dance, which brings a community together, occurs with or without a belief in spirits. The physical connection that occurs through movement when individuals move in unison creates a group unity that is kinesthetically felt. This kinesthetic energy led to Hironaka's assertion that community connection is a strong aspect of the bon dance in Lahaina.

LAHAINA BON DANCE:
REFLECTION, MIGRATION, AND RESILIENCE

When reflecting on the past and present bon dance, the sense of community expands beyond West Maui. This is highlighted with a following of bon dance participants who continue to travel around the island, from one bon dance to the next, every weekend of the season.[44] Imai recalled, "Since everyone was poor, [bon dance] provided good, clean fun."[45] Individuals looked forward to the relief from everyday hardships it provided. Moreover, the community was not limited to one side of the island but rather included the entire island.

The existence and consciousness of a bon dance community that travels from one bon dance to the next, affects the bon dance season schedule. When creating a season's schedule, the Hongwanji council tries to avoid possible conflicts with the Lahaina Hongwanji bon dance. This is illustrated in the way that the Hongwanji bon dance schedule changes every year based on Lahainaluna High School's student exchange.[46] During the exchange, students from Japan go to Maui to learn English, Hawaiian culture, and the bon dance. The students attend one of the Honpa Hongwanji churches located in Kahului, Makawao, Wailuku, and Lahaina. While some of the other church bon dance are consistently set for a particular weekend in a month, the dates for the Lahaina Hongwanji bon dance is dependent on the student exchange schedule. This schedule consideration occurred after the student exchange was established. However, the bon dance has had additional transformations that have occurred through the years.

Although current bon dance music is recorded, during the plantation era live music was played. Back then, if there were two nights of bon dance, one night included Okinawan dance.[47] On the other night, the dances were mainly Betcho or Fukushima Ondo and Iwakuni Ondo.[48] In fact, Asai Aotaki recalled that when she was young, "there was only Betcho and Iwakuni."[49] Betcho is similar to Fukushima Ondo in rhythm, but with slightly different hand motions.[50] As described at the beginning of this chapter, Fukushima Ondo is upbeat and performed to the intricate rhythms of taiko drums and flute that accompany a singer. The distinguishing mark of Fukushima Ondo is the "use of the *minteki* (flute) and the fast and furious tempo of the incessant drum beating."[51] The dance consists of five movements followed by a clap.

The Iwakuni Ondo stands in contrast with Fukushima Ondo in tempo and style. According to Onishi, Iwakuni Ondo is, "named from the city of Iwakuni in Yamaguchi prefecture."[52] In Iwakuni Ondo, there are several drummers that dance in a circle in front of one drum, taking turns hitting the drum. A characteristic that is unique to Iwakuni Ondo is a chanter would stand in the yagura holding an umbrella while singing.[53] Depending on the song, the dancers would call out, *dokkoi-sho*, after a verse. After three or four verses, again depending on the song, dancers would join in with the refrain, *Arya-sa korya dokkoi to-na*.[54] During the early years, Iwakuni Ondo was a popular dance with six or seven hundred dancers, "in three or four large rings so close together that to make a complete circuit may take [a full] hour."[55] However, the popularity of Iwakuni Ondo has changed since those early years. Tasaka heard that some of the people did not like one of the Iwakuni songs since it had sixteen verses and the dance had only five moves to a slow tempo.

According to Tasaka, there was a period of eight or nine years between the late 1990s–early 2000s that Iwakuni Ondo did not exist.[56] This was in large part because many of the older drummers passed away and no one carried on the tradition. Tasaka, who had been an Iwakuni drummer, decided to bring Iwakuni back to the bon dance. For about ten years he has been singing songs of his teacher, sensei Tokunaga.[57] Tokunaga was Tasaka's drumming teacher and leader of the Iwakuni on Maui. There are other songs that he is trying to revive as well.

A unique transformation of the Iwakuni Ondo on Maui was that drummers are not part of one particular group. The drummers are called O-bon drummers and are not required to attend a particular bon dance. If a drummer(s) attends a bon dance, they will play the drum. Another aspect to being an O-bon drummer is that they accompany some of the recorded music. Tasaka said that there is an unwritten rule that if the bon dance is at one drummer's church then that drummer has priority to beat the drum for their favorite song. They might even request a song be played for the bon dance. This is unlike Iwakuni groups on O'ahu where each group has their own drummers and they beat the drum only during Iwakuni songs.

During World War II, churches and all cultural activities came to a halt. After the war, plantations were still going strong.[58] It is not certain as to when recorded music was first used at the bon dance, however, one dance to recorded music that has traversed time and space is Tanko Bushi, the "Coal Miners Song." Tanko Bushi is performed at the bon dances throughout the islands and in several bon dances in Japanese communities in northern California.[59] There are four basic movements in the dance that depict the work of mining coal. The motions imitate digging the coal, throwing it over the shoulder, wiping the brow, and finally pushing the coal. Although it is a simple dance, Tanko Bushi remains popular at the bon dance.

When looking back at the bon dance during the 1960s, S. Thompson recalled that the music took on some of the plantation life.[60] For example, an older dance performed for one season, "Hore Hore Ondo," was recorded by Shimakura Chiyoko.[61] Hore hore is the Japanese Romanization of hole hole, which is the Hawaiian word for stripping of the dried leaves of the sugar cane.[62] Ondo is the Japanese word for dance. Songwriters in Japan composed Hore Hore Ondo, which tells of the hard work in the sugar fields, but Hawai'i is still a wonderful place. This stands in stark contrast to the hole hole bushi, which were songs composed by women, often depicting the hardships and experiences of plantation workers.[63] One hole hole bushi, "likened the early morning plantation work call to birds crying and temple bells tolling—both associated with misfortune and death, especially a family member."[64] Another reflected a mother's lament, as she had to work up until the time she gave birth, and after birth, take the infant with her to the fields.[65] The words in yet another hole hole bushi reflected the endurance of hardship.

> Starting out so early
> Lunches on our shoulders
> Off to our holehole work
> Never seems to be enough.[66]

The dismay of the Japanese workers with the situation they found themselves in is especially captured in this hole hole bushi:

Wonderful Hawaii, or so I heard.
One look and it seems like Hell.
The manager's the Devil and
His lunas are demons.[67]

According to S. Thompson, the dance for Hore Hore Ondo had motions of cutting the cane stalk and used a tenugui to indicate the hard work. While somewhat reflective of plantation life, it also was reflective of the way in which the tourist industry portrayed Hawai'i as a beautiful paradise.

S. Thompson added that other dances from the past were Tokyo Ondo, Sakura Ondo, and Yagi Bushi.[68] O-bon drummers accompany Yagi Bushi. At one time, one person played the entire song, now the drummers will rotate with each verse.[69]

During the 1960s, S. Thompson recalled that the Tokyo Gorin Ondo, sung by Minami Haruo, was performed in preparation for the 1964 Olympics, which was hosted by Japan. This was a big event for Japanese communities, including in Hawai'i, since it was the first time an Asian country hosted the Olympics. In anticipation for the 2020 Olympics, Japan has begun reviving the Tokyo Gorin Ondo with new choreography to reach both older and younger generations.

Interestingly, Tokyo Gorin Ondo provides an example of ways in which social media has become instrumental in moving cultural events and dance across borders. For example, Toshiye Kawamura, director of Sakura Minyo Doo Koo Kai, received a post on her Facebook feed that Japan released music videos to teach the bon dance. According to Kawamura, Gorin Ondo oogis (fans), tenugui, and yukata are being sold. Kawamura received the following description of the song from Facebook:

> Exactly three years from now, the Olympic Games Tokyo 2020 will be in full swing. We are looking forward to meeting people from all over the world and seeing them enjoy themselves at the Games. In fact, this was one of the main motivations behind the remaking the Olympic Song. The singers were Sayuri Ishikawa, Yuzo Kayama and Pistol Takehara. The song lyrics and the dance routine have been remade especially for the 2020 Games. This summer, the song might be playing at summer festival near you, so why not go along and dance the night away. The concept of the song and dance is *happy* and *peace*.

In response, Sakura Minyo Doo Koo Kai in Sacramento, California and in other communities on the U.S. continent are learning the new choreography for the 2020 Olympics in Tokyo.[70] Here, the bon dance community extends beyond the boundaries of Hawai'i and includes other national and international Japanese communities. In addition, the opportunity to capitalize on products such as, yukata, oogi, and tenugui, are available for purchase internationally. At the time of writing this chapter, it is not certain whether the Tokyo Gorin Ondo will be performed in West Maui, however, this is mentioned to emphasize two important aspects of bon dance experience in West Maui. The first is that several of the participants in this project emphasized that bon dance in Lahaina has retained a tradition passed on through the years that differ from the transformations of bon dance in Japan. The second point is that the bon dance has become a venue for raising funds.

The bon dance as fundraiser stands in contrast to the original function of the bon dance. In fact, during the plantation era, Imai and Aotari recalled giving out musubi (rice balls) and takuan (pickled daikon radish) to participants as a gesture of appreciation. Now that there are concession stands that sell food at the bon dance, this practice was discontinued. Both Imai and Aotari have suggested starting it up again but received resistance from the church event organizers. Although they are unable to pass out food, Aotari continues providing a gesture of appreciation by giving handmade tenugui to participants.

There was a decline in the bon dance that began around the 1970-80s. According to one individual interviewed for this project, the bon dance community was not only strong during the plantation era, but also the church was central to the community.[71] Reverend Shinri Hara provided reflections of this when she explained, during the Obon service at Lahaina Jodo Mission, that preparations began weeks before the bon dance.[72] She remembered that it was a time of cleaning the pavilion area, building the yagura, and preparing food. The community was like family. However, one individual explained that with the closing of the sugar plantation the community demographics changed.[73] The congregation has gotten smaller and when they meet, only about twenty people attend. This decline in the congregation was not limited to one church. In fact, participants in this project stated that there were significant declines in all three churches in Lahaina. In addition, with the change in the community and congregation, there was less interest in the bon dance. Although there was a decline in congregation membership, there has been a resurgence of bon dance in recent years. According to one individual, after a

Tenugui given to dancers. Courtesy of Diane Letoto.

change to upbeat music combined with community outreach, the bon dance has experienced a revival and now there are many of young participants.[74] The individual believes that Maui Taiko has a following of supporters, which has increased attendance at Lahaina Jodo Mission bon dance.

The popularity of Maui Taiko was seen at the bon dance that I attended in Lahaina—Shingon Mission, Lahaina Jodo Mission, and Lahaina Honpa Hongwanji. As described at the Shingon Mission bon dance in the beginning of this chapter, the upbeat tempo of Fukushima Ondo and Ei Ja Nai Ka brought more participants into the circle to dance. In Fukushima Ondo, younger dancers would take liberty to either skip or prance for the first two movements instead of taking the traditional step-together-step. Others might even be free form on their hand movements for five beats. Traditionally the sixth beat is a single clap, however many of the dancers would modify the clap by clapping hands with another dancer. The songs played by Maui Taiko are popular. This was evidenced when I wanted to join in the dance and had a difficult time finding space in the circle of dancers.

With the increase of younger participants in the bon dance, "Beautiful Sunday" is yet another popular dance because of its upbeat tempo. As described at the beginning of this chapter, the dancers sometimes prance from one move to the next. There is more freedom in the movement in that there is little attention to codified movements. In addition, since it is not considered a traditional bon dance, the dance is performed at the end of the evening.

Another nontraditional dance played only at the end of the evening at Lahaina Jodo Mission and Lahaina Hongwanji is "Pokemon Ondo." Bishop Dean Okimura of Koboji Shingon Mission in Honolulu choreographed this dance.[75] The music is about an anime character that sets out to get dragon balls, symbolizing the attainment of eternal life.[76] "Pokemon Ondo" traveled from Oʻahu to Maui where it has gained popularity.

In addition to the upbeat dances of "Beautiful Sunday" and "Pokemon Ondo," another favorite among the younger generation is "Shiwase Samba." Reverend Okahashi in Osaka choreographed "Shiawase Samba" and taught the dance in Seattle.[77] On his return to Japan, he stopped in Honolulu where he taught the dance. The dance has since traveled to Maui and has become one of the favorites of the bon dance at Lahaina Jodo Mission and Lahaina Hongwanji Mission.

Although the more upbeat dances have gained popularity among a younger generation of bon dance followers, there is tension between those who want to keep the bon dance more traditional with older dances and those who prefer the contemporary, upbeat dances. At one time the traditionalists attempted to restrict the younger dancers from jumping, however they are now merely asked to be careful. S. Thompson recognizes the desire to keep the dance more traditional by some of the participants and organizers. When he creates the music line up at Lahaina Jodo Mission and Lahaina Honpa Hongwanji, he reserves the modern upbeat music, such as "Pokemon Ondo" and "Beautiful Sunday," for the end of the bon dance. Recently, those who would like to keep the dance more traditional have been more receptive to the upbeat dances since they are popular among the younger generation.

The increase of younger dancers at Lahaina bon dance in recent years comes after years of decline. With the influx of foreign residents, the outflow of the younger generation, and the increase of tourism in West Maui, there are concerns regarding the future of the bon dance.[78] In the past, preparation for the bon dance at Lahaina Jodo Mission brought neighbors and long-time supporters together to set up the yagura, clean the area, and prepare the food.

There was a strong sense of community and extended family during the plantation era, which is weakening with the changes that are occurring, especially in demographics, in Lahaina. Although there is a weakening of community as compared to the past, the attraction of upbeat dances for a younger crowd provides hope for the continuance of bon dance.

The resiliency in Lahaina's bon dance stands in contrast with the bon dance on Lānaʻi. The Lānaʻi experience provides a glimpse of how the island's socioeconomic situation affected the Japanese community and its bon dance.

LĀNAʻI BON DANCE:
A REFLECTION OF CAPITALISM'S DESTRUCTIVE FORCE

Since the pineapple industry came to a halt, the majority of the land on Lānaʻi is unused and undeveloped. Currently, the population on Lānaʻi is around three thousand, of which Tasaka guestimates that 70 percent of the people work for the county or state and around 30 percent for the hotels.[79] There have been subsequent attempts to find other uses for the land on Lānaʻi. According to Tasaka, one such attempt was the production of macadamia nuts, however, that endeavor failed. Without the availability of jobs, the younger generation of Japanese left the island.[80] Some left for jobs on Honolulu or Lahaina. Subsequently, aging families also left Lānaʻi to live with their children.[81]

Hideko Saruwatari, a ninety-one-year-old resident of Lānaʻi, recalls some of her experiences and memories of bon dance during plantation days. She remembered the days when "there were only public baths with no roofs. There was no running water. Transportation was horseback."[82] She then told me how her mother, Aiko Murakami, who was a very young girl when she first went to Lānaʻi, could bear to stay on Lānaʻi only two to three months before going back to Lahaina. She said it was too hard.[83] Eventually, her mother was taken back to Lānaʻi, where she married and settled.

Saruwatari remembered that the Lānaʻi Hongwanji was originally located at the current site of Lānaʻi Union Church. When it was the site of the Lānaʻi Hongwanji, members built the church and the small building across the churchyard where the bon dance and sumo were held. During World War II, the church closed. Since the church was on leased land, the building was returned to the company. After the war, Lānaʻi Hongwanji was forced to relocate and was reopened at its current site. [84]

Saruwatari felt that there was a strong sense of community at the bon dance during plantation days. She felt the bon dance was a time when everyone turned out and the men "came with the drums. At that time, there was no recorded music, only drums. The men played drums for the bon dance."[85] According to Saruwatari, the two main bon dances were Fukushima Ondo and Iwakuni Ondo. At intermission, the women of the church served rice balls and pickled vegetables to all the participants. Like the Lahaina example, this was a gesture of appreciation that is also prevalent in Japanese culture.

Saruwatari explained that church organizers discontinued the free food given to the participants at intermission. However, there are active members who continue to cook and serve food after the bon dance to the individuals who help put the bon dance event together. In recent times, Saruwatari has received resistance to continue the practice of providing free food for the people who help put the event together. Most of the free food is donated, which led Saruwatari to believe that the resistance is due to the lack of cultural understanding.

In addition to a different cultural perspective as it pertains to providing food for volunteers, there is a lack of interested supporters of the bon dance on Lānaʻi. At the July bon dance that I attended, the most popular aspect of the event was the food stands. The long line of residents waiting to buy the local favorites disappeared after they purchased their food. However, the decline in the bon dance on Lānaʻi could be reflective of a decline in the population and lack of a vibrant economy as well.

With a dwindling population, the Lānaʻi bon dance is at risk of discontinuing. During the past few years, supporters from Lahaina have been going to Lānaʻi to perpetuate bon dance. Clyde Tasaka, Jane Imai, and Asai Aotaki, to name a few, have organized groups of people from Lahaina to attend Lānaʻi's bon dance. In fact, at the July bon dance, the dancers were primarily from Lahaina. With the bon dance dependent on individuals who live elsewhere, Saruwatari's lament is don't know if going to have bon dance in the future.

This grim future of the bon dance on Lānaʻi, follows a history of strong community involvement, at a time when the pineapple industry was thriving. Here, the bon dance is reflective of the economic influence that went from one of abundance to one of depletion. As tourism on Lānaʻi develops, the transformation in the landscape and ethnoscape brings further uncertainties regarding the future of the bon dance on Lānaʻi.

Yagura on Lānaʻi. Courtesy of Diane Letoto.

Concession stand at the bon dance on Lānaʻi. Courtesy of Diane Letoto.

Lānaʻi Bon Dance, 2017. Courtesy of Diane Letoto.

Lānaʻi Bon Dance, 2017. Courtesy of Diane Letoto.

CONCLUSION

This ethnological survey of bon dance in West Maui began with colonization and capitalist endeavors that brought Japanese immigrants to Hawai'i. They immigrated to Hawai'i to work on the plantations and brought with them bon dance, which created a sense of community as well as a connection to a homeland. Wearing yukata or happi coat at the bon dance became a signifier, initially for home, and eventually the community.

After the closure of the plantations in West Maui and a shift to tourism industries, the demographics of the community changed. The economic transformations that occurred on the island of Lāna'i affected the rise and fall in the participation of bon dance. In Lahaina, the closure of the plantations also brought a change to the bon dance. The bon dance participation decreased, as did the sense of community. The remembrance of plantation days and the strength of community is why some wish to keep the bon dance more traditional. However, there are tensions that exist between those who wish to keep bon dance more traditional, with those who feel that it is necessary to keep the younger generation of participants interested and engaged in bon dance. As such, livelier choreography and music is used. This notion is exemplified with the shift in popularity from Iwakuni Ondo during plantation days to Fukushima Ondo in current day.

For the island of Lāna'i, the uncertain economic future has one longtime resident of Lanai troubled about the future of bon dance. Through the embodiment of dance during my participation in the bon dance on Lāna'i, I felt a connection to land and community even as an outsider. When I heard Saruwatari's story, I shared her concern of the uncertainties that lie before her, the bon dance, and the future of the island. As the bon dance continues to travel across boundaries continually engaging participants, albeit in different ways, the resilience of the bon dance transforms and morphs into newer forms as highlighted in Lahaina. There is nostalgia for the past but at the same time, the resilience of the bon dance is dependent and central to its community. As the community changes, so will the bon dance. With these changes, there are conflicts between those who believe that the tradition of bon dance is one thing and those who blur the boundaries of tradition with contemporary innovations. Yet, the true tensions lie not in the interpretations of tradition and contemporary innovations, but rather with the silent practice

Maui Minyo Dance Group, date unknown. One of the first minyo groups to lead the bon dance on Maui. Courtesy of Dan Thompson. Standing (*left to right*): Grace Thompson, Sadako Miyabara, Miyuki Kawabata, Teruyo Sato, (?) Tanaka, Helen Kondo, Tomiko Amine, Unknown, Aotaki Asai, Pat Agena, Nancy Agena, Sadako Shiotsuyu, Jane Nagasaki, Unknown. Sitting (*left to right*): Sumiko Iwamura, Fumie Shinyama, Chiyono Ayawa, Vivian Ichiki, Miyoko Yamamoto, Sueko Masuda, Anita Yamafuji.

of politics and capitalist interests that continue to change the landscape and ethnoscape on West Maui.

As I bring this chapter to a close, it is my hope that this is not a closure to the study of bon dance on West Maui. The difficulty in writing this chapter is that there are many more stories to be told and recorded, as well as other histories that need uncovering.

NOTES

1. Yano, Christine. "Japanese Bon Dance Music in Hawaiʻi: Continuity, Change, and Variability". Thesis. (Honolulu: University of Hawaiʻi, 1984). Christine Yano defines O-bon as a Buddhist festival of the dead.

2. Kimono is a traditional garment of Japan made of silk work by men and

women. Nowadays the kimono might be made of polyester or some other synthetic blend. Yukata is a cotton kimono worn by men and women during the summer and on casual or festive occasions such as the bon dance.

3. Happi is a straight-sleeved short jacket styled similar to the yukata.

4. Christine Yano defines the yagura as a tower. Typically, the tower is built with four legs and a platform elevated several feet above ground. From the platform, priests might speak to the crowd or chant to begin the dance, singers would chant to one of the dances, or as in the case of Lahaina Hongwanji, the DJ or music/dance announcer would sit or stand.

5. I have been a participant at bon dances on Oahu for over thirty years. From around 1981, I was a member of the Yamada Minyo Group and the Iwakuni Bon Dance Club, which led minyo and Iwakuni dances at Moʻiliʻili Hongwanji Mission, Kailua Hongwanji Mission, Koboji, and Honpa Hongwanji bon dances.

6. O-bon can also be written as O-bon.

7. The date of the O-bon is the fifteenth day of the seventh month of the lunar calendar. There are however, variations of when the O-bon is celebrated. Yano explains, for example, in some areas of Japan the festival may start on the twelfth day and continue as long as the seventeenth day of the seventh month of the lunar calendar, which often falls in the eighth month, or August of the solar calendar.

8. Mauka means mountain. In this reference, the altar was on the mountainside of the island, which is opposite the ocean.

9. Tasaka, Clyde, Personal cnterview, February 12, 2018. The first dance differs from church to church and referred to as the church song.

10. This tradition of playing a song reflective of the church teachings or one of the teachers to start the bon dance was a norm, which differs from one sect to another. For example, the first song at Jodo Mission might be Shinran Ondo, a song about Shinran who was a disciple of Hōnen, founder of the Jodo Mission.

11. At the bon dance, dancers who danced in the innermost circle are usually associated with the minyo (folk) dance group leading the particular bon dance. In some bon dances, these leaders could also be attendees of the church or regular participants who know the dance.

12. Fukushima Ondo is a traditional bon dance song with drummers, a flute, and singers. Fukushima Ondo is from Fukushima prefecture and one of two dances performed at bon dance on plantations.

13. Ei Janai Ka is a drumming arrangement and bon dance choreographed by PJ Hirabayashi of the San Jose Taiko. According to Nancy Zionkowski, dancer and member of the Nakayama Minyo Group, Hirabayashi is a good friend of Kay Fukumoto, founder of Maui Taiko, and taught Ei Janai Ka to Maui Taiko.

14. Silva, Noenoe K. *Aloha Betrayed: Native Hawaiian Resistance to American Colonialism*. (Durham and London: Duke University Press, 2004).

15. Buck, Elizabeth. *Paradise Remade: The Politics of Culture and History in Hawaii.* (Philadelphia: Temple University Press, 1993) 71.

16. Collins, Lance. "Wahikuli: Crown Lands in the Time of Tourism," *Tourism Impacts West Maui.* (Honolulu: North Beach-West Maui Benefit Fund, Inc., 2016) 11.

17. The Lahaina Restoration Foundation project is a 501(c)3 Hawai'i nonprofit organization founded to "restore, preserve, and protect the physical, historical and cultural legacies of Lahaina." (http://lahainarestoration.org/about/) At their website, it is possible to view an interactive map of the West Maui's plantation camps. See http://lahainarestoration.org/plantation-camp-maps/. Site accessed February 19, 2018.

18. Nordyke, Eleanor C. and Y. Scott Matsumoto. "The Japanese in Hawaii: a historical and demographic perspective". *Hawaiian Journal of History*, Volume 11, 1977. Honolulu: Hawaiian Historical Society, 163.

19. Conroy, Hilary and T. Scott Miyakawa, ed., *East Across the Pacific.* (Santa Barbara, California: American Bibliographical Center Clio Press, 1972) 25–29. Cited by Nordyke and Matsumoto.

20. Nordyke and Matsumoto, 163.

21. Fuchs, Lawrence H. *Hawai'i Pono: An Ethnic and Political History.* (Honolulu: The Bear Press, Inc., 1961) 106.

22. Takaki, Ronald. *Strangers from a Different Shore: A History of Asian Americans.* (New York: Back Bay Books, 1998) 156.

23. Jane Imai, telephone interview, February 19, 2018.

24. Takayuki Meguro, Rev., personal communication, July 5, 2017.

25. Takaki, 1998,167. Lunas are the boss or supervisors of the plantations.

26. Meguro, 2017.

27. Anderson, Benedict. *Imagined Communities.* (London: Verso, 1991) 133.

28. Ibid.

29. Ibid.

30. United States Census Bureau: The Fourteenth Census of the United States Taken in the Year 1920. Volume III. Population 1920 Composition and Characteristics of the Population by States. Outlying Possessions, 1172.

31. Meguro, 2017.

32. Takaki, 1998, 164.

33. G. Hara became minister at Lahaina Jodo Mission in 1963.

34. There are other works written on the origin of bon dance such as, Christine Yano's "Japanese Bon Dance Music In Hawai'i: Continuity, Change, and Variability", Judy Van Zile's *The Japanese Bon Dance in Hawai'i*, and " 'Bon' and 'Bon-Odori' in Hawai'i." to name a few, however I chose to use Hara's version as a participant in this project and in respect for the hours he spent talking with me.

35. Ibid.

36. Liu, Youlan. Lecture notes by Liu Youlan. Honolulu: University of Hawaii, 1989.

37. Gensho Hara, personal communication, July 6, 217. In addition, excerpts were taken from Hara's program for Lahaina Jodo Mission's O-bon Festival.

38. In Motoyoshi's lecture on bon dance on Kauai, she explains that the lanterns can be placed in an ocean if there is no river and if there is no ocean, then it can be burnt. Motoyoshi, Yukiko. "A History of Bon Dance on Kauai: a lecture". (Kauai: Kauai Historical Society, 2012).

39. Anonymous, personal communication, July 6, 2017.

40. Shinnyo-en is a spiritual practice founded by Ito and Tomoji Shinjo rooted in Shingon Buddhism. Ito Shinjo was training to become a Shingon priest, but believed that the esoteric practices of Buddhism should not be limited to an elite group of priests. Although Shinnyo-en is rooted in Buddhism and follows its tenets, it is not limited to Buddhist practitioners. Through my personal experience I have found that Shinnyo-en practitioners are from diverse religious backgrounds and many continue to practice those religions as a complement to Shinnyo-en. The Lantern Festival Hawaii is held annually on Oahu at Magic Island in Ala Moana Beach Park on Memorial Day.

41. Ai Hironaka, personal communication, July 6, 2017.

42. In my family, yasumi meant vacation or a break. According to the online Japanese-English Dictionary, yasumi also means recess, respite, and suspension. http://www.kanjijapanese.com/en/dictionary-japanese-english/yasumi. Accessed March 17, 2018.

43. Interview, Hironaka.

44. Jane Imai, telephone interview, February 19, 2018.

45. Imai, 2018.

46. Clyde Tasaka, telephone Interview, February 18, 2018.

47. Almost everyone that I spoke with recalled that if a church held bon dance on two nights, one night had Okinawan dance.

48. Dan Thompson, personal communication, July 6, 2017.

49. Asai Aotaki is 92 years who not only participated in bon dance but also was a member of the Maui Minyo Kai, a folk dance group that led the bon dance for many years.

50. D. Thompson, 2017.

51. Onishi, Katsumi. "Bon and Bon-Odori in Hawai'i", *Social Process in Hawii*. Douglas Yamamura, ed., Volume IV. May, 1938, 53.

52. Onishi, 52.

53. The tradition of holding the umbrella has since changed with the use of microphones.

54. This is the pattern of the cadence and refrain that we use in the Iwakuni Bon Dance Group on Oahu. Onishi grouped the refrain for Betcho, Iwakuni, Oki-

nawan dance together when she said, "Every once in a while, the dancers shout in chorus, *Betcho-betcho, dokkoi-sho, Arya-sa korya dokkoi to-na,* or *Tenyo-tenyo-ichiriki-ye-sa-sa,* depending on the dance."

55. Onishi, 51.

56. Tasaka, 2018.

57. Clyde Tasaka, telephone interview, February 12, 2018. Tasaka knows him as sensei Tokunaga. Sensei is honorific for teacher.

58. Jane Imai, telephone interview, February 19, 2018.

59. I have been to the bon dance in several cities in northern California where they danced Tanko Bushi.

60. Sherman Thompson, personal communication, August 5, 2017. Thompson selects and plays recoded music for Lahaina Jodo Mission and Lahaina Hongwanji bon dance. He introduces the songs live in a DJ style. Thompson was born and raised in Lahaina, but currently lives in Honolulu.

61. S. Thompson, 2017.

62. Okihiro, Gary. *Cane Fires: The Anti-Japanese Movement in Hawai'i, 1865–1945.* (Philadelphia: Temple University Press, 1991) 29.

63. Ibid.

64. Okihiro, 31.

65. Okihiro, 32.

66. In Okihiro's chapter on hole hole bushi, he recognizes Franklin Odo's collection of *hole hole bushi,* which was unpublished at that time.

67. Ibid.

68. S. Thompson, 2017 and Asai Aotaki, personal communication, July 8 2017.

69. Tasaka, February 12, 2018.

70. E-mail communication with Toshiye Kawamura. April 1, 2018.

71. Anonymous, 2017.

72. Reverend Shinri Hara, daughter of G. Hara gave the Dharma message at the O-bon service held on Saturday, July 1, 2017. Part of her message was her recollection of preparing for the bon dance, and the importance of community and family during this period.

73. Anonymous, 2017.

74. Anonymous, 2017.

75. Michi Takemoto, telephone Interview, January 30, 2018. Takemoto has been teaching minyo as an exercise class at the Manoa Japanese School ever since the 1980s and at Honpa Hongwanji in Honolulu from 1993–2002.

Joyce Araki, telephone interview, February 4, 2018. Araki (Professional name, Bando Mitsumasa II) is a professional classical dance teacher of the Bando Japanese school of dance. She began learning from the Bando School in 1954 and took over the school as the head instructor in 1996. Araki and her students lead the bon dance for recorded music at Honolulu's Honpa Hongwanji.

76. Takemoto, 2018.
77. Araki, 2018.
78. Anonymous, 2017.
79. Tasaka explained this while he drove me around Lanai. Also cited in the World Population Review. http://worldpopulationreview.com/states/hawaii-population/. Accessed March 31, 2018.
80. Hideko Saruwatari, personal communication, July 9, 2017.
81. Saruwatari, 2017.
82. Saruwatari, 2017.
83. Saruwatari, 2017.
84. Hideko Saruwatari, telephone interview, February 19, 2018.
85. Saruwatari, 2017.

Works Cited

Anderson, Benedict. *Imagined* Communities. London: Verso, 1991.
Buck, Elizabeth. *Paradise Remade: The Politics of Culture and History in Hawai'i.* Philadelphia: Temple University Press, 1993.
Collins, Lance. "Wahikuli: Crown Lands in the Time of Tourism", *Tourism Impacts West Maui.* Honolulu: North Beach-West Maui Benefit Fund, Inc., 2016.
Fuchs, Lawrence H. *Hawai'i Pono: An Ethnic and Political History.* Honolulu: The Bear Press, Inc., 1961.
Hatta, Kayo, Mari Hatta, Diane Mei Lin Mark. *Picture Bride.* Videotape. California: Miramax films in association with Thousand Cranes Filmworks, 1994.
Nordyke, Eleanor C. and Y. Scott Matsumoto. "The Japanese in Hawai'i: a historical and demographic perspective", Hawaiian Journal of History, Volume 11, 1977. Honolulu: Hawaiian Historical Society.
Okihiro, Gary. *Cane Fires: The Anti-Japanese Movement in Hawai'i, 1865–1945.* Philadelphia: Temple University Press, 1991.
Onishi, Katsumi. "Bon and Bon-Odori in Hawai'i", *Social Process in Hawaii.* Douglas Yamamura, ed., Volume IV. May 1938.
Silva Noenoe K. *Aloha Betrayed: Native Hawaiian Resistance to American Colonialism.* Durham and London: Duke University Press, 2004.
Yano, Christine. *Japanese Bon dance Music in Hawai'i: Continuity, Change, and Variability.* Thesis. Honolulu: University of Hawai'i, August 1984.

Internet sites

United States Census Bureau: The Fourteenth Census of the United States Taken in the Year 1920. Volume III. Population 1920 Composition and Characteristics of the Population by States. Outlying Possessions. https://www2.census.gov/library/publications/decennial/1920/volume-3/41084484v3ch10.pdf
http://www.kanjijapanese.com/en/dictionary-japanese-english
http://worldpopulationreview.com/states/hawaii-population/

https://tokyo2020.org/en/news/event/20170816-01.html
https://www.youtube.com/watch?v=il3ouYJlTYc

Interviews

Anonymous. Personal interview. July 6, 2017.
Aotaki Asai. Personal interview. July 8, 2017.
Araki, Joyce. Telephone interview. February 4, 2018.
Hara, Reverend Gensho. Personal Interview. July 6, 2017.
Imai, Jane. Telephone interview. February 19, 2018.
Meguro, Reverend Takayuki. Personal interview. July 5, 2017.
Saruwatari, Hideko. Personal interview. July 9, 2017.
Takemoto, Michi. Telephone interview. January 30, 2018.
Tasaka, Clyde. Personal interview. July 7, 2017.
Tasaka, Clyde. Personal interview. February 12, 2018.
Tasaka, Clyde. Telephone interview. February 18, 2018.
Thompson, Dan. Personal interview. July 6, 2017.
Thompson, Sherman. Personal interview. August 5, 2017.
Zionkowski, Nancy. Personal interview. August 12, 2017

REGIONAL PLANNING EMERGING FROM A PLANTATION WORLD

The Case of West Maui

Brian Richardson

Economic and political histories of the islands of Hawai'i are often narrated as a series of stages that move through changing systems of economic dominance connected to external forces. The economic focus has shifted from harvesting sandalwood and supplying whaling ships, to expansive plantations of sugarcane and pineapple, to tourism and military support. Similarly, the political history of the islands has moved to, and then from, a native monarchical system, to an exclusionary republican system dominated by settler European missionaries and capitalists, to a broadly-based democratic system dominated by strong party institutions. The shift from the republic-plantation system to a democratic-tourism system, which occurred primarily in the late 1950s and through the 1960s, has been described in at least two very different ways: as the creation of a modern political and economic system based on tourism, where Hawai'i emerged out of the closed world of the plantation society into a free and democratic future, or as the reconfiguration of the plantation society in terms of tourism, where the dominant power relations, which make Hawai'i dependent on local property owners, global capitalism, and American imperialism, remain in place and may even have become more entrenched.

Competing ways of understanding the political order is relevant to broader social debates during periods of significant socioeconomic transition, such as with the rise of tourism. The occurrence of key changes in the islands are fairly uncontroversial: hotels were constructed, airports were expanded, plantations ceased to operate and were converted into resorts or suburban housing. But it is not as easy to characterize the global economic connections and their impact on local political structures and ideals. Nor is it easy to offer a straightforward reading of documents created during the time, documents that often show, even if they do not reflect upon, the political and conceptual tensions at play. Instead, such historical documents often illustrate a much muddier intellectual and material landscape, where people are responding to political, cultural, and economic dynamics that are sometimes recognized but unspoken, sometimes hoped for but unrealistic, and sometimes unavoidable and only partially understood. The documents are products of their times. As such, there is value in recovering the ambiguities that are at play in such documents, insofar as they help illustrate the complexities of the issues that were being faced.

THE PLANTATION PERIOD

In the late nineteenth century, and until the 1970s, the West Maui region was dominated by a plantation economy focused on sugar production. Pioneer Mill Company, the first sugar plantation in the region, began in the late nineteenth century as an early investment of James Campbell, who became one of the wealthiest people in Hawai'i during its territorial period. He sold the Lahaina plantation in 1877 to Henry Turton, one of his investment partners. By the First World War, Pioneer Mill was owned by Heinrich Hackfeld and James Pflueger. In 1918, the company was confiscated by the government based on the owners' German descent, and sold to a group of local businessmen. The company, which was later renamed American Factors, and then Amfac in 1966, was one of the so-called "Big Five" companies that dominated Hawai'i during its territorial period. The Big Five included Amfac, Castle and Cooke, Alexander and Baldwin, C. Brewer and Co., and Theo H. Davies and Co. The five companies were a closely-knit web of shared officers, executives, and directors who were all integrated with the Republican Party that then ruled the islands. The government was an overt arm of the corporations and many prominent oligarchs and their families also served in key government posts.

Pioneer Mill controlled large areas of land in West Maui that were devoted to sugar cane production. Not only did their holdings include agricultural lands, but also the areas needed to maintain the infrastructure and administration of sugar production, such as railroads, irrigation systems, office space, and accommodations for the plantation workers. The planning for the region was focused on the economic goals of the company, with most of the planning done with little input or external oversight. Infrastructure would be improved based on business goals and technological developments, such as a railroad, which the company built in the late nineteenth century, or the expansion of port facilities to accommodate larger freighters. The first well on Maui was drilled by the company in 1883. Between 1948 and 1951, the company engaged in an extensive rock removal and landscape improvement program that allowed an additional three thousand acres of land to be mechanically planted, cultivated, and harvested. At its height, Pioneer Mill controlled thirteen thousand acres of agricultural land in West Maui, which is close to half of the agricultural land in the region, and it was also connected to key parts of the infrastructure, such as the power company, the ice company, general stores, the theater, and the hospital.

The closed character of the economic and political system of West Maui was enhanced by the geographic character of the region. West Maui is almost completely separated by land from the rest of the island by mountains. There is a coastal road that goes to the north of Lahaina, but the winding and often single-lane route is impractical for large-scale transportation. The only viable terrestrial connection is a coastal route to the south of Lahaina that joins with Mā'alaea and Kahului. The route parallels to an ancient trail which, over the last century, and particularly with the rise of the mass-market tourist economy, has been expanded, flattened, and paved to allow for cars, trucks and buses. But during the plantation period, this road was narrow and often steep and poorly maintained. It was not until 1951 that a tunnel was constructed to provide a more level road. One implication of this geological situation was that West Maui's primary connection to the outside was the ocean and that its primary activities were largely internal, except when sugarcane was ready for export.

The local government in West Maui developed alongside the rest of the islands of Hawai'i. Lahaina had been the capital in the early part of the nineteenth century, during the reigns of Kamehameha II and III, although the capital shifted to Honolulu as the islands became more connected to global economic systems. In 1905, seven years after Hawai'i became a U.S. Territory, the island of Maui, along with the other major islands in the territory, was organized as a separate county. Maui's political structure had been a combination of government agents from Honolulu and, in areas such as West Maui, of power structures tied to the plantation companies. Maui did not have a mayor until 1969, although the chairman and chief executive of the board of supervisors was informally called *mayor* from 1905 to 1969. The plantation economy was based on interactions among landowners, the county, the Territory, and outside factors that included the American government, experts, technological developments, and the economic structures that supported the use of Maui as a source of sugar for global markets. The corporatist system offered little space for political discourse. As a result, planning for the region was closely tied to the needs of the landowners and the power structures of the plantation economy.

The primary economic function of the territorial government was maintaining social order, organizing trade, and developing infrastructure, specifically major roads, airports, and government buildings. In 1951, for instance, the territorial government acquired federal funds to help construct the tunnel south of Olowalu, which improved the ability to take cars and trucks between West and Central Maui. Kahului airport opened in 1952, but would not be significantly expanded for years, in part because the airport, unlike the ports, did not serve the dominant industries on the island. The primary airport in the Territory was on Oʻahu. In the *1953 Territory of Hawaii Public Works* report, the total budget for the state was roughly $5.5 million, of which more than half was related to highway maintenance and construction "for commuters" (Department of Public Works, 1953, 7). This 1953 document makes little mention of tourism, hotels, travel, or the tourism industry in general. The only mentions of Waikīkī are for a seawall, some dredging, and a contract to build a new, onshore aquarium to replace the one that had been there since 1904. The only mentions of Maui are tied to buildings at the Maui Vocational School: one that was completed in 1953, and three more that were planned for 1954. Likewise, the document makes no direct mention of sugar or pineapple production, although two references to irrigation projects are tied to diverting water to the plantations. In this case, the general silence towards infrastructure is explained, in part, by the existing plantation infrastructure that was well established, and thus needed little maintenance. The silence can also be explained, in part, by the separation of jurisdictions between the companies who controlled the internal infrastructure of the plantations, and the government who controlled the infrastructure beyond the plantations, such as island-wide irrigation systems, airports, and major roads. Likewise, in the 1950s there was little oversight of the internal activities of the plantations. The state's Land Use Law was not passed until 1961, and federal environmental regulations would not be passed until the 1970s. Planning was not a civic activity and people outside of the corporate structures were not part of the process. Planning within the plantation spaces was largely done in-house and was controlled by the companies rather than the government or the people.

THE MAUI ECONOMIC DEVELOPMENT ASSOCIATION'S 1958 PLAN

The Maui Economic Development Association (hereinafter referred to as the Association) was created in 1957. As the *Maui News* noted, the organization was composed of "thirty-nine citizens voluntarily banding together for the purpose of stimulating new job opportunities" (*Maui News*, 12). The following year, the organization began work on a master plan and completed it in 1958. Written by Virginia Keyser, the document was typed and copied but not professionally published. At the same time, the Association printed and distributed a twenty-two-page booklet, designed like a slideshow that provided an outline of the plan.

Much could be written about the Association's 1958 plan. *The Maui Plan* is written as a hardship narrative that personifies Maui as a woman who requires greater exploitation in order to survive. Readers may notice the casual racism, including the claim that, "Those with an Oriental background in particular make excellent employees—intelligent, adaptable and loyal" (Keyser, 52). In addition, the proposed model for long-term development solves unemployment by increasing the population, which increases the number of people seeking employment and, though they fail to point this out, could thus increase the rate of unemployment. Finally, there is a failure to accurately predict the potential growth of tourism in Waikiki and elsewhere on the islands, which ballooned due to intense high-rise hotel development and the expansion of jet passenger travel. As a specific plan, the document has minimal value. As a political document that connects to the debates of the time, however, the plan is significant insofar as it establishes a sense of who were supposed to be involved in the decision-making process.

Of specific interest here is the political framing of the plan itself. The Association was quasi-governmental, much like the Committee of Safety had been during the 1893 overthrow of the Hawaiian Kingdom, and had acquired key planning and support roles in the overall transformation of Maui. The group was composed of powerful members of the community, who used their positions to direct Maui's future in ways that were consistent with their personal power and their visions of what a desirable future would look like. The Association's self-appointed roles included contacting potential investors, restoring Lahaina—which focused on slum clearance, rehabilitation, and the enforcement of building codes (Keyser, 101)—developing parks and recreation areas, and educating the citizens. A more detailed analysis of the membership and activities of the Association remains to be done. What is relevant here is how the Association created a single, authoritative voice describing Maui's goals. Ostensibly, the Association created the plan with the input of four groups: "private citizens," "business and professional people," "property owners," and "leaders of industry." There is no mention of Native Hawaiians or of any claims to land use based on historical ties to the land. There is no mention of who counts as a private citizen, or of the relative importance of private citizens compared to the other citizens or noncitizens who were given status in the plan. Thus, while there are periodic claims that the plan was created with widespread input, there is little evidence that the input was widespread, that it was equitable, or that it had an impact on the plan itself.

The authoritative tone of the document is in part formed by its description of the present and future as if they were objective facts. There are no uncertainties or controversies, and thus few real decisions. The document simply describes the situation and treats the plan as obvious. There is a good sandy beach in Kāʻanapali where the, "number of sunshiny days is high and the climate is superior even for Hawaii" (Keyser, 32). Likewise, "Lahaina presents the greatest potential for exploitation" (Keyser, 41). The question of whether a resort should be built in Kāʻanapali is not even addressed. It is simply a fact that there ought to be one. Whatever its claims to including input, the *1958 Plan*, published a year before statehood and several years after the start of the Democratic Revolution, essentially transcribes the worldview of the landowners, the businessmen, and the developers, as if their view was obvious and unchallengeable.

The *1958 Plan* is partly concerned with selling itself to people who had little or no input into its content or implementation. Thus, one of the responsibilities of the Association's Education and Public Relations Committee is the "Establishment of effective lines of communication to the public, to government officials, and to high level decision-making businessmen" (Keyser, 118). The quality of communication is not the same, and the connections with those who are less important is much more one way. For instance, one goal for the Human Resources Development Committee is "Indoctrinating new retired residents to Maui into some useful community participation" (Keyser, 111). The authoritarian voice that unfolds the plan is thus tied to a political strategy of salesmanship and indoctrination. In other words, it is an overall planning strategy in keeping with the plantation structures of the territorial period, where plans, if they are public at all, are presented as a given and promoted as a collective good, even if the true benefactors are the self-selected members of the Association and their peers.

AMFAC'S 1966 PLAN

In 1966, Amfac Properties published its *Master Plan for the Town of Lahaina Maui, Hawaii,* which was formally submitted by Adam Krivatsy, an employee in the firm of John Carl Warnecke and Associates, and sent to the Maui County Planning and Traffic Commission by Amfac president Robert Midkiff. While the *1958 Plan* focused on exploitation and saving Maui from her dire situation, the *1966 Plan* relied on creating a sense of benevolence in Amfac's relationship to the West Maui region. It can also be read as a veiled attempt to ensure Amfac's dominance over the process, but that goal is not explicit. Rather, the planning ought to be done, "in public and with community cooperation," and while it ought to respect "the plantation and the plantation's needs," (John Carl Warnecke and Associates, 1) the plantation is seen as a static entity that will neither profit from nor challenge the new development.

The plan periodically emphasizes that it ought to include broad public input. For instance, "It is everybody's interest that the community participate in the establishment of the planning goals and objectives. The Development Plan, which will be built upon these policy decisions and will reflect them, can only be successful if the greater majority of the Lahaina residents is behind the proposals" (John Carl Warnecke and Associates, 54). Likewise, "Not the planners, not the government agencies, but the people shape a community. Once a good plan has public support, Lahaina's future will be promising" (John Carl Warnecke and Associates, 99). The process, however, remains one where descriptions of the current situation and of the future are framed in such a way that public input is minimal, at best. Instead, the plan is framed by unquestioned goals, statistics, expert descriptions, and self-evident explanations of how the world works. Topics that are not open to public discourse include potential changes in the economy, in tourism, in employment, in population, and in locations of development. Likewise, future projections of everything from hotel rooms to income levels are used to forestall community decision-making, insofar as the projections have already dictated the decisions to be made.

It is worth noting that while these future projections are given as uncontestable facts, in hindsight they can be seen to be wildly incorrect. For instance, the number of visitors to Maui is projected to rise from 157,000 in 1965 to 525,000 in 1980. In fact, in 1980 there were almost 1.4 million visitors to Maui (State of Hawaii, 174). The objective tone of the plan precludes the reader to explore how the projections might be wrong or, more importantly, what might have been done differently to adjust the numbers, even if the projection would have been accurate had nothing been done. The whole frame of Amfac's plan, as with the Maui Economic Development Association's plan, is to indicate what has to be done, not to create a place to explore and debate alternatives.

In fact, so much about the region is presented in a self-evident and unchallengeable way, making it difficult to see how there could be any meaningful public input at all. The real input occurred prior to the plan, and it has all been formed into a single, monolithic voice. As noted in the introduction to the *1966 Plan*, the document, "reflects the concerted efforts of economists, planners, architects, engineers, marine geologists, landscape architects and many local residents" (John Carl Warnecke and Associates, iii). The local residents are one of many different inputs. Elsewhere, the document notes that the public good, itself, must be balanced by "the rights of the individual property owners and developers" (John Carl Warnecke and Associates, 83). Property owners and developers, in turn, do not have to be residents and may not even have to be citizens. The scope of public input, then, is highly proscribed, not only in the creation and expression of the plan, but also in the formation of Maui's future development. Experts and landowners dominate, just as they did in the plantation system.

Ultimately, Amfac dominates. Amfac's plan emphasizes that it is important to ensure that sugarcane production is not threatened by tourist development itself. Interestingly, the fact that Amfac owned the primary tourist resort in West Maui is not mentioned. Moreover, at no point in the document does Amfac, the major landowner in the region, admit to the profits it stands to make through the plan. Amfac's plan, in other words, is an attempt to maintain the oligarchic economic and political system, even as it recognizes the need to carve out some space for tourism as a new part of that system. Amfac is both positioned to dominate tourism in the region and has situated itself as deserving of compensation for any loss of sugarcane land. Whether the economic activity is in terms of sugarcane or tourism, the plan ensures that Amfac will command the field.

THE PIVOT TO TOURISM

It was against the oligarchic economic system centered on the Big Five that the so-called Democratic Revolution began in the mid- to late-1950s. In basic outline: Japanese Americans returning from the battlefields of World War II joined forces with emerging unions and external industrialists to take control of state and local government. At the same time, there was a significant pivot in the economic priorities of the territory and, as of 1959, the state. The traditional plantations, focusing on sugarcane and pineapple, were in decline and, by the early 1960s, tourism was quickly expanding.

On Oʻahu, the development of the tourism industry did not supplant the plantation system, at least in terms of immediate land use. Waikīkī, which had not played a significant role in the plantation system, was developed as a physically separate area of economic activity. Waikīkī had already been a tourist area, although on a much smaller scale and combined with residential and agricultural uses. With the rise of mass tourism, the primary changes on Oʻahu were in land use in the Waikīkī and airport areas, and in governmental priorities, including laws and public funding. Where once the primary way to reach Hawaiʻi was by cruise liner, airplanes began to dominate travel in the 1950s, especially with the advent of the commercial jet airliners that became commonplace by 1960. By the early 1950s, Trans-Pacific Airlines, later called Aloha Airlines, was regularly flying between the islands. In 1950, the company had created a family fare plan to encourage neighbor island flights. By the middle of the 1960s, traveling between and within the islands had become so convenient that the economic threat of a circle tour was recognized, where visitors travelled so quickly that their economic impact in any particular place was negligible. Day trips were no longer profitable. The practices and scale of economic activity were much greater. Tourism was no longer about offering lunch, some gasoline, or a tour guide to small groups, as was the case when tourism was dominated by rich travelers before the Second World War. The middle class belonged to a system of mass consumption tourism and needed to be encouraged, if not required, to consume throughout their travels.

Greater urban engineering was necessary. Infrastructure was needed that existed beyond the areas directly controlled by the hotels. At the Honolulu Airport, a new terminal was built in 1962 and an expansion program ran from 1970 to 1978. Many hotels were being built during this time, primarily in Waikīkī. The first hotel in the Hilton complex opened in 1955, the Outrigger Waikīkī opened in 1967, and the Sheraton Waikīkī opened in 1971. The state and county planning focused on the development of Waikīkī, in part due to the increasing influence of land developer and industrialist Henry Kaiser, and on a few outlying tourist destinations, such as the Polynesian Cultural Center, which opened in 1963. There was a corresponding effort to promote Waikīkī as a travel destination, specifically to potential off-island, middle-class tourists, initially from the United States and Canada. Creating tourism depended in part on creating Hawai'i as a modern state with standardized regulations, transportation systems, rules governing such things as car rentals and taxis, and construction and labor standards. Creating the tourist economy, in other words, depended to a large degree on creating a North American-style exotic space that could accommodate large numbers of visitors.

While the creation of a tourism economy focused on the areas around Waikīkī and the Honolulu airport, derivative discussions and economic developments were also occurring in places throughout the state. Tourism development in Maui occurred later and was typically expressed in ways where Honolulu remained the hub of the system. Some people argued that tourism development should remain focused on Waikīkī, with certain high-interest areas in the outer islands, such as Volcanoes National Park on the Big Island, included in the strategy as short-term destinations. Maui would then be positioned as a destination for short trips, such as to historic Lahaina, the Haleakalā volcano, or Hāna.

Other groups, including Amfac, argued that Maui ought to develop as a tourism location in its own right. One location designated as a place to pivot to longer-term tourism was West Maui and the area north of Lahaina in particular. The first phase of the Kā'anapali resort area opened in 1961. At the same time, Lahaina was imagined as an historic district, which included the downtown area being designated as a federal National Historic Landmark in 1962. Where the National Park at Haleakalā offered tourists an experience of nature, Lahaina offered tourists an experience of a past. At the same time, other parts of the region were developed into resorts. In December 1962, the Royal Lahaina Beach Hotel, which included an 18-hole golf course, was dedicated. In January 1963, *The Maui News* celebrated the opening of the Sheraton's $4 million resort in Kā'anapali as the first hotel in the outer islands owned by a national chain (*Maui News*, 2013).

That the first closed, self-contained resort in Hawai'i was created in Kā'anapali has much to do with the development of tourism on O'ahu and the ability to move that model, refined to be a closed system, to an even more completely controlled and isolated plantation property. A development project like the Kā'anapali resort would have been very difficult to undertake on O'ahu at the time because land ownership and governance, while dominated by an oligarchic system, was still too fragmented to allow resort-level development. Henry Kaiser purchased eight acres in Waikīkī for

$3.5 million in 1954 to build the Kaiser, later called the Hilton, Hawaiian Village. He had purchased an existing hotel development that first opened in the 1920s, which itself had replaced vacation cottages. In West Maui, on the other hand, Amfac controlled a huge portion of the region and could plan changes with little concern for other landowners or stakeholders. The Kāʻanapali Resort area, for instance, was built on a two thousand-acre site, most of which had earlier been tied to the plantation system. The entire development plan and execution depended on a single large-scale landowner who could control the process from start to finish. Thus, Amfac's development of Kāʻanapali, as with the framing of its *1966 Plan*, would only be viable at a time when the statewide economic goals (and laws and regulations) were pivoting to tourism, and when the control of land and political discourse in the neighbor islands was still based on a plantation style system with little or no civic engagement.

THE 1968 PLAN

In the 1960s, the expectations of political engagement changed as the closed structures of the plantation system were transformed in Hawaiʻi. State and local governments became more important in creating and maintaining the economic infrastructure, and the population was becoming a greater player in political discussions. It is in this context that the 1968 *A General Plan for the Lahaina District* was produced. The *1968 Plan* was written for the recently-created Maui County Planning Commission by Hiroshi Kasamoto, along with Muroda and Tanaka, Inc. This was not a private planning document, nor one created by a private economic group; it was intended for public distribution and designed in part to encourage public debate.

The final report was written by Anthony Hodges, who would later become the executive director of Life of the Land, one of the groups trying to create a more locally focused sense of planning (Nakaso). In 1972, the *Maui News* noted that Hodges fought against plans for development in Wailuku-Kahului (10/7/1972, A5) and argued that the island's population should be limited (9/4/1971, A2). Along the same lines, in the early 1960s, Kasamoto had been Hawaiʻi County Planning Director and, according to Cooper and Daws in *Land and Power in Hawaiʻi*, "wanted to control development and stop speculation" (Cooper and Daws, 260). The goal for the *1968 Plan*, as will be explored, was as much about using government to help manage poorly planned development as it was an actual plan for developing the region. Government, particularly the local government, was positioned as an integral player in the creation of the physical and social order. Companies may still be responsible for much of the organization that occurs within their own resorts, but people were placed in a better position to challenge some development. The government was more concerned with the infrastructure, overall appearances, building codes, and permissions.

In contrast to the *1966 Plan*, the *1968 Plan* acknowledges that sugarcane and pineapple will experience increased international competition. However, there is no mention of the possibility that plantations will close or lose their dominance, nor that the land controlled by those corporations will convert to tourist-based development. Rather, in a somewhat evasive way, the *1968 Plan* recommends that the government should, "assist them in the future to maintain a viable position relative to the increasingly competitive mainland and foreign markets" (Hodges, 2). The remainder of the plan offers no specific ways to help the plantations, which encourages the reader, at least by implication, to imagine the end of the plantation system: "Is the Lahaina District as good a place to grow sugar and pineapple as it was five years ago? Will it be better or worse five years from today?" (Hodges, 18) The plan asks the same, open question about tourism, but the emphasis of the remainder of the plan is on developing the region for tourism, not on enhancing agriculture. The shift is implied. The real question is how best to plan in a way that creates the best outcomes for landowners if the plantations retract or close and the plantation order disintegrates.

Unlike speculative or private real estate development, planning in a plantation system tends towards long-term stability of land, people, and governance. The idea that the society needed to, "control development and stop speculation," would have seemed redundant because the plantation system was based on stability. A plantation system is not organized for short-term exploitation—the investment in infrastructure and the possibilities for long-term profit are too important. Land development, on the other hand, especially at the point where the infrastructure is being created out of the remnants of the prior plantation system, depends less on stability and more on the flexible and intense changes in land and people to increase short-term profits. Hotels and resorts may want stability after they are built, but developers operate within a different time frame, typically wanting to keep the amount of land available for development at a moderately low level to increase prices, but also to develop that land as quickly as possible with minimal cost or concern for externalities. The *1968 Plan* arose, then, partly as a response to the problems and opportunities created by the imminent change in Maui's primary economic activity, from agriculture to tourism, a change that threatened to bring unwanted instability, profiteering, and poorly conceived development.

The *1968 Plan* was not written for a corporate audience. It was written for the community. The region had been dominated by a single plantation company for almost a century, creating a situation where the ideals of an open or effective democratic system, including public discourse and representative government, did not exist. West Maui was a company town, run like any other company town, where corporate power and submission to the company were more important than expertise or obtaining public input. In the conditions created by the plantation system, the 1968 planning document can be positioned as a rejection of the plantation's closed political and economic system through a twofold, if oblique, viewpoint. On the one hand, the plan appeals to the expertise of the city planner. On the other hand, it appeals to the value of public discourse. It is not simply, as *The Maui News* would have it, that newspapers ought to be the source of information, "in the Interests of the People," which are likely to be depicted as coinciding with the narrow interests of those who own the newspapers. Rather, according to the *1968 Plan*, the public-at-large ought to become engaged in public discourse (Hodges, 19). The plan advocates that the region ought to contribute to cultural and personal growth: "this is a plan for people," (13) and it is the people, rather than land development, who ought to be served (14). In these terms, the *1968 Plan* is a document of civic empowerment.

> If the County of Maui does not act now to secure for its people their rights to keep an environment which is as good as or better than that which they now have, then no matter what type or amount of employment, no matter what type or how many new people or how many dollars the development of the District may bring, the County will have failed those who now support it with taxes. (14)

The *1968 Plan* is as much an attempt to create a desire for planning in the residents, or those who pay taxes, as it is an attempt to offer a plan. It was a desire, in some way, to create a sense of community that could play an effective political role in discussing the future. With the rise of tourism and the decline of plantations, different futures had become possible. The first step was to create political conversations of any kind. West Maui needed to develop the necessary political culture, which, for the *1968 Plan*, involved creating a structure that connected experts, residents, public decision-making authorities, and land owners.

The Expert

As with prior plans for post-plantation West Maui, the expert is a central figure of the 1968 planning process. Future planning in the West Maui region, for instance, ought to be based on a "comprehensive inventory of all vistas, micro-environments, topographic and landscape elements, historic structures or sites and other points of interest that might potentially be protected, enhanced, created or preserved by the establishment of an appropriate scenic road corridor." Likewise, there should be design review boards that focus on "special treatment districts," such as Lahaina, which has a historical charm that should be preserved as part of the general environment of the region. While creating a space for public discourse, however, the *1968 Plan* does not advocate for the spread of democracy. Rather, the plan imagines a political landscape that is dominated by planning itself, with public input being only part of the process.

In terms of urban design, the *1968 Plan* spends considerable time discussing generalized aesthetic principles, or what are referred to as "landscape controls" (Hodges, 28), for modern roads more so than it does discussing road construction and where to locate public facilities. Signage (both temporary and permanent), guard rails, fences, overhead utility wires, lighting, and landscaping along the side of the road, are all considered. Roads are not simply about moving people and commodities from one place to another, they have become part of the lived space. One goal of the plan is to establish guidelines to ensure that the roads create an enhanced experience for the driver, who is assumed to be sitting fifty-two inches above the road grade and for someone on a bus, who would be 112 inches above the road grade, without affecting the experiences of the people who are not using the roads. The roads should be organized around *meander lines* that include the slope areas and points of interest that are organized to create a "visual corridor" (Hodges, 28). The document likewise considers the use of trees, the best kinds of lighting, and sign controls. One recommendation is for the County of Maui to give "serious consideration to the eventual use of international signs on all of the public roads" (Hodges, 30), a suggestion that is notable insofar as it connects the local plans to global practices. Taken together, these suggestions move many of the planning discussions away from political discourse and into a list of professional statements of how things ought to be done. At least in these areas, expert knowledge dominates the discussion while other political groups are left to either accept the professional advice or create a landscape by making bad decisions.

The larger issue, however, is the conflict between private desires to exploit land and the public interest in the quality of the lived environment. One solution to the dangers of greed in land development is for special assessment districts to be created to help pay for infrastructure projects, such as utilities and sewage. Another is to set up a system of positive controls that encourage developers to maintain public sight lines to scenic areas such as beaches and vistas (Hodges, 24). The focus throughout the plan is on what might now be called sustainability. The report notes, "growth of the district will come, and it is encouraged, but not at the expense of the environment on which that growth ultimately depends. Instead, growth of the district is encouraged only so long as it improves—not simply maintains—the quality of life that residents can have there" (Hodges, 19). The appeal to the quality of life, which is something that the experts would measure, was first raised in the introductory section of the plan, where one goal is to "encourage landowners—both large and small—to coordinate development efforts among themselves and with the government, in order to provide the community maximum benefits—not only in terms of economic gains, but relative also to the securing of a fuller and more satisfying life" (Hodges, 3). The vision here is distinct from the political structures of the plantation system. The fact that the plan even includes a discussion about community members' quality of life shifts the terms of reference away from plantation production, which would only be concerned with meeting basic needs, or, in the case of the *1958 Plan*, employment. People lived in communities in the plantation system, but their quality of life was not a central concern for planning. In the late 1960s, on the other hand, the residents became an important part of the overall structure, in part because tourism labor was understood to be local and somewhat intransient. If this is true, then the focus on the category of residents may be a way to emphasize the importance of those who have lived in the region because, it is assumed, they are the ones who will continue to live in the area and should be protected from development plans that are only designed to appeal to tourists and increase the profits of land developers. The plan thus expands whose input should be included, and how it should be included. Experts, however, still create the agenda and the terms of discourse prior to the public joining the conversation.

Residents

While there are constant references to residents, there is a general lack of a concern for an active citizenry. In the cover letter, Muroda and Kasamoto write that "this book, and process of thinking to which it might introduce you, will better enable you to know where your real alternatives for action lie—and where, on the other hand, they are not to be found" (Hodges, 2). Their hope, however, does not extend to political engagement and remains focused on expressing personal preferences. The residents are not experts, they are more like consumers who are offered different products and allowed to provide feedback so that the experts and developers can make better decisions. There is no discussion of voting. Residents have opinions, but they have no civic function. In fact, while the *1968 Plan* includes a discussion of the role of government agencies such as the public approval authority, there is no concern for the state legislature or other elected officials. Rather, the system is based on a local corporatist structure that separates landowners from planning experts, and urges that surveying the preferences of residents is crucial to deciding which types of development to pursue.

The calls for residents to become actively engaged exist alongside a system where active engagement is highly circumscribed. The plan does not call for citizens to participate in their government to establish legitimate rulers. Rather, the plan calls for residents to be consulted, or, more accurately, the plan assumes that the process wants the residents to participate and calls on them to become actively engaged. The reader ought to be "involved in the planning for your region which is, after all, your home" (Hodges, 2). The idea of home, which is not found in the other plans, is not necessarily tied to land ownership, but it is based on the capacity to reside in the region, which has nothing to do with citizenship, civic engagement, or historical connections. The *1968 Plan* does not consider who counts as residents, which means that the foundational participants in the process are unknown, especially given the imminent dissolution of the plantation-based sugarcane communities and the corresponding rise of the resort and vacation system. The concept of resident becomes less clear with the rise of seasonal occupants in the area, the rise of Kīhei as a separate tourist destination, and the displacement of workers in the tourism industry to places beyond West Maui. Neither homeowners nor workers are obviously residents. If workers, tourists, and landowners come into West Maui from the outside, who is left to reside there? And if there are no residents, then what happens to political discourse, however narrowly understood? That is, even as it hailed residents as a fixture of West Maui's planning horizons, the plan is empty of any commitment to the actual people living there.

Just as the *1968 Plan* is based on an account of political membership disconnected from civic engagement, the plan is also based on an account of membership that obscures any connection to the past, which has implications for the status and rights of Native Hawaiians. There is no discussion of such things as sacred places, ancestral bones, or disputed land titles. In fact, Native Hawaiians are not mentioned in the document at all. At best, some of the Native historical sites are deemed relevant, so long as they have a present value to the tourist economy. Even then, the focus of the historical preservation is on Lahaina's brief whaling period. The exclusion of Native Hawaiians is an example of the plan's general tendency to constitute the political space of West Maui by dissolving any but those with the most immediate ties to the region. Belonging is flattened to a technical designation, but one in which people are easily disenfranchised. People who own land in the region are included in the process, while at the same time people who work in the region but live elsewhere are not. Even former plantation workers would have no stake in the community if they ever move away. The criteria for belonging, under the plan, are satisfied whether the landowner arrived months ago or was part of a worker's family that had lived on the plantation for generations.

Public Approving Authorities

For all of its advocacy for community involvement through government, the *1968 Plan* makes almost no reference to governmental power separate from corporate power, with the exception of the public approval authority and some unnamed departments, agencies, and commissions (Hodges, 17, 22). At one point, there is recognition that the current situation in West Maui could be understood in political terms, but this is only mentioned once, and only as part of a list that also includes economic, aesthetic, and social perspectives (Hodges, 16). The narrative is dominated by the passive voice, by technocratic questions, and by unnamed or abstracted actors. The county, and other levels of government, are referenced and at one point there is a call for popular participation, for the public-at-large to be part of the process. The author writes:

> Quality—whether it be quality of life or quality of environment—is a
> question of value. Hence, the first proposals are concerned primarily with
> creating an atmosphere in which the community's real sense of value

can be elicited, nurtured and grown. Only in this way can it be decided
what type of development, what type of government, what type of a
life is desired—and, moreover what type of each of these things can be
had. There is only one way to find these things out for sure: Get people
involved (19).

The details of the text here are important. The author is not saying that the
public can decide what happens, but only that public involvement (presum-
ably through polling, interviews, or forums) is necessary for a decision to be
well-made. The planning structure is thus obscured through a passive voice
where the transition from plantations to tourism is decided through a process
where input from residents at specific points in the process suffices for political engagement.

Land Owners

Experts, residents, and approving authorities have wrestled with how the process is still dominated by land owners, who are able to set the agenda even
if other groups may be able to guide the decisions in some minimal ways.
Even experts need to convince those in power, although different audiences
will be convinced by different reasons. At times, the plan reads like a missive
to an abstracted king, hoping to supplicate him into granting a more open
and reasonable development plan. The authors write, for instance, of the wisdom of Amfac and Alexander and Baldwin, who have decided to "develop
at a moderate to low density, since this will protect the quality of the district's environment" (Hodges, 17). The thoughtfulness and benevolence of
the large-scale landowners is contrasted with the impatience and greed of the
developers (Hodges, 9), who are trying to "max out" the development sites.
The latter are said to lack both civic virtue and reasoned plans. In passages
such as these, the *1968 Plan* supports the plantation companies, and the slow,
internal deliberative processes of a plantation industry, against the incursion
of external, impatient development that has no ties to the community.

The obscure status of the landowners further obscures whether the planning system allows for a proactive citizenry to shape the landscape, or whether
the landowners remain the dominant force for determining the future of the
region. In the *1958 Plan*, there is no pretense for widespread input. In the *1968
Plan*, there is some space created for input, but the agenda is set by those who
own the land, whose potential greed creates a constant pressure towards deca-
dence and poor decisions. While the experts and the residents ought to warn

public decision-making authorities, the empowerment recommended by the *1968 Plan* does not challenge the basic power structures or development discourse and, by failing to offer a grounded account of who the residents are, and how they might have more significant connections to the land than mere residing, the plan undermines the potential for real political dialog, even if the tone of the document differs significantly from the authoritarian tone of the *1958 Plan*.

CONCLUSION

While *A General Plan for the Lahaina District* is ostensibly an infrastructure development plan, it also offers a political vision that purports to empower the residents of West Maui in ways that were unavailable in the oligarchic, plantation system that had been in existence for almost a century. Land developers, public approving authorities, residents and planning experts are all located in a political system where planning ought to be public and ought to take into account the overall quality of life in the region. However, the plan does not advocate changing the power relations themselves. If anything, the power of the primary landowners is reinforced because they exist outside of the public political process. The plantation system is not the problem, speculative development is.

The goal of the plan is thus to moderate the excesses of development by creating a space where residents can provide input. That input, however, is likewise limited—people are not able to assert political rights, but may offer suggestions in an attempt to influence either the landowner or the government. In these terms, the plan reasserts the stability of the plantation system, with moderate economic developments and a minimal concern for workers. Appeals to the opinions of residents and the quality of life in the community, in other words, become useful ways of countering speculative development to ensure that the "wise" development undertaken by the old plantation companies, such as Amfac and Alexander and Baldwin, can be used to rework the plantation fields into resorts, golf courses, and other places for tourists. The plan does not need civic engagement, it needs public input as a way to temper the chaos created by greedy, shortsighted developers. As with the plantation system, it is still up to the large-scale landowners and the experts to ultimately decide what the plan is. Thus, while the *1968 Plan* ostensibly frames the discussion of development in terms very different than the 1957 and 1966 plans, there is very little practical difference between them. While the first focuses on the necessary exploitation of the island, the second focuses on the benevolence of the plantation company, and the third focuses on the value of community empowerment, the results are not very different. The plantation remains the dominant force and the same groups, including workers and Native Hawaiians, are marginalized from the process, even while the residents are asked for their input.

WORKS CITED

Callies, David. (2010). *Regulating Paradise : Land use controls in Hawai'i* (2nd ed.). Honolulu: University of Hawai'i Press.

Center for Oral History (2003). *Pioneer Mill Company: A Maui Sugar Plantation Legacy.* Social Science Research Institute, University of Hawai'i at Mānoa.

Cooper, George and Gavan Daws. (1990) *Land and Power in Hawaii: The Democratic Years.* Honolulu: University of Hawaii Press.

Department of Public Works, Territory of Hawaii (1953). *Annual Report to the Governor.* Honolulu, Hawaii: Territory of Hawaii.

Hodges, Anthony. (1968). *A General Plan for the Lahaina District.* Wailuku, Maui: Maui County Planning Commission.

John Carl Warnecke and Associates. (1966) *Master Plan for the Town of Lahaina Maui, Hawaii.* Honolulu, Hawaii.

Kent, Noel. (1993). *Hawaii: Islands Under the Influence.* Honolulu: University of Hawai'i Press.

Keyser, Virginia. (1958). *A Perspective on the Economic Development of the island of Maui.* Honolulu, Hawaii: Child & Waters, Inc.

Maui Economic Development Association (1958). *The Maui Plan.* Wailuku, Hawaii.

Maui News. "MEDA Commended for Promotional Progress." *Maui News* (Wailuki, HI), April 24, 1957.

———. "Hodges Suggests Population Limit." *Maui News*, September 4, 1971, A2.

———. "Battle Lines Drawn Over Wai-Kahu Plans." *Maui News.* October 7, 1972, A5.

———. "50 years for Sheraton Maui." *Maui News* (Wailuku, HI), January 24, 2013. http://www.mauinews.com/page/content.detail/id/569192/50-years-for-Shera-ton-Maui.html.

Nakaso, Dan. "Tony Hodges." *The Honolulu Advertiser* (Honolulu, HI), August 16, 2009. http://the.honoluluadvertiser.com/article/2009/Aug/16/ln/hawaii908160329.html.

State of Hawaii (1981). *The State of Hawaii Data Book 1981: A Statistical Abstract.* Honolulu, Hawaii: Department of Planning and Economic Development.

SIX THESES ON THE PROBLEM OF GENTLEMEN'S ESTATES IN WEST MAUI

Bianca Isaki

INTRODUCTION

This chapter interrogates the conventional logic governing the problem of gentlemen's estates.[1] They are fake farms, elitist spatial practices, gendered organizations of labor and property, and vehicles of gentrification, but they are also emblematic of the "institutional incorporation of [Hawaiian] lands into/as the domestic space of [the U.S. for people] who recreate this space as home through that ongoing imperial (re)production of nation-making, the settler state[.]"[2] Key to this last point is interrogation of settler home-making and settler sexualities that are key to the reproduction of disrepaired structures of relating to West Maui's land, farming, and food.

I take an oblique view on gentlemen's estates by asking what they are, how they might actually fit with criteria that permeates state discussions of land use, and how the ways they are problematized are anyway defective for decolonization. This vantage on *the problem* of gentlemen's estates also emphasizes the problem as one of Native sovereignty, but not only of a sovereign power to dispel the disempowerment associated with an inability to feed oneself, a nation, a community, or a people (although sovereignty must also entail that ability). Part I offers an overview of what is identified as gentlemen's estates in West Maui. Part II outlines the conventional formulations of gentlemen's estates as a problem. Part III enumerates six theses on the problem of gentlemen's estates.

Signs outside of a gated community in Kaua'ula, West Maui. Courtesy of Jonathan Scheuer.

Part I: Overview of West Maui gentlemen's estates

Historically, the "gentlemen's estate" referred to the manor houses of British landed gentry, and in the U.S., homes like Jefferson's Monticello. Maui Realtor Association's David DeLeon noted the term "gentlemen's estate" was taken up in Maui as a way of identifying hobbyist farmers who gentrified agricultural lands, raising their values beyond a level at which farming could be feasible.[3] In today's West Maui, the usual referent is a gaudy luxury mansion with attached swimming pool on a handful of acres of agricultural lands.

To conform with agriculturally zoned district requirements, gentlemen's estates are nominally considered "farm dwellings" and conduct agricultural activity. The effort to flout the intention and purpose of laws governing agricultural land uses has resulted in claims that multimillion dollar mansions replete with pools are "farm dwellings," and sod-farming is an "agricultural activity." In Launiupoko, for example, the 454 Wailau Place "farm dwelling" comes with a pizza oven, a golf cart, a Tesla car, and a Vantage home fire suppression unit. At a recent state Water Commission meeting, an attorney for Steve Strombeck, a homeowners in Makila Plantations, described Strombeck as a "sod farmer" who had hired two or three local workers.[4] Strombeck's five-acre "sod farm" has an assessed value of $3,299,500, and is a short term rental with a pool, according to the county property tax database.

Between 1997–2006, 2,600 acres were removed from the Maui county agricultural district.[5] Thousands of the remaining acreage are slated for development of market rate agricultural lots and more densely-developed affordable housing. In 2005, the majority of agricultural subdivisions or condominium lots under development were on Maui.[6] Agricultural subdivisions in Pu'unoa, Launiupoko, and Ukumehame were specifically derided for having little to do with agriculture and were challenged for violations of state land use law.[7]

Maui's agricultural zoning ordinance is codified at Maui County Code (MCC) Chapter 19.30A, which provides that the maximum developable area of a lot is ten percent of the total lot area and the minimum area of a lot of two acres.[8] MCC §19.30A.050.B(10) provides for accessory uses, including short term rentals with an approved farming plan. However, Maui's short term rental ordinance was not enacted until 2012, so TVRs operating prior to that time were eligible to be grandfathered under the new law.

Gentlemen's estates are primarily located in mauka agricultural lands of Kapalua, Kā'anapali, Launiupoko, Kaua'ula, Kahoma, and Olowalu. The white areas in Figure 1 indicate lands zoned for agriculture by the state Land Use Commission (LUC).[9] The county left Lahaina as "interim zoned," and therefore there are no lands zoned agricultural under county ordinances in West Maui.

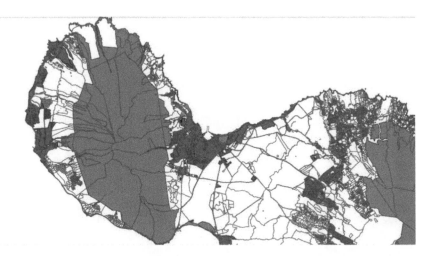

State of Hawai'i Land Use District Boundary map, Maui. Map layers from Land Use Commission, State Land Use Boundary Amendment Map (accessed Sep. 4, 2017) available at: http://files.hawaii.gov/luc/maps/maui_slud_2012.pdf.

West Maui Land Company is responsible for much of the development in West Maui on 4,500 acres from Kahoma through Olowalu. In 2001, Makila Land Company, which is a subsidiary of West Maui Land Company, bought about 4,500 acres between Lahaina and Olowalu from former sugar plantation, the Pioneer Mill Company.

Many West Maui Land Company developments are planned for lands south of Lahaina town. The agriculturally zoned home sites in Launiupoko begin at two acres, and the gated Puʻunoa Estates community at five acres. These developments include: Mahanalua Nui (also known as Launiupoko), Puʻunoa, Makila Plantation, Makila Ridge, and Makila Nui, and Olowalu Makai/Mauka (completed projects) and Kahoma Residential, Makila Rural, and Olowalu Town (in process).[10]

To the north, Kapalua Plantation Estates includes "Billionaire's Row" of mansions, also on lands zoned for agriculture. In Kapalua Mauka, the Mahana Estates consist of "luxury homes on sites ranging from .64 to 4.3 acres" situated between the Plantation golf course and Village walking trails. "The views are spectacular."[11] Nearby, the Kapalua Plantation Estates on agricultural lands in Kapalua surround the PGA Tour Plantation golf course and "command some of Maui's highest prices."[12] Currently, only two transient

Puʻunoa Estates, a gated community in Kauaʻula, West Maui. Courtesy of Jonathan Scheuer.

vacation rentals are advertised for Kapalua agricultural lands. Karen Mayuiers claimed to have the only TVR permit for a TVR in Kapalua Plantation Estates at an average of $2,286 per night.[13] However, Beachfront Avalon by the Sea is also operating in this area at an average of $2,595 per night.[14]

The "fake farms" problem of gentlemen's estates is readily apparent in the many luxury vacation home rentals existing and planned for the mauka agricultural lands of Kaua'ula and Launiupoko. Brief review of transient vacation rental (TVR) advertising sites showed at least nine vacation rental properties on State Land Use District (SLUD) agricultural lands in Kaua'ula alone.[15] Currently, only two transient vacation rentals are advertised for Kapalua agricultural lands.[16]

Further, many real property owners of parcels in Kaua'ula and Launiupoko agricultural subdivisions are entities and individuals who do not have addresses in West Maui. Maui communities suffer from these islands of capital accumulation within their agricultural lands.

From 2008–2015, home sales on Maui to nonresidents outnumbered sales to residents, 51.7 percent to 48.3 percent.[17] For West Maui, nonresident sales compared to resident were 72 percent to 28 percent.[18] The average price of homes sold to local residents was $761,280, as opposed to $1,804,155 for foreign buyers, and $1,184,414 for U.S. continental buyers.[19] Maui communities suffer from these islands of capital accumulation within their agricultural lands. Many real property owners of parcels in Kaua'ula and Launiupoko agricultural subdivisions are entities and individuals who do not have addresses in West Maui. Such absentee ownership has been problematized as

Table 1. Airbnb TVRs in Kaua'ula, West Maui

TVR NAME	SIZE	PRICE/NIGHT	KAUA'ULA LOCATION
Maui Life	4 bds	$349	N. Lauhoe Pl.
Paradise Plantation Hawai'i	4 bds	$839	Makila reservoir/ S. Lauhoe
Sunset oasis	3 bds	$545	Kai Hele Ku St
Luxury Maui Home	4 bds	$680	Pa'ia Pohaku St.
Pohaku Beauty	4 bds	$795	Pa'ia Pohaku St.
Your Private Oasis	8 bds	$1,800	Kawaiku St.
Hale Makoa Kai Estate	4 bds	$1,973	Haniu St.
Paradise Cabana	4 bds	$1,400	Wailau Pl.
Maui Sunset	6 bds	$650	———

Source: AirBnb website (accessed Sep. 1, 2017).

Table 2. Owners of Kaua'ula and Launiupoko agricultural lots

ADDRESS	OWNER	OWNER LOCATION	VALUE	ACREAGE
454 Wailau Pl.	WoweeMaui, LLC	Connecticut	$6.4m	27.76
0 Launiupoko St.	WoweeMaui, LLC	Connecticut	$1.82m (no bldg.)	25.019
0 Launiupoko St.	Bianco Revocable Trust	Washington	$1.68 (no bldg.)	25.868
0 Launiupoko St.	Wild West Condo.	Kīhei	$2,900	29.233
0 Launiupoko St.	Makila Heights Condo	Kihei	$100	27.341
0 Launiupoko St.	Sanford & Irma Katz Trust Everett Lewis	California	$1.69m (no bldg.)	26.416
64 'Iliahi Way	Farren Family Trust	Texas	$1.2m	62.75
325 Hokiokio Pl.	Douglas Salisbury	Lahaina	$2.74m	5.14
0 Hokiokio Pl.	Ann Perrick	California	$0.986m	11.061
0 Mele Komo	J. Todd Erickson	Vancouver	$0.217m	5.008
0 Mele Komo	Barnes Family Trust	Canada	$1.08m	5.025
0 Mele Komo	Rosendo Valenzuela	California	$1.0765m	5.007
36 Wili Okai Way	Richard Siler	Washington	$1.06m (no bldg.)	5.584
65 Wili Okai Way	Cirrus Family Trust	Lahaina	$4.169m	5.114
55 N Lauhoe Pl.	Strombeck Family Trust	California	$4.74m	5.033
24 S Lauhoe Pl.	Lot 2 Makila Plantation	California	$3.07m (bldg.)	5.821
431 Punakea Lp.	Phase III, Condo Kenneth & Michelle Moore Trust	Pukalani	$2,600	26.477
0 Punakea Lp.	Aloha Plantation Condo Wallis Family Trust	Washington	$1.86 (no bldg.)	15.47
0 Punakea Lp.	Kenneth McPhee Trust	California	$100	12.96
225 Punakea Lp.	James Ward	Toronto	$1.55 (no bldg.)	15.656
67 Punakea Lp.	Mary Whitney	Lahaina	$1.06m (bldg.)	12.953
0 Hainu St.	3SFF Family Trust	Lahaina	$2.17m (bldg.)	15.15
0 Hainu St.	James & Maria Kato Trust	Wyoming	$1.53m	15.164
80 Hainu St.	Donald Johnson	California	$0.60m	15.497
60 Hainu St.	4 Too Many Family Trust Sunset Winds Condo	Lahaina	$0.754 (bldg.)	15.931
0 Hainu St.	Gregory Howeth	Lahaina		
70 Wai Kulu Pl.	Coconut Farm Condo		$2.729 (bldg.)	16.193
	Richard Hoehn	Washington	$1.538 (no bldg.)	15.226
80 Wai Kulu Pl.	Kalaheo Condo	Vancouver BC	$100	5.059
79 Wai Kulu Pl.	LeBruns LLC	Lahaina	$.802	310,548 sf
88 Hainu Pl.	Blue Makai Condo	Lahaina	$100	3.793
25 Hainu Pl.		Kīhei	$1.917 (bldg.)	16.905
91 Hainu St.		Lahaina	$100	16.055
147 Haniu St.		California	$5.293 (bldg.)	16.21
———		Lahaina	$100	19.21

Source: Maui Real Property Database (accessed Aug. 2, 2017).

a "freedom from the duty to contribute to daily life and the perpetuation of the community."[20] West Maui suffers from these islands of capital accumulation that do not reinvest in them. When people express their desire to control lands apart from obligations to the communities who also live there, they express imperial desires.

PART II: CONVENTIONAL APPROACHES TO THE PROBLEM OF GENTLEMEN'S ESTATES.

Gentlemen's estates occupy lands that were legally zoned for agriculture. These lands were so zoned to implement a state scheme under which Hawai'i could become less dependent on US continental markets, exploitative food production practices conducted "elsewhere," and Matson freight shipping. Rapidly rising prices and overwhelming demand for more affordable homes in Hawai'i created pressure to develop houses on agricultural lands. This is partly because it is generally quicker and less costly to subdivide agricultural lands for residential use. So-called "Farm dwellings" have included luxury mansions and vacation rentals that drive up the price of other farmland that becomes cost-prohibitive for bona fide farmers. Further, many agricultural developments have been excused from traditional housing developer fees that help finance public facilities, such as schools, parks, and roads.[21] As with transient vacation rentals and other gentrification processes, development of gentlemen's estates increases land values, property taxes, and the cost of land around it.

Hawai'i Land Use regulations

Since it was enacted in 1961, Hawaii's land use law has expanded permissible uses of agricultural districts to include sixteen uses, including hydroelectric facilities, retail food operations, and wind farms.[22] Counties are required to enforce the state land use law, including a duty to investigate subdivision proposals that "will in all likelihood not be used for agricultural purposes and may be an attempted circumvention of the land use district amendment procedure and controls" on "prime agricultural land."[23] This provision indicates the argument that much of Hawaii's agricultural lands are not "prime agricultural land" and may not be suitable for agriculture at all. The Lahaina District contains approximately 31,373 acres of conservation, 24,381 acres of agricultural, 271 acres of rural, and 5,257 acres of urban SLU lands. Of the 5,257 acres of urban lands, 2,149 acres of that land has an improved valued of over $100,000 per acre.[24]

The county's agricultural zoning envisioned that agricultural lots would be used by yeomen farmers who would actually grow crops or animals on them and maintain a pastoral lifestyle.[25] The rift between concept and reality has been identified in the fact that "real farmers" cannot afford to buy and maintain a "farm" on two-acre lots that go well over $180,000.[26]

For much of the 1980s and 90s, Maui County remained frustrated by the obvious disconnect between that agricultural zoning concept and the result, which became known as "gentlemen's estates." This term did not grow out of a historical reference to landed gentry, but rather that a new phenomenon of hobbyist farmers on agricultural plots amounted to a sort of gentrification of rural Maui.[27] The concept of escaping crowded urban conditions has been attractive to newcomers and local residents. As one agricultural subdivision resident stated, "It's the best of Maui, out in the country, quiet, peaceful, the tradewinds blowing, with no neighbors breathing down your neck, but close to the ocean and mountain and with all the modern facilities minutes away. It's truly special."[28]

Through the county's community planning process, West Maui communities early identified several key problems that touch on the use of agricultural lands for gentlemen's estates. These key problems include threats to open spaces, specifically on agricultural lands and gulches; failed implementation of land use controls, noting projects "have been permitted that were inconsistent with the Community Plan and agriculturally designated lands are being used for other than agricultural purposes[;]" inadequate infrastructure; unconstrained growth; instabilities in the economy due to overreliance on tourist industries; a lack of affordable housing; increasing crime rates; and a lack of protection for cultural diversity and remaining rural lifestyles within the region.[29] Community plan objectives and policies sought to maintain land acreage required to sustain present and future agricultural operations and open space; prevent urbanization of agricultural lands; encourage maintenance and development of water sources for agricultural activities; and discouraging use of agricultural lands for non-agricultural purposes.[30] Gentlemen's estates can conform to all of these policies by, for instance, conducting some agriculture and maintaining large lot sizes. WoweeMaui, LLC, whose mailing address is Greenwich, Connecticut, owns a $6.4 million property on 27.76 acres of agricultural land just south of Launiupoko Beach Park.

While gentlemen's estates exacerbate most of these problems, the problem posed by gentlemen's estates was never explicitly called out by the 1996 community plan. Part of the reason was the failure to articulate the region's de facto population: the residents who live here, the tourists who stay here, and the commuters who travel back and forth to jobs in the region.[31] Rather, the kind of population that lives in gentlemen's estates are marked by wealth. These include vacation rental owners, new in-migrants from outside of Hawai'i, in-migrants from O'ahu, seasonal tourists, and Maui residents.

The incursions of this hobbyist farmer into agricultural land markets inflated the value of that land and displaced other potential owners, including those who would otherwise have acquired such lands by custom, intestate succession, or other forms of inheritance. This applies to many of West Maui's kuleana land parcels. Pioneer Mill, and other large landowners, took over kuleana parcels under claims of adverse possession, quitclaim deeds, amongst other relatively questionable legal means. After Pioneer Mill closed in 1999, lands that it had claimed went to Amfac, Kā'anapali Land Corporation, West Maui Land Co., Makila Land Co., Maui Land and Pineapple Co., and other developers.

Native Hawaiian members of the organization Kuleana Ku'ikahi LLC, and who farm taro in Kaua'ula, sought to stop fake agricultural developments, and specifically the use of agricultural lands for the Pu'unoa I, II, and III and Kaua'ula Subdivisions in Kaua'ula valley. During a 2003 Land Use Commission (LUC) meeting, they called attention to impacts of these new developments on their water sources and the kalo farming and other cultural practices that depended on those water sources.[32] They pointed out that no nonpotable water source had been identified for the subdivisions prior to the county granting building and subdivision permits; the local water source was Kaua'ula stream, which Kuleana Ku'ikahi members used for lo'i kalo, traditional and customary, and domestic uses; and use of agricultural lands for these subdivisions would harm lands along Kaua'ula Stream and Kuleana sought protection for them. Many of the Pu'unoa agricultural subdivision are built with pools and water features. "There will be no Hawai'i if this place looks like Honolulu," Kaua'ula valley resident Albert-Dall Napahi Dizon told LUC members.[33] Dall-Dizon is amongst many living in mauka areas of West Maui who have seen too many homes that look like leisure estates rather than farm dwellings.[34] The LUC ruled that the subdivisions were lawful and Hawaii's Intermediate Court of Appeals affirmed that decision.

In 2007, a bill was proposed in the Hawai'i senate explicitly to ensure agricultural land is used for farming and not for fake farms, and thereby implement constitutional provisions requiring the same.[35]

Some of the best agricultural lands in the state are also lands that, because of topography, location, and climate, are desirable for development of upscale housing. The legislature finds that, in the recent past, hundreds of acres of agricultural land have been converted into developments that feature luxury homes and a lack of agricultural activity, agribusiness, or subsistence farming. While the homeowners may cultivate a few fruit trees or an herb garden, no meaningful agricultural activity takes place, even though the developments are sometimes called "agricultural subdivisions."

The legislature further finds that the loss of agricultural lands to "fake farms" results in the loss of ability of the State to develop sustainable agriculture that could increase food and fuel self-sufficiency for Hawaii's people.

The purpose of this Act is to comply with the requirements of article XI, section 3, to protect the State's agricultural land by ensuring that agricultural land is used for agricultural activities, agribusiness, or subsistence farming and not for "fake farms".[36]

In 2015, the State Office of Planning published its State Land Use System (SLU) Review.[37] The SLU Review noted, "over the years, the permissible uses for the Agricultural District have been a mended repeatedly to broaden the uses allowed in the Agricultural District—from 5 uses in 1965 to 21 uses currently—which has weakened the nexus to agricultural production and bona fide farming. The Special Permit has been increasingly used to permit non-agricultural uses, notably vacation rentals, in the Agricultural district."[38] West Maui has seen its share of increased nonagricultural uses of its agricultural lands. Lahaina's Kauaʻula and Launiupoko areas have seen an increasing number of vacation rentals in recent years. Kahoma Ranch LLC obtained access easements over state agricultural lands, which easements are now used to site their ATV Tours. These commercial uses may be deemed accessory to agricultural operations under more recent statutory changes to Hawaiʻi land use laws.

Rural districting for pastoral lifestyle communities

Rural land districts are characterized by relatively low density residential lots, usually at least a half an acre in size. Rural districts explicitly also include golf courses, golf driving ranges, golf-related facilities, and geothermal resources exploration and geothermal resources development.[39] Given this legal definition, agricultural subdivisions that are planned for West Maui's Makila,

Launiupoko, Olowalu, and Ukumehame would rather fall under "rural" as opposed to agricultural land uses.

Since 2007, the Realtors Association of Maui has taken the position that agriculturally zoned properties should be upzoned to "rural" lands. Rural lands can be two-acre, five-acre, or ten-acre lots, allowing an increase in density without requiring subdivision. Under a rural designation, state laws requiring owners to farm would not apply and "[the County] Planning Department would no longer be required to force owners to pretend to be farmers."[40] Maui realtors identify as a problem the subterfuge imposed on owners by the county in regard to agricultural lands. This position is based on the presumption that the owners are not going to be farmers and increased density of Maui land use is a good thing. Nearly 35 percent of new property owners in Maui were nonresidents.

Although rural district land uses seem to fit proposals for agricultural lifestyle communities, developers have apparently deemed the process for redistricting lands too burdensome to bother with. In September 2015, Makila Land, LLC (MLL) sought to make the State Land Use Commission (LUC) the accepting agency for an EIS to be prepared for a proposed 271-acre, 150-unit Makila Rural Community development ("Makila Rural development) that included parcel segments currently proposed for the project. MLL planned to develop the Makila Rural development on 231 acres located at TMK Nos. (2) 4-7-013:001, 002, 003, 004, 005, 006, 007, 008, 009, 010, 011, 012.[1] MLL's Makila Rural Development included a proposed reclassification of forty acres from Agricultural to Urban SLU districts. The LUC agreed to become the accepting agency, but in April 2016, MLL announced that it determined not to pursue the Makila Rural development at that time and requested that the LUC terminate its docket.

Subsequently, lands that would have comprised the Makila Rural development were split up into at least three parts: Polanui Gardens (TMK Nos (2) 4-7-013:001 and 002); Makila Kai project (TMK Nos (2) 4-7-013:003, 004, and 005); and Makila Rural East (TMK Nos (2) 4-7-013:006, 007, and 008). Makila Kai, LLC proposed to build a 49 unit development on 79.5 acres of the agricultural lands that previously comprised part of the Makila Rural development proposal. In late 2017, a West Maui community group,

---

1 Makila Rural development that included parcel segments currently proposed for the project. MLL planned to develop the Makila Rural development on 231 acres located at TMK Nos. (2) 4-7-013:001, 002, 003, 004, 005, 006, 007, 008, 009, 010, 011, 012.

Nā ʻŌʻio o Makila, filed a complaint against the Makila Kai development for failing to adhere to several environmental review laws and other required procedures. Later, in November 2017, the Maui County Council decided to table the Makila Kai, LLC's request for a district boundary amendment, which was required for a portion of its development. West Maui residents, and their representatives, took note of the developers' apparent attempt to evade state LUC processes and comprehensive environmental review by splitting the larger project into three segments. The developers' primary response was to highlight the affordable housing component of the Makila Kai proposal, which would utilize about a third of the lands slated for residential development, with the rest devoted to gentlemen's estates. The developer's attempt to hold together gentlemen's estates and affordable housing is aligned with the neoliberal state's obstinate refusal, and inability, to address structural disrepairs that give rise affordable housing crises.

Economic contradictions and gentlemen's estates.

The economic impacts of West Maui's gentlemen's estates on housing costs are far from unique. "In a world of burgeoning tourism, rampant property development and booming markets for island havens (tax and finance) and retreats (from hyper connectivity), island gentrification research and policy analyses will not suffer from lack of raw material for fieldwork."[41] Researchers of Swedish archipelago gentlemen's farms compiled a non-exhaustive inventory of worldwide rural gentrification phenomena.[42]

Repeatedly, government and public policy advocates have agreed with the conventional wisdom that the problem of fake farms is that they do not produce food, constitute and end run around land use laws, and disproportionately raise land values. This approach is overly descriptive and fails to apprehend the complexity of the issue. Actual gentlemen's estates as they have existed historically and now, including those in West Maui, *have* referred to small-scale, diversified farming operations, albeit usually run by propertied white men. Martin's observation is correct in many instances. Retirees and others with ready capital, often from Canada and the U.S., are eager to buy a few acres on which to grow vegetables, raise honeybees, and a few chickens. These aspirations conform to an agenda for local agriculture and sustainability without, however, addressing displacement of Hawaiian tenant farmers and local communities.

Actual farming on gentlemen's estates does not remediate the problem of inflating costs of agricultural land.

Similarly, in Södra Skärgården, which is an island in the Swedish archipelago, a surfeit of interest in summer homes has increased housing costs for local communities, but avoiding the problem is not easy: "people complain about others who sell to summer guests, and say they would never do that. But later, when they move, they do the same thing. You are a fool not to take the market value. That is just to give the difference to the next owner."[43] Skärgården's example points to the deep-seated economic contradictions that condition the possibility for gentlemen's estates and gentrification.

In Hawaii's law and policy circles, the problem of gentlemen's estates has been discussed in terms of what the "best uses" of agricultural lands, particularly those that do not have highly productive soils. Hawai'i attorney Adrienne Suarez wrote of the issue, "[t]here is a balancing process involved in agricultural preservation. The forces of conservation and control must give in to the forces of development and growth, and vice versa…"[44] Suarez concludes, "[t]here is a balancing process involved in agricultural preservation."[45] This balance would best be achieved, according to Suarez, through a clear policy governing compromise.[46] Suarez's balance, however, distinguishes between prime or "productive" agriculture intended to be built out into agricultural subdivisions.[47] In Kaua'ula and Launiupoko, however, marginal agricultural lands are only such when they are not irrigated. Makila Land Company argued that they were not providing irrigation and therefore the loss of these lands to de facto residential subdivisions was not a loss of food production capacity. This argument, however, required restricting the memory of these lands to the post-plantation era. Prior to Pioneer Mill, these valleys, and indeed most of Lahaina, were hugely productive.

Hawai'i attorney Nathan Roehrig countered by citing concerns even higher grade agricultural lands have been turned into de facto residential subdivisions. This "misuse" of state agricultural lands is seen in questionable luxury developments replete with golf courses on agricultural lands meant to be protected for agricultural purposes.[48] This leaves aside that even higher grade agricultural lands have been turned into de facto residential subdivisions and that developers divert waters from places like Mākila and Kaua'ula, which officially rendered those soils less productive.[49]

More generally, legislators and other politicians call out the problems of fake farms, which are that they do not produce food and raise agricultural land values outside the reach of the typical farmer.

Accordingly, the primary objection to gentlemen's estates has been that they are fake farms, peopled by vacation home renters and profiting rich people and trusts in Hawai'i (sometimes) and in the continental U.S. (more of the time). The agenda of food sovereignty, particularly in its opposition to fake farms, has enabled important alliances between and across concerns with Hawaiian independence, agribusiness practices, health, and healthy ecosystems. In its 2013 report, the UN Commission on Trade and Development (UNCTAD) predicted that small-scale, organic farming, as opposed to chemical-intensive monocrops by large agribusinesses, will be key in the future. The cover of the UNCTAD report displays in full capital letters "WAKE UP BEFORE IT IS TOO LATE: Make agriculture truly sustainable now for food security in a changing climate."[50] The report was based on contributions from more than 50 international experts weighing in on "the inter-related problems of hunger and poverty, climate change, economic, social, and gender inequality, poor health and nutrition, and environmental sustainability."[51] UNCTAD urged that farmers must see themselves not only as food producers, but as managers of ecological systems that include energy, soil, water, and biodiversity. The expansive view articulated by UNCTAD conjoins food production and environmental renewal in innovative and needed ways. Like UNCTAD, British geographers developed "post-productivism" to discuss more holistically changes in South Africa's countryside.[52] Post-productivism is used, neutrally, to describe a shift in focus from the quantity of food production to the quality of food production; the emergence of nonfood-producing farm jobs and activities for income (known as pluriactivity); a return to traditional, environmentally sound and sustainable farming techniques; increasing environmental awareness and regulation of agriculture; the gradual removal of state support for agriculture; counter-urbanization, leading to social and economic restructuring; the creation of consumptionist countryside; the demand for amenity value from rural landscapes; agriculture that does not occupy a central role in the countryside anymore; and a widening of the agricultural community to include emerging farmers, organic farmers and hobby farmers.[53] Yet, even these broader perspectives fail to extend answers to the disrepairs consequent to West Maui's fractured colonial history, of which gentlemen's estates are one symptom.

Here, the "gentlemen's estate" is a strawman in debates over fake versus real farmers, or even over farmers who could be doing more. Development of a more affordable, ecologically-beneficial version of the farming estate would not respond to the crucial question of *who* will populate any housing on Hawaii's lands, agricultural or otherwise. Unasked the answer is that they will be populated by people with ready capital and to whom this agricultural lifestyle appeals.

Formulations of gentlemen's estates as a matter of ecological, aesthetic, or food-production failings fail to acknowledge, much less address, gentlemen's estates as symptoms of settler colonial domination and capitalist markets. The state, the housing market, the buyers, and even the typical farmer originate outside of West Maui and, together, make gentlemen's estates possible through in-migration and capital investment.[54] Instead of these approaches, I offer the following six theses on the problem of gentlemen's estates in West Maui.

Part III: Six Theses

Thesis No. 1: I take my first thesis from Dr. Kawika Winter, Director of Lima-huli Garden and Preserve on Kauaʻi, who observed Hawaii's agriculture needs to be restored to "the motivational driver of ancient times: the honor of the place and the well-being of its people."[55] Winter reminds us that agriculture is not only about food production, and that the problem with fake farms is not only that they do not produce food but the host of systems that take agricultural lands out of local food production. The possibility of the gentlemen's estates is conditioned on laws that increasingly expand permissible uses of agricultural lands, condominium property regimes that allow for non-subdivided subdivisions, calls from realtors to cash in on opportunities to build dream homes and vacation rentals, and of course, the settler colonial state's convenient forgetting of native systems of land use that flourished prior to plantation agribusiness and persist today.

I want to get behind Winter's directive. Doing so means getting beyond the question of better and worse uses of state agricultural lands. Winter's restoration calls for a multifaceted redoing of our relationships with land, food, and farming. Realtors, developers, politicians, and their attorneys' talk as if West Maui's vacant agricultural lands are evidence only of the absence of plantations and further that this absence is an invitation to make better use of those lands. As I'll discuss, this kind of talk seeks to silence desires for a different world and the difference already existing, historically and now, in this world. Scholar Fred Moten wrote, "…I believe in the world and want to be in it. I want to be in it all the way to the end of it because I believe in another world in the world and I want to be in that."[56] Moten's affirmation of his desire to be in a world in this world denies a messianic temporality that stymies discussions of decolonization as something that opens up in a deferred future. This is what I read in Winter's formulation—a doing away with a schedule of land use reforms and directly seeking to restore purposeful agriculture. Winter's call intervenes in the state's schedule of land use policy and towards motivations, honor of place, and well-being. Directing us towards such ready-to-hand sites relocates agency into a broader project of restoring agriculture.

Thesis No. 2: The problem with the gentlemen's estates is "a lack of thought." I take this thesis from the 1867 report from the committee appointed to research the cause of famine in Lahaina. This report underscored that the problem with institutions like the gentlemen's estate is not only that it does not grow (enough) food, but that they continue a settler colonial capital extraction from West Maui's land and water.

Historically, West Maui saw agricultural successes nearly unimaginable today. In 1793, foreign traveler Archibald Menzies traveled throughout the valleys and mountains of Lahaina, and observed "irrigated agricultural fields extending from near-shore to the mountains" and plants unlike others seen in the islands.[57] As late as 1846, Lahaina magistrate D. Kahaulelio remembered Lahaina was not a town, it was the food garden for the island of Maui."[58] By 1867, however, Kahaulelio wrote, "before, I never saw them bringing produce from Waipio, Hawaii to feed the people of Lahaina. But in this time, the hull of the schooner, Halawa, and other boats, is often filled with the produce of Waipio, to feed those of Lahaina…"[59]

Soon thereafter, a committee, including Kahaulelio, was appointed to investigate the cause of the famine. They attributed it to sugar plantations that took the land, labor, and water previously devoted to traditional subsistence farming.[60] "[Sugar mills] do not farm, but instead, they burn up the food of the kalo lands." Lahaina's many loʻi and dryland sweet potato fields had been turned over to planting cane.

Water, which had been sufficient before, had all gone to sugar cane. The sugar plantations took stream waters and consequently the taro lands of the kuleana were dry. "Before the building of the sugar mills in Lahaina, water was seen flowing through the streams of Kauaula, Kanaha and Kahoma. Taro was seen growing abundantly, and on the terrace banks, there was growing cabbage, bananas and such. The people of Lahaina were always seen planting taro. Thus, it was known that the famines were set aside, and the abundance of the land made this clear…. Thus it is right that the people of Lahaina, plant these foods, that they may end these famines…"[61]

In regard to labor, the committee found "those who once cultivated taro, sweet potato, and gourds have switched to sugar because they want more money… but there is not ample food, and that is the mistake." The committee found the labor of the 250 men who work the sugar mill in Lahaina goes towards sugar and not to farming. Other strong people were not cultivating food, but gathering pulu (tree fern down), pepeiao (forest mushrooms), and such, to earn money.

And "many of the people have left the planting of their *Kuleana* lands— the *kalo, uala, maia, uhi*, and such—with expectations that they shall satisfy their hunger by this work."[62] The young people went to the sugar mills and left farming to their elders. Further, the number of people farming and cultivating food had diminished while the population, increased by settlers, meant "there are as many to eat food as in the time of Kamehameha III."

The committee identified the deterioration of traditional food production, specifically the displacement of ulu, by sugar. "[A] food which once protected (sustained) the people in times of famine has been mistreated. It is the *ulu* (breadfruit).... But now, with the extensive planting of sugar cane, many of the bread fruit trees have been cut down and the wood become fuel for the mill." In ancient times, "this cutting down of the breadfruit, would lead to one probably being cast away to some isolated land, just like Kaululaau who was banished to Lanai, because he had cut down the breadfruit trees."[63]

Finally, the committee found, "God is not the reason for this lack, nor is it because there is a lack of rain instead it is the lack of thought by men."[64] The committee's thoughtful approach to the lack of food in 1867 that should be brought to West Maui's fake farms problem today. West Maui is not suffering a famine, but the 1867 committee report shows the linkage between settler colonial monopolization of agricultural land and water is not a new one. It also helps to underscore what is settler colonial about economies set up around land capitalization by sugar, then, and gentlemen's estates, now.

The problem of gentlemen's estates as fake farms repeats certain structures of the 1867 famine, as another method of settler resource extraction from land—then by sugar and now by realtors and developers. But it is also caused by a "lack of thought" that also outlines the ways colonialism takes form, historically and materially in indigenous social contexts. In this way, the committee noted what postcolonial scholar Ashis Nandy characterized in colonial subjecthood, "As a state of mind, colonialism is an indigenous process released by external forces. Its sources lie deep in the minds of the rulers and the ruled. Perhaps that which begins in the minds of men must end in the minds of men."[65] There is a kinship between a call to address this affirmative adoption of colonial processes and, and Winter's call to realize, again, traditional motivations that honored this place and ensured the well-being of its people.[66]

Thesis No. 3: Gentlemen's estates are still a problem when they *are* farms. In 2005, Rick Holt, an Oregon developer sought a solution by combining residential development with farming on 240 acres of land once planted in pineapple at Peʻahi, above the famed surf break also known as Jaws. Holt located the problem with the hypocrisy of planning officials, who allowed farm-dwelling subdivisions without enforcing the requirement to farm.[67] Similarly, in the same year, Amfac successor Kaanapali Development Corporation sought to sell 108 house lots amid 500 acres of existing coffee trees above Kaanapali Resort. Stephen Lovelette, Kaanapali Development executive vice president, said the company wants to sell the marginal asset but help ensure it is kept in agriculture. "This is keeping people employed and keeping a product coming out of the ground," he said, "It will still look like it is—nice and green and forested."[68] Today, Kāʻanapali Coffee Farms consists in 500 acres of "spacious island-style farm houses with swimming pools" with actual coffee farming accomplished by "master growers" who are sort of like sharecroppers. But agricultural operations like the coffee farm cannot restore the importance of place and dignity of farming that Winter called for. This is rather a return to the settler plantation, which was key to Hawaiian dispossession.

Historically and not just in Hawaiʻi, agriculture functioned as a colonizing force.[69] Frieda Knobloch described the ways agriculture was integral to settler colonialism in the American West between 1862 and 1945. She observed, "[c]olonization is an agricultural act. It is also an agricultural idea."[70] The word "colony" comes from the latin word *colonus* meaning "farmer."[71] Farmers were not only instruments for developing land, but are further crucial to U.S. agrarian ideals that were built around the Jeffersonian belief that "farmers make the best citizens."[72] Thomas Jefferson described this agrarian republican vision for America in his *Notes on the State of Virginia* (1781), "Those who labour in the earth are chosen people of God, if ever he had a chosen people, whose breasts he has made his peculiar deposit for substantial and genuine virtue." The city, by contrast, he characterized as populated by a dirty "mob" who "add just so much to the support of pure government, as sore do to the strength of the human body."[73] Much like current exhortations towards "off-the-grid" living and food sovereignty, Jefferson faulted city living for placing its subjects in a dependent relationship and depriving them of contact with land.[74]

The relative isolation and stateliness of the gentlemen's estate is a consequence of its aesthetic development. Not only respite held away from the "city mobs," the gentlemen's estate was also an architectural means of registering disgust for the country cottage and its denizens.[75] The gentlemen's estate also conveyed a political perspective, specifically the late eighteenth century English view that "disinterestedness was necessary for parliamentary members to vote in the natural interest and this disinterest could be guaranteed by hereditary landholding."[76] This disinterestedness was marked by the gentlemen's distance from agricultural work, and therefore the gentlemen's estates' scenic improvements were not to "seem to be in any way determined by, or even understood in relation to, agricultural improvements for fear of besmirching their liberality."[77] This effort towards liberal disinterestedness from agricultural operations would come to distinguish the English and U.S. architectural engagements with the country manor.[78] Even within English contexts, however, contradictions arose between agriculture theorists who posited housing as a utilitarian, disciplinary tool and aesthetes "picturesque theorists, who valued visual forms from older agricultural practices."[79] Hawaii's plantation agriculturalists infamously utilized working housing and the plantation structure more generally as means of worker discipline.

Around the turn of the eighteenth century, the gentleman farmer figured in efforts to articulate a uniquely U.S. identity. In the United States, the gentleman farmer was deemed to be the epitome of the self-sufficient man. He had a "special competence" through which he could purchase agricultural lands through his own accumulated wealth.[80] Second, his close involvement with managing his land was deemed to mean he was also "very effective in exploiting the land he farmed" and, additionally, "he would also be more able to rent land out well, since his intimate knowledge of the land's possibilities would allow him to pick appropriate tenants."[81]

> In short, the burgeoning market for land moved land to the highest value user, the competent gentleman farmer. And as he became more familiar with it, his ability to generate value only increased so that he was, given the circumstances of the times, far and away the most economically efficient owner of the land. Unlike the great lord, the intrinsic value of the land he owned would be far less if the gentleman farmer were expropriated for his skills would then be unavailable to manage it. It would be better for a far-sighted government to negotiate a steady tax from each of these farmers than to expropriate any one of them. In addition, security of property would enhance the taxes the gentleman farmer would pay because he would then have a greater incentive to invest in the land and create value.[82]

American nationalism also integrated agrarian ideals into the premise that it would be successful as a "republic of freeholders—self-sufficient, morally virtuous, politically independent, free-thinking and freedom-loving 'yeomen.' "[83] In this sense, critique of the lack of farming on the gentlemen's estate has its origins in the development of a uniquely American identity. In his 1857 essay "Landscape and Its Treatment," Wilson Flagg urged the American people not to aspire to gentlemen's estates because they oriented British landscapes and to rather concern themselves with real farming.[84] Americans, by contrast with the British owner of the gentlemen's estate, "should be governed by a republican feeling, and not endeavor to distinguish their own grounds from those around them, for the vain purpose of indicating the extent of their domains[.]"[85] Flagg went on to decry preoccupation of the British with gentlemen's estates over "the general aspect of the county" although the former "are not to be regarded as more important than laborers' cottages."[86]

> As we live in a republic, our rules for the improvement of landscape must be republican; and the less we copy the examples which are exhibited to us in a foreign land, and the more we govern our practice by general principles, the more useful and delightful will be the result. It would be no great gain to the beauty of the country, that a few rich men had fine gardens and estates, laid out in a costly style of decoration, if the principles of this art were neglected by all the rest of the community.[87]

Flagg's discussion reminds us that opposition to the gentlemen's estate has a basis in these early campaigns for the American yeoman farmer and searching for a uniquely American identity based in the American landscape. Flagg's critique, however, did not address how agrarian ideals themselves operated as settler colonial instruments.

The republic of yeoman became a template for U.S. nationalism that had to work over the contradiction that arises from confrontation with indigenous farmers. Not only did American Indians farm, but early English colonists found themselves dependent on the Indians' harvests.[88] However, the notion that Indians did not farm was necessary to white settlers' conception of superiority, and therefore farming became, over time, racialized in ways that color both farming and the concept of the yeoman-citizen today.[89] Western industrial agriculture that characterized the nineteenth century would be alien to both the agrarian yeoman ideal and traditional Hawaiian farming practices.

Settler farming was critical to creating (racialized) settler subjects, and also to subjecting Native peoples.[90] Zoe Matties, in her article on u"Unsettling Settler Food Movements" referenced Canadian state officials' historical use of the regulation of foodways to "streamline the colonization process."[91] They sought to regulate access to meat to transform the Blackfeet peoples "from hunters to herders, from barbaric predators preying on the plains' ownerless stocks of animal capital, to civilized producers subject to Anglo-American standards of labor, property, and land tenure."[92]

When we fault gentlemen's estates only for being fake farms our criticism leaves aside the singularly U.S. vision of yeomen farmers inhabiting homesteads across Hawai'i was part of integral to the colonial imagination of the 1901 U.S. Organic Act. Hawai'i has seen this in the 1895 Land Act,[93] which provided for homesteading lands under 999 year leases but excluded non-citizen, Asian settlers and made those leases inalienable or devisable.[94] In practice, however, only 527 homesteads were applied for and of those, only 337 were patented, and many of the initial benefits to Hawaiians were lost by the onset of the twentieth century. In 1910, an amendment to the U.S. Organic Act, which was designed to encourage homesteading, ironically ended up facilitating further transfer of prime sugar lands to plantations.[95] By 1951, fewer than 10 percent of the homestead leases remained in Native Hawaiian hands, owing in large part to a lack of available capital to fulfill a development condition of the leases and the prohibition against testamentary dispositions.[96]

Today, the colonial history of settler farming continues to contextualize West Maui's agricultural subdivisions. This means we cannot only approach the problem of gentlemen's estates, but the ways that they have been formulated as a problem. Restricting our analysis to the ways they are fake farms, raise property values to dissuade farming we want to happen, or even criticisms of the gendered insularity of their spatial practices risks reproducing a historically American homestead agenda that has driven settler colonialism in Hawai'i and elsewhere.

West Maui Land Co. is responsible for much of the planned development on 4,500 acres from Kahoma through Olowalu.[97] It credits itself with "revitaliz[ing] the sugar lands abandoned in the mid to late 1990s."[98] West Maui Land Co. also thus identifies itself as holding the legacy of West Maui's plantation—the Pioneer Mill Company, and its land consolidation and holding practices. West Maui Land Co. goes further, describing a vision of West Maui populated by families occupying a reenergized plantation infrastructure.

> By restoring and augmenting preexisting plantation infrastructure sys-
> tems in Olowalu and Launiupoko areas, these lands and communities
> are being reenergized with the goal to facilitate small-scale farming and
> ranching. A growing trend toward diversified agriculture, farms in opera-
> tion include tomatoes, avocados, bananas, papayas, and plants including
> herbs, cut flowers, landscaping plant stock, palms and native plants. More
> and more families are finding that lot sizes and evolving trail systems
> complement their love of horses. Family farms and equestrian pursuits
> serve to cultivate a variety of products for the Maui community and foster
> the spirit and benefit of local business and the private sector.[99]

Here, West Maui Land Co. offers its vision of how to live in the aftermath
of the plantation. The distribution of land and water uses begins from where
Pioneer Mill left off, which troublingly forecloses live questions about whether
Pioneer Mill properly held those lands and waters. That is, West Maui Land
Co.'s version of West Maui is based on the thin premise that a new commu-
nity can arise without first reckoning with the wrongs wrought by Pioneer
Mill—and all those institutions that enabled it.

In 2003, Jim Gribaudo, a buyer of one of West Maui Land Company's agricultural subdivision lots, commented, "common sense tells me we
should never discourage any amount of agriculture."[100] The "common sense"
instructing Gribaudo instanciates Mark Rifkin's "settler common sense."
This concept "suggests the ways that legal and political structures that enable
non-Native access to Indigenous territories come to be lived as given, as
simply the unmarked, generic conditions of possibility for occupancy, association, history, and personhood."[101] In other words, Gribaudo's "common
sense" observation that any amount of agriculture is good structures and is
structured by experiences of a *non-relation* with place and history that "takes
shape around the policies and legalities of settlement but that do not specifically refer to them as such or their effect on Indigenous peoples."[102] Here,
Gribaudo's okay-ness with his market rate agricultural lot pronounces a
non-relation to West Maui's extensive history of colonial agriculture. That
it appears to him as common sense demonstrates how settlement comes to
be lived in quotidian forms of non-Native being.[103] I return to this concept
below.

Thesis No. 4: The problem with gentlemen's estates is not only that they raise
the value of agricultural lands. As summarized by a 2005 news article: "Con-

troversial residential projects on land zoned for agriculture are nothing new in Hawai'i, but the state's superheated housing market is driving more creation of so-called agricultural subdivisions with buyers building luxury homes on land a typical farmer could never afford."[104] Here, again, the state, its housing market, buyers, and even the "typical farmer" originate outside of West Maui and function as vectors of settler colonialism within it.

Within this traffic of Western property rights, Hawaiian land rights tend to be confined to a mere duty to consult and accommodate.[105] The archetypal farmer has been displaced by a brand of agricultural lifestyle as the capitalist produce of West Maui lands. This is made most obvious in West Maui's contemporary property regime, which is described by West Maui Land Company's Peter Martin, "People buy the land for the lifestyle.... What they really want is the opportunity to farm."[106]

Martin, through West Maui Land Company's website, identifies a saleable agricultural lifestyle that includes, according to his websites for the Mahanalua Nui project in Launiupoko and Pu'unoa Estates in Kaua'ula valley, a luxury "farm dwelling," a pool, soccer fields, land to grow food, or to have someone else grow it for you, hiking and cycling trails horseback riding, gated entry, and private water provision.[107] The Mahanalua Nui project area in Launiupoko "includes a network of trails for hiking, horseback riding and cycling as well as a streambed park area in the Launiupoko valley."[108] Families living on these 153 agricultural lots that are served by Launiupoko Water Company receive private potable and nonpotable water service.[109] The lots are described as "ideal for entrepreneurial families interested in small scale farming or ranching." Similarly, the Pu'unoa Estates in Kaua'ula valley are networked with hiking, horseback riding and cycling trail systems and "ideal for individuals who dream of pursuing equestrian or farming endeavors."[110]

Real estate consumers are here called to experience self-possessed containment in single-family homes, agricultural plots, and gated communities. These describe a settler state spatial imaginary that produces "forms of affective interiority," which "normaliz[e] certain modes of selfhood and experiences of space that reiterate the obviousness of settler jurisdiction."[111] The West Maui Land consumer pitch is premised on and innovates from a settler spatial imaginary.

Casting these 153 lots as waiting to be filled by hiking, horseback riding, cycling, or park recreating families reiterates a version of the colonial principal of *terra nullius*, meaning "nobody's land" and available for state occupation.[112] Audra Simpson points out that *terra nullius* is based on the concept of "empty land" and an imposed dualism onto settler civilization and indigenous land tenure structures.[113] This difference, and the "differential power" of how difference is accounted for defines "not only difference but establishing *presence*, by establishing the terms of even being seen[.]"[114]

West Maui Land Co. and Kāʻanapali Land Co.'s offering up histories of the becoming of the community repeats strategies used by developers to sell the suburbs to middle class white workers.[115] Yet, the full account of this agricultural landscape concerns the transaction between developer and its market subject. W.J.T. Mitchell notes, "landscape is a social hieroglyph that conceals that actual basis of its value. It does so by naturalizing its conventions and conventionalizing its nature."[116] Power relations and inequalities get writ large onto the material landscape of West Maui's agricultural lands and are made legible through, for instance, developer descriptions of unit lots for sale.[117] Proposals for the Makila Rural and Makila Kai developments portrayed West Maui's mauka lands as dry, rocky, and unirrigated. New settler discourses on these lands' idleness are a stark counterpoint to the histories of abundant production on agricultural lands. Under the developers' logic, if not gentlemen's estates, what else could make these waste lands productive? Developers pose this rhetorical question, confident that the response will not be to seek ways to restore these lands to support traditional Hawaiian farming and to return people to their kuleana parcels.

The conditions of possibility for West Maui Land's kind of people, lifestyles, and opportunities populate a settler state spatial imaginary and in so doing, produce "forms of affective interiority." These forms are further highlighted in the kind of person described in residential estates, which are good for hiking, cycling, equestrian, entrepreneurs. The hailing of this kind of person is identified with "biopolitical marketing" strategies that mobilize certain creative, entrepreneurial, and competitive capacities of real estate consumers. These strategies constitute a form of neoliberal governmentality because they regard lifestyle and consumer decisions as investments and a means of governing others' "ethical deficiency and economic incompetence."[118] The very production of such forms of affective interiority instanciates an intimate complicity between gentlemen farmers with the reproduction of settler colonialism.

Gentrification, as a socioeconomic process, was first identified by Ruth Glass in her 1964 study of urban change in London. Friedrich Engels, however, earlier articulated the underlying political economic dynamics of gentrification in *The Housing Question* (1975 [1872]).[119] The chronic lack of affordable housing, which is the primary reason gentrification becomes an issue, is a symptom of capitalist relations and therefore only abolition of the later could solve housing crises. Engels therefore denounced the "gospel of harmony between labor and capital" which posited that "[i]f the capitalists knew their true interests, then they would give the workers good houses and put them in a better position in general, and if the workers understood their true interests they would not go on strike, they would not go in for Social Democracy, they would not take part in politics, but docilely follow their superiors, the capitalist." Specifically, Engels took aim at reformist proposals to transform rent into lease payments towards the acquisition of the rented property. "The cleverest leaders of the ruling class have always directed their efforts towards increasing the number of small property owners in order to build an army for themselves against the proletariat."[120]

Understood as an artifact of capitalist relations, it is apparent that *West Maui* does not have a gentlemen's estate problem. Gentlemen's estates in West Maui happen because *other places* have problems—colonial desires for stately mansions, a lack of education and ethics around land speculation, and a defective imagination of the good life—resulting in gentrification, increasing land values, and displacement of existing communities by rich newcomers. "Gentry" comes from the British "landed gentry," a propertied class that owned thousands of acres of land.[121] They took little interest in farming, and rather focused on "gentlemanly pursuits such as hunting, shooting, charitable activity and public affairs."[122] They are an aspirational class of wealthy people seeking to join the upper class through the acquisition and use of land and housing to increase social standing.

Like the concept of gentry, gentlemen's estate organizes gender. Patriarchal power is inscribed in the ownership and identity of these agricultural manors.[123] The Swedish term for a gentlemen's estate is *herrgard*, which translates to the master's country estate. They are gentlemen's estates because of a masculinized relationship to nature, land, and home. They been static concepts. Shaunna Wilkinson, for instance, marked a new image of masculinity: "a man who mediated between earlier aristocratic and landed ideals of masculinity and his new middle-class, professional, and merit-based identity"—that emerged through the new confluence of industrialization and the home in nineteenth century England.[124] Katarina Bonnevier has approached the gendered dimension of manor houses through architecture.

Like other gentlemen's estates across Hawai'i, those in West Maui tend to adopt plantation style architecture, which is marked by low profile wood frames, exposed rafters and vertical plank siding, with wide-hipped, split pitch roofs. In the nineteenth century, planters and missionaries started constructing plantation houses that were adapted from the New England frame houses. They were particularly popular at the height of the sugar and pineapple plantation era in the early to mid-1900s. Plantation architecture grew out of the industrial plantations' need to house new workers. In the mid-nineteenth century, Pacific whaling grounds were becoming depleted and petroleum was replacing whale oil. At the same time, the 1850 Masters and Servants Act legalized the importation of contract laborers to Hawai'i.

West Maui gentlemen's estates incorporate the aesthetic of earlier plantation house architecture. They typically had an open verandah along one side, with a sloped roof, window louvers, and raised floors.[125] Since the 1970s and 80s, the plantation-style home has been popular in moderate to upscale Hawai'i housing. After WWII, these houses were often painted with whatever excess paint was available. On Kaua'i, many exteriors were painted with the dark battleship grey surplus paint, and interiors of some homes were painted with bright aqua and yellow, because those were available in Hawai'i at the time.[126]

The plantation aesthetic is incorporated into West Maui's gentlemen's estate as a means by which West Maui's propertied settler developers narrate people's dream of a tropical good life.[127] Here, the "good life" flags Lauren Berlant's cruel optimism, which is a form of setting people up to fail by disregarding the material circumstances in which they live. What is cruel about this optimism is its "relation of attachment to compromised conditions of possibility."[128] "Cruel" is not the same as disappointing. Optimism is cruel when the kind of relation or attachment (to something) impedes the flourishing that motivated the initial attachment. The dream of a mansion, or even just a single family home with "breathing room" in West Maui, funds the drive to densify agricultural lands outside of planned development, and the consequent snarls of traffic, crowded beaches, and struggles for water resources. Attachments to the good life promised by West Maui Land's lifestyle communities are cruel because their development makes that almost life impossible.[129] A synonym for wanting is desiring, and desire, or the lack thereof, is constitutive of sexuality. John MacArthur's research on the British early nineteenth century aesthetic engagements with agricultural reforms described a similar image in desires for "the small house in its own garden" held by UK settlers headed for North America and Australasia. "The material and social technologies of the cottage became not only equipment for the colonial enterprise, but a kind of colonization of the home by a new kind of family."[130] The point is that aspirations clustered around images are also structures for settler colonial desires. I next approach sexuality and gender at the heart of disrepaired optimisms clustered by the gentlemen's estates.

Thesis No. 5: Gentlemen's estate lifestyles are infrastructures of settler heteronormativity. Crucially, above Martin articulates the desire for gentlemen's estates as also a desire for a certain lifestyle. What this means is that the gentlemen's estate constellates property regimes, the single family, the single-family home, *jus sanguinis* doctrines of citizenship that create family ties to the settler state, and personal things, such as bodies, feelings, and family, that are supposed to mean the most to and about us. These are the substrates of a settler sexuality instructs the reproduction of settler colonialism in everyday life. Because the operative form is sexuality, it puts that which is supposedly most within one's reach—personal things, such tastes, inheritance, home, and, apparently, aptitudes for equestrian pursuits, into a relationship with colonial administration.

Settler sexuality parallels Lauren Berlant and Michael Warner's 'national heteronormativity', a jumbled normalizing script that embeds sex into the everyday. "The citizen's paradigmatic lifestyle is rife with signs of public sexual culture: 'paying taxes, being disgusted, philandering, bequeathing, celebrating a holiday, investing for the future, teaching, disposing of a corpse, carrying wallet photos, buying economy size, being nepotistic, running for president, divorcing, or owning anything "His" or "Hers." '[131] Part of what makes public sexuality's imbrications with the colonial so elusive is that it takes up concepts, categories, and emblems of normative domesticity (driver licenses, residences, and waged-employment) that organize settler society and implicate sex practices but do not turn us on. It means examining "forms of institutionality involved in sustaining the existence of the settler state" that "generate practices of inhabitance and social interaction (such as those around property holding)."[132] Attending to settler society as an organization of sexuality calls attention to the ways a particular configuration of homes, families, and lifestyle are naturalized and administratively implemented.[133]

Pausing to name the normal ways of participating in settler sexual cultures alerts us to the highly intimate forms through which colonialism reproduces itself. Such attention centralizes the constitutive relation of the domestic space of the U.S. nation-state and normative modes of settler selfhood.[134] Rifkin argues that a colonial concept of indigenous peoples is incorporated as a feature of settlers' *sensation* of normative, self-possessed containment as part and parcel of the project of neutralizing the jurisdictional crisis created by indigeneity.[135] This relationship between the settler nation's story of itself and the non-relations between its' citizens and the contradictions of that story takes place within a process, or rather, multiple processes, providing for the historical and persistent deferral of Native sovereignty.[136] Rifkin points to the historical co-production of an expanding governmental role for "making possible forms of non-Native residence, production, and movement while simultaneously articulating, validating, and implementing such policies in ways that proliferate a sense of selfhood and occupancy as preceding/exceeding the terms or influence of the government."[137] Settlers of the American West operated within the U.S. government's trade and land transfers with Native Americans. Here, the template for everyday experiences of settler dwelling, relations to Native others, and the settler state was "anchored in settler sovereignty, in the sense of being dependent on forms of state jurisdiction and policy that themselves subsume and displace Indigenous presence and territoriality."[138]

West Maui's gentlemen's estates draw on this template. The occupant-consumer achieves a desired sensation of self-possession and individuality within a political economy dependent on, at its base, U.S. imperial authority over Native peoples. What gets worked over, however, is the sense that these have anything to do with each other.[139] Rifkin's literary research describes connections between the displacement of indigeneity and the everyday life of non-Natives in order to posit ways "non-Native feeling takes shape within and helps naturalize the exertion of US imperial authority over Native peoples."[140] Similarly, I argue that scoping gentlemen's estates as settler sexual and domestic practices marks non-Native authority as saturating "quotidian life in ways that are not necessarily present to settlers as a set of political propositions or as a specifically imperial project of dispossession."[141] This identity with the project of settler domesticity and selfhood marks gentlemen's estates as also a problem of settler colonial affect. The desire for gentlemen's estates should not feel right.

Thesis No. 6: The problem of gentlemen's estate is a problem of undoing settler futurity. Settler futurity is premised on the "elimination of the Native" and the erection of "a new colonial society on the expropriated land base[.]"[142] Refusing gentlemen's estates, and the host of presumptions about land, property, and community that they require, is also a matter of refusing our common participation in these regimes. As set forth in Thesis No. Five, key to this refusal is a patient parsing out the acts and investments that constitute participation. Here, I argue for refusal and negation as modes of decolonial resistance to the problem of gentlemen's estates.

Rachel Flowers outlined a politics of refusal for Indigenous women in part by drawing upon Foucault's response to Immanuel Kant's "What is Enlightenment?" (1982), "Maybe the target nowadays is not to discover what we are but to refuse what we are. We have to imagine and to build up what we *could be* to get rid of this kind of political 'double blind,' which is the simultaneous individualization and totalization of modern power structures."[143] Flowers' refusal specifically addresses settler authorities' attempts to define the terms on which indigenous futurity will be set.[144] Similarly, Chickasaw scholar Jodi Byrd observes, "power and transformation can be found in the tearing down of walls as much in the building of them."[145] "In the end," Byrd commented, "the quality of our struggle against the structures of colonialism will be determined by what we chose to dismantle."[146] Importantly, these negative approaches also instruct us to look for the decolonized world that exists in this one.

Lee Edelman's reproductive futurism[147] targets what the fantastic family anticipated by the gentlemen's estate brackets *now*. Swimming pools amidst declining water resources, watered lawns occupying the space of farmlands, individual fireproofing systems poised against wildfires produced by periodic drought produced by climate change, pretending away traffic, and of course, a society fractured by U.S. occupation. This is a schedule of terms that counsel against reproducing a futurity.[148] It is not a decolonial temporality, however, but a way of making way for one. Realtors, developers, and their attorneys talk as if West Maui's vacant agricultural lands are evidence only of the absence left by the plantations and as if this absence is an invitation to "make better use" of agricultural lands. This kind of talk ignores that the historical productivity of West Maui is also a future for it. Here, "indigenous peoples and nations... are continually deferred into a past that never happened and a future that will never come."[149]

Native studies scholars have criticized Edelman's call for no future because the call excludes those for whom actual reproduction is a material bulwark against genocide and because his theories are untethered from engaged political struggle. This is true and also a reason that I parse Edelman's no future unevenly against *settler* reproduction. As Andrea Smith has cogently argued: "if the goal of queerness is to challenge the reproduction of the social order, then the Native child may already be queered."[150] Edelman's *No Future* can also be read more narrowly because it argues that liberal politics inserts itself as a fantasy that the slippage between meaning and signifier can be unified in what gets called the Child. Edelman calls for queering this "reproductive futurism" as a way of intervening in what gets reproduced.[151]

Scholar and activist Fred Moten described how his intellectual concerns with Black genocide in the academy align with those of French critical philosopher, Gilles Deleuze, "Like Deleuze, I believe in the world and want to be in it. I want to be in it all the way to the end of it because I believe in another world in the world and I want to be in that."[152] Moten's affirms a desire to be in a possible world in the world that denies the messianic temporality that stymies discussions of decolonization as something that opens up only in a deferred future. As with Byrd, Moten talks about ends as substrates of a difference already existing, historically and now, in this world. Moten's desire is also not a facile call to belong to this world together. "Just because we are in the room together does not mean we belong to the room or each other: belonging is a specific genre of affect, history, and political mediation that cannot be presumed and is, indeed, a relation whose evidence and terms are always being contested."[153] As indicated by Byrd, resistance it in its own time even as it is against the settler colonial structures it dismantles. Both registers must be operated—against the everyday means through which denizens of gentlemen's estates reproduce settler futurity and towards the refusal to cede that traditional motivations that honored this place and ensured the well-being of its people in this time.

The lack of thought that plagued Lahaina in 1867 were desires for sugar capital, new economies, and the fate of traditional food systems. 150 years later, I am arguing for more thought about desires for gentlemen's estates, the policing of those desires, and the traditional motivations that honored this place and ensured the well-being of its people.[154] The restoration Winter calls for is, and is more than, a call to harken back towards the pre-history of Hawaii's plantation days. It is also a way of believing in a decolonized world in the world, and one that we should want to be in.

NOTES

1.   This chapter was presented as part of a panel at the West Maui Pacific Peoples and their Environment Conference held in Lahaina, Maui, October 13–14, 2017.

2.   Mark Rifkin, "The frontier as (moveable) space of exception," 4 *Settler Colonial Studies* 176, 177 (2014).

3.   David DeLeon, "Real Agriculture vs. Gentleman Farms: Zoning Changes Altering Rural Maui," (accessed May 16, 2017) *available at*: http://www.maui -style.com/Articles/Gentleman%20Farms_article.htm.

4.   Testimony of Sarah Tsukamoto on behalf of Steve Strombeck and the Strombeck Family Revocable Trust, Item B-2, Regular Meeting of the Commission on Water Resource Management, State of Hawai'i (Jun. 19, 2018).

5.   Long Range Planning Division, County of Maui, Maui General Plan 2030, Agricultural Resources Technical Paper, at 24 (Sep. 2007).

6.   Andrew Gomes, "Farming finds no home on agricultural land," *The Honolulu Advertiser* at 1, 6 (Sun. Jun. 12, 2005).

7.   Andrew Gomes, "Farming finds no home on agricultural land."

8.   Maui County Code § 19.30A.030.D.

9.   Source: Map layers from Land Use Commission, State Land Use Boundary Amendment Map (accessed Sep. 4, 2017) *available at*: http://files.hawaii.gov /luc/maps/maui_slud_2012.pdf.

10. *See* Maui County Department of Public Works subdivision files for Makila Nui, County of Maui Subdivision File No. 4.957; Makila Ranches—Phase 2 No. 4.927; Makila Ranches—Phase 1 No. 4.924; Makila Ridge No. 4.888; Makila Plantation No. 4.868; Makila Plantation Phase 2 No. 4.838 Makila plantation No. 4.928; Makila Plantation No. 4.825; Mahanalua Nui No. 4.580, No. 4.724; Mahanalua Nui Phase I, No. 4.730; Mahanalua Nui Phase II, No. 4.731; Mahanalua Nui Phase V, No. 4.909; Puunoa Subdivision No. 4.776; Launiupoko Large Lot Subdivision No. 2, 4.837, 4.824; Olowalu Makai—Komohana Subdivision Nos. 4.758, 4.760; Olowalu Makai—Hikina Subdivision No. 4.834; Olowalu Mauka No. 4.766; Ukumehame Subdivision 4.738; Ukumehame Agricultural Subdivision Phase 1, 4.875; Ukumehame Agricultural Subdivision Phase 2, 4.876.

11. Luxury Real Estate Maui, "Mahana Estates" (accessed Oct. 5, 2017) *available at*: http://www.luxuryrealestatemaui.com/mahana-estates.php.

12. Luxury Real Estate Maui, "Plantation Estates" (accessed Oct. 5, 2017) *available at*: http://www.luxuryrealestatemaui.com/plantation-estates.php.

13. *See* County of Maui, Bed and Breakfast Operation Permit No. BBWM2009/0008.

14. VRBO website (accessed Oct. 5, 2017) *available at*: https://www.vrbo.com/65549 and https://www.vrbo.com/4027539ha.

15. Land Use Commission, State of Hawai'i, SLU Agricultural maps (updated 2012) *available at*: http://files.hawaii.gov/luc/maps/maui_slud_2012.pdf.

16. Karen Mayuiers claimed to have the only TVR permit for a TVR in Kapalua Plantation Estates (Maui Permit No. BBWM2009/0008) at an average of $2,286 per night. However, Beachfront Avalon by the Sea is also operating in this area at

an average of $2,595 per night. *See* VRBO website (accessed Oct. 5, 2017) *available at*: https://www.vrbo.com/65549 and https://www.vrbo.com/4027539ha.

17. Dep't of Business, Economic Development and Tourism, Research and Economic Analysis Division, State of Hawai'i, Residential Home Sales in Hawaii: Trends and Characteristics: 2008–2015, 5 (May 2016) *available at*: http://files .hawaii.gov/dbedt/economic/data_reports/homesale/Residential_Home_Sales _in_Hawaii_May2016.pdf ("DBEDT Home Study").

18. DBEDT Home Study at 6.

19. Ibid, at 21.

20. Zygmun Bauman, *Globalization: The Human Consequences*, 9 (Cambridge, Polity: 1998).

21. Andrew Gomes, "Farming finds no home on agricultural land," *The Honolulu Advertiser* at 1, 6 (Sun. Jun. 12, 2005).

22. HRS §205-2(d).

23. Haw. Op. Att'y Gen. No. 75-8 (1975) citing HRS § 205-12.

24. Hawai'i State Office of Planning, Dep't of Business, Economic Development, and Tourism, "Report on Urban Lands in the State of Hawai'i, Part I: Supply of Urban Lands," Tables 1 & 2 (May 2006) *available at:* http://files.hawaii.gov /dbedt/op/spb/Urban-Lands-Project_compiled_Final.pdf.

25. David DeLeon, "Real Agriculture vs. Gentleman Farms: Zoning Changes Altering Rural Maui," (accessed May 16, 2017) *available at*: http://www.maui -style.com/Articles/Gentleman%20Farms_article.htm.

26. Ibid.

27. Ibid.

28. Ibid.

29. Planning Dep't, County of Maui, *West Maui Community Plan*, 9-10 (1996).

30. West Maui Community Plan, 24.

31. West Maui Community Plan, 10.

32. Gary Kubota, "Land use debate mushrooms on Maui," *Honolulu Star-Bulletin* (online) (Thurs. Jan. 2, 2003) *available at*: http://archives.starbulletin.com /2003/01/02/news/story6.html.

33. Ibid.

34. Ibid.

35. S.B. 1236, §1, H.D. 1, S.D. 1, 27th Hawai'i Legislature, 2007 quoting article XI, § 3, Hawai'i Constitution, "The State shall conserve and protect agricultural lands, promote diversified agriculture, increase agricultural self-sufficiency and assure the availability of agriculturally suitable lands."

36. Ibid.

37. Office of Planning, Dep't of Business, Economic Development, and Tourism, State of Hawai'i, State Land Use System Review: Draft Report (May 2015) *available at:* https://planning.hawaii.gov/wp-content/uploads/2015/05/SLU

-Review-Report_FINAL-DRAFTv2_05-05-2015_POSTED_TO_WEB.pdf
("SLU System Review").

38. SLU System Review at v.

39. HRS §205-2(c).

40. Realtors Association of Maui Website, "Historical Context—How Did We Get Here?" (accessed Jul. 2, 2017) *available at*: http://www.ramaui.com/content/504fa8756c401/Agricultural_to_Rural.html

41. Clar et al., "Island Gentrification and Space Wars," 505.

42. Peaks Island, Maine, USA: "a working class island feeling the grip of gentrification" (Bouchard, 2004). The Maine coast: "All along the coast, land values are skyrocketing due to second-home ownership and gentrification" (Snyder, 2006). New England: "The process of gentrification and coastal transformation is accelerating in New England as it is in most coastal areas of the US" (Hall-Arber *et al.*, 2001). Smith Island, Maryland: "working waterfront, threatened by gentrification" (Horton, 2005). St. Simons Island, Georgia: "'Developers are sweeping through this island....They've got a plan in place, and it does not include us'" (Jonsson, 2002). Hilton Head and other islands in Beaufort County, Georgia: "Now they are involved in an ongoing conflict wherein their land is quickly being taken away by wealthy elderly people and multimillion-dollar resort companies" (Yagley *et al.*, 2005). Salt Spring Island, British Columbia, Canada: "'In the future, the people who contribute to the uniqueness of Salt Spring...won't be able to afford to live here'" (Shilling, 2004). Vieques, Puerto Rico: "'I'm sure it can turn into a place that the land can be out of reach to the locals'" (Román, 2003). "Speculators from New York and San Juan are buying, buying, buying" (Dreifus, 2004). Tenerife, Spain: development pressure from the tourist industry has generated gentrification of whole districts involving evictions of over 5,000 residents and over 200 businesses (Garcia Herrera & Smith, 2005). In places like the Penghu Islands (Pescadores) in the Taiwan Strait, as with much of the South Pacific, traditional forms of land tenure, together with memory literally vested in the land (ancestors being buried on family land), have constituted the main barriers to gentrification. Clar et al., "Island Gentrification and Space Wars," 504-05.

43. Eric Clar, Karin Johnson, Emma Lundholm, and Gunnar Malmberg, "Island Gentrification and Space Wars," Chapter 14 in *A World of Islands: An Island Studies Reader*, Godfrey Baldacchino, ed., 501 (Media Centre, Blata I-Bajda, Malta 2007).

44. Adrienne Suarez, Avoiding the Next Hokulia: The Debate over Hawaii's Agricultural Subdivisions, 27 *U. Haw. L. Rev.* 441, 447 (2005) citing Rory Flynn, "Seeing Through the Fog of 'Fake Farms,'" *Hawai'i Reporter*, Jan. 30, 2007, *available at* http://www.hawaiireporter.com/seeing-through-thefog-of-fake-farms/123.

45. Ibid.

46. *Suarez* quoting Myrl Duncan, Agriculture as a Resources: Statewide Land use Programs for the Preservation of Farmland, 14 *Ecology L. Q.* 401, 409 (1987).

47. Suarez, at 446.

48. Nathan Roehrig, "Urban Type Residential Communities in the Guise of Agricultural Subdivisions:" Addressing an Impermissible Use of Hawaiʻi's Agricultural District, 25 *U. Haw. L. R.* 199, 200-01 (1999).

49. Roehrig, "Urban Type" at 200-01.

50. UN Commission on Trade and Development, Trade and Environment Review 2013 (Sep. 18, 2013) *available at*: http://unctad.org/en/PublicationsLibrary /ditcted2012d3_en.pdf.

51. Ibid. (Foreword).

52. Manfred Spocter, Rural gated developments as a contributor to postproductivism in the Western Cape, 95 *South African Geographical J.* 165-186 (2013).

53. Spocter, at 167.

54. Sutherland, at 569.

55. Fern Rosensteil, "From Syngenta to Hartung Brothers: Better stewardship expected?," *The Garden Isle* (online) (Sep. 30, 2017) *available at*: http:// thegardenisland.com/news/opinion/guest/from-syngenta-to-hartung-brothers -better-stewardship-expected/article_6a282563-f51c-55d0-9f56-4e03102e464c .html.

56. Stefano Harney and Frank Moten, *The Undercommons: Fugitive Planning and Black Study*, 118 (Minor Compositions: New York, 2013).

57. Kepā Maly and Onaona Maly, *He Wahi Moʻolelo No Kauaʻula a Me Kekāhi ʻĀina o Lahaina i Maui: A Collection of Traditions and Historical Accounts of Kauaʻula and Other Lands of Lahaina, Maui*, prepared for Makila Land Co. & Kamehameha Schools, Vol. 2, at 31 (Jun. 1, 2007) ("Maly V.2").

58. Maly V.2 at 930.

59. Ibid, at 932.

60. Maly V.2 at 931 translating *Nupepa Kuokoa*, Apelila 12, 1867 (aoao 4) "No ka Wi" (About the Famine) (by D. Kahaulelio).

61. Ibid, at 934.

62. Ibid, at 932.

63. Ibid.

64. Kahaheulio went beyond the committee report to prescribe solutions to the famine, including filling kuleana with planted foods, planting native foods, and maintaining other customary rules around eating. Maly V.2 at 932.

65. *Ashis Nandy Intimate Enemy:* The Intimate Enemy: Loss and Recovery of Self Under Colonialism, *at 3 (Oxford UP, rev'd 2010).*

66. Rosensteil, "From Syngenta."

67. Andrew Gomes, "2 subdivisions make effort to tie in farming plans," *The Honolulu Advertiser* at 6 (Sun. Jun. 12, 2005).

68. Ibid.

69. Commenting on agriculture in the American West between 1862 and 1945, Frieda Knobloch observed, "Colonization is an agricultural act. It is also an agricultural idea." Frieda Knobloch, *The Culture of Wilderness: Agriculture as Colonization in the American West, (Chapel Hill: Univ. North Carolina Press, 1996),* 1.

70. Knobloch, at 1.

71. Ibid, at 5.

72. *See* Paul B. Thompson, *The Agrarian Vision: Sustainability and Environmental Ethics,* (Lexington: University Press of Kentucky, 2010).

73. Thomas Jefferson, *Notes on the State of Virginia,* ed. Frank Shuffelton (New York, Penguin 1999 reprint), 170–71.

74. Janet Fiskio, "Unsettling Ecocriticism: Rethinking Agrarianism, Place, and Citizenship," 84 (2) *American Literature* 301, 303 (2012).

75. *See* John Macarthur, *The ornamental cottage: landscape and disgust,* ProQuest Dissertations Publishing, (University of Cambridge (United Kingdom) 1989).

76. John Macarthur, "The Heartlessness of the Picturesque: Sympathy and Disgust in Ruskin's Aesthetics," 32 *Assemblage* 126, 130 (1997).

77. Ibid.

78. Ibid, at 131.

79. Ibid, at 130.

80. Raghuram G. Rajan and Luigi Zingales, *Emergence of Strong Property Rights: Speculations from History,* Nat'l Bureau of Economic Research Working Paper Series, No. 9478, at 18 (Jan. 2003) *available at*: http://www.nber.org/papers /w9478.pdf.

81. Ibid.

82. Ibid.

83. Angela P. Harris, "(Re)Integrating Spaces: The Color of Farming," 2(1) *Savannah Law Review* 157, 164 (2015).

84. Wilson Flagg, "Landscape and Its Treatment," 34 *The North American Review* 151 (Jan. 1857).

85. Flagg, "Landscape and Its Treatment,"173–74.

86. Ibid.

87. Ibid, at 175.

88. Bethany R. Berger, "Red: Racism and the American Indian," 56 *UCLA L. Rev.* 591, 607 (2009).

89. Angela P. Harris, "(Re)Integrating Spaces: The Color of Farming," 2(1) *Savannah Law Review* 157, 170 (2015).

90. In her "Unsettling Ecocriticism: Rethinking Agrarianism, Place, and Citizenship," Janet Fiskio proposes an "agrarianism of the margins" in answer to whether the concept of place can be reformulated in ways that are inclusive of

communities who travel the borders of the food system. Janet Fiskio, "Unsettling Ecocriticism: Rethinking Agrarianism, Place, and Citizenship," 84 (2) *American Literature* 301, 303 (2012).

91. Zoe Matties, "Unsettling Settler Food Movements: Food Sovereignty and Decolonization in Canada," 7(2) *Cuizine* ¶8 (2016) *available at*: https://www .erudit.org/en/journals/cuizine/2016-v7-n2-cuizine02881/1038478ar/.

92. Matties, ¶8.

93. The Land Act of 1895 (Act of August 14, 1895, Act 26, [1895] Hawaii Laws Spec. Sess. 49-83).

94. Neil M. Levy, "Native Hawaiian Land Rights," *Berkeley Law Scholarship Repository*, 848, 863 (1975) *available at*: http://scholarship.law.berkeley.edu/cgi/viewcontent .cgi?article=3093&context=facpubs.

95. Act of May 27, 1910, ch. 258, § 5, 36 Stat. 443. This Act directed the Territory to open land in a given locality when 25 or more qualified homesteaders. This motivated sugar planters to secure their lands against potential homesteaders by striking a deal with the Hawaiian Homes Commission, under which the Hawaiian Homes Commission would receive certain, mostly second class lands, and the sugar planters were assured that lands under sugar cultivation would be withdrawn from homesteading.

96. After overthrowing the Hawaiian Kingdom's monarch, the Republic of Hawai'i expropriated Crown lands and disposed of some of these lands for homestead farming under Hawaiians were technically eligible for these homesteads, but white settlers ended up being the main beneficiaries. Neil M. Levy, "Native Hawaiian Land Rights," *Berkeley Law Scholarship Repository*, 848, 864 (1975) *available at*: http://scholarship.law.berkeley.edu/cgi/viewcontent.cgi?article =3093&context=facpubs citing G. Luter, *Report on Homesteading in Hawaii 1839–1961* (Jan. 3, 1961) at 15, on file Hawaiian State Dept. of Land and Natural Resources.

97. These developments include: Mahanalua Nui (also known as Launiupoko), Pu'unoa, Makila Plantation, Makila Ridge, and Makila Nui, Olowalu Makai/ Maukaand Peahi Hui, Kahoma Residential, and Olowalu Town (not Makila Rural).

98. West Maui Land Co., Real Estate Division Website (accessed Dec. 15, 2017) *available at*: http://www.westmauiland.com/realestate/contact-2/about-us/.

99. Ibid.

100. Gary Kubota, "Land use debate mushrooms on Maui," *Honolulu Star-Bulletin* (online) (Thurs. Jan. 2, 2003) *available at*: http://archives.starbulletin.com /2003/01/02/news/story6.html.

101. Ibid.

102. Ibid.

103. Ibid.

104. Gomes, "Farming finds."

105. Dawn Hoogeveen, "Sub-surface Property, Free-entry Mineral Staking and Settler Colonialism in Canada," 47 *Antipode* 121, 129 (2014); *see also Ka Pa'akai o ka Aina v. Land Use Commission*, 94 Hawai'i 31, 7 P. 3d 1068 (2000).

106. Gary Kubota, "Land use debate mushrooms on Maui," *Honolulu Star-Bulletin* (online) (Thurs. Jan. 2, 2003) *available at*: http://archives.starbulletin.com/2003/01/02/news/story6.html.

107. West Maui Land Co., Mahanalua Nui Subdivisions/ Launiupoko, (accessed Oct. 1, 2017) *available at*: http://www.westmauiland.com/realestate/our-listings/mahanalua-nui/.

108. Ibid.

109. Ibid.

110. Ibid.

111. Mark Rifkin, "Settler States of Feeling," in *A Companion to American Literary Studies*, 346 (ed. Caroline F. Levander, Robert S. Levine) (2015).

112. Captain Cooke invoked this doctrine when he encountered people in what is now Australia to claim that these aboriginal peoples' land was available for possession because land belonged to no one. Australia's High Court did not overturn this doctrine until 1992, with the *Mabo* decision.

113. Audra Simpson, "On Ethnographic Refusal: Indigeneity, 'Voice,' and Colonial Citizenship," 9 *Junctures* 67, 69 (Dec. 2007).

114. Ibid.

115. *See* Dennis Wood, "Selling the Suburbs: Nature, Landscape, Adverts, Community," 5 *Transformations* No. 5 (Dec. 2002) *available at*: http://www.transformationsjournal.org/wp-content/uploads/2017/01/denniswood.pdf.

116. W.J.T. Mitchell *Landscape and Power*, 2-3 (Chicago, 1994).

117. Nancy Duncan, *Landscapes of Privilege: The Politics of the Aesthetic in the American Suburb*, 44 (Routledge, 2003).

118. Detlev Zwick and Yesm Ozalp, Chapter 10: "Flipping the Neighborhood: Biopolitical Marketing as Value Creation for Condos and Lofts," in *Inside Marketing: Practices, Ideologies, and Devices*, 237 (Oxford UP: 2011).

119. Clar et al., at 482.

120. Engels, *The Housing Question* (Part I).

121. Lee-Ann Sutherland, "Return of the gentleman farmer?: Conceptualising gentrification in UK agriculture," 28 *J. Rural Studies* 568, 568 (2012).

122. Ibid.

123. Katarina Bonnevier, *Behind Straight Curtains: Towards a Queer Feminist Theory of Architecture*, 280 (Axl Books, 2007).

124. Wilkinson, Shaunna, "(Re)making the gentleman: Genteel masculinities and the country estate in the novels of Charlotte Smith, Jane Austen, and Elizabeth Gaskell," Marquette University, ProQuest Dissertations Publishing, 5 (2014).

125. Cleveland Salmon, *Architectural Design for Tropical Regions,* 45 (Wiley & Sons, 1999).

126. The Historical Colors of Hawaii Plantation Housing (accessed Nov. 1, 2017) *available at:* https://www.colormatters.com/color-and-design/historical-color -matters

127. Nancy S. Cook, "Doomed Developments in the Desert: Re-reading Land Development, the American Family and Ordinary Paces in a Time of 'Cruel Optimism'," in *Affective Landscapes in Literature, Art, and Everday Life,* (eds. Christin Berberich, Neil Campbell, Robert Hudson) Chap. 5, 85. Cook describes conventional depictions of developers who "figure only as soulless rapists of land who exploit working people's dreams of the good life in a safe place."

128. Lauren Berlant, "Cruel Optimism," 17(3) *Differences: A Journal of Feminist Cultural Studies* 20, 21 (2006).

129. By contrast, Berlant's concept is based on a more psychoanalytic analytic and thus discusses an optimism comprised by attachments to "self-interruptions as utopias of structural inequality." Berlant, "Cruel Optimism," at 35. Here, I extend the concept to address structural disrepairs consequent to the utopic fantasies hailed by developer dream homes.

130. John MacArthur, Colonies at Home: Loudon's *Encyclopaedia,* and the architecture of forming the self, 3 *Architectural Research Quarterly* 245 (Sep. 1999).

131. Lauren Berlant & Michael Warner, "Sex in Public," 24 (2) Critical Inquiry 547, 556 (Winter, 1998).

132. Mark Rifkin, "Settler States of Feeling," in *A Companion to American Literary Studies,* 346 (ed. Caroline F. Levander, Robert S. Levine) (2015).

133. Mark Rifkin, "Settler common sense," at 323.

134. Mark Rifkin, "Settler States of Feeling," 344.

135. Mark Rifkin, "Settler common sense," at 346–47.

136. Ibid. at 326.

137. Ibid. at 330.

138. Ibid. at 330.

139. In his "Settler States of Feeling," Rifkin targeted this working over in Henry David Thoreau's *Walden* and William Apess' "Eulogy on King Philip." Mark Rifkin, "Settler States of Feeling," in *A Companion to American Literary Studies,* 344 (ed. Caroline F. Levander, Robert S. Levine) (2015).

140. Rifkin, "Settler States of Feeling," at 344.

141. Mark Rifkin, "Settler common sense," at 323.

142. Patrick Wolfe, "Settler colonialism and the elimination of the Native," 8(4) J. of Genocide Research 387, 388 (Dec. 2006).

143. Michel Foucault, "The Subject and Power," in *Michel Foucault: Beyond Structuralism and Hermeneutics* (H. Dreyfus and P. Rabinow, eds) 336 (Chicago UP: 1982).

144. Rachel Flowers, "Refusal to forgive: Indigenous women's love and rage," 4(2) *Decolonization: Indigeneity, Education & Society* 32, 35 (2015).

145. Jodi Byrd, Structures and Events: A Monumental Dialogue.

146. Specifically, Byrd was talking about the renewed push to remove statutes of confederate officers in public spaces. More broadly, she hoped for the Chickasaw Nation to come to "an expansive understanding of grounded relationality that resists settler state power." Jodi Byrd, Structures and Events: A Monumental Dialogue, *Bullybloggers* (Sep. 20, 2017) *available at*: https://bullybloggers.wordpress.com/2017/09/20/structures-and-events-a-monumental-dialogue/.

147. In *No Future*, Lee Edelman argued that liberal politics inserts itself as a fantasy that the slippage between meaning and signifier can be unified in what gets called the Child. Lee Edelman, No Future: Queer Theory and the Death Drive (Durham, NC: Duke University Press, 2004). Edelman calls for queering this "reproductive futurism" as a way of intervening in what gets reproduced.

148. Native studies scholars have criticized Edelman's call for "no future" because the call excludes those for whom actual reproduction is a material bulwark against genocide and because his theories are untethered from engaged political struggle. This is true and also a reason that I parse Edelman's "no future" unevenly against settler reproduction. As Smith has cogently argued: "If the goal of queerness is to challenge the reproduction of the social order, then the Native child may already be queered." Andrea Smith, Queer theory and Native studies: the heteronormativity of settler colonialism, 16 (1-2) *GLQ: A Journal of Lesbian and Gay Studies* 41, 48 (2010).

149. Jodi Byrd, *The transit of empire: Indigenous critiques of colonialism*, 211 (University of Minnesota Press, 2011).

150. Andrea Smith, Queer theory and Native studies: the heteronormativity of settler colonialism, 16 (1-2) *GLQ: A Journal of Lesbian and Gay Studies* 41, 48 (2010).

151. Lee Edelman, No Future: Queer Theory and the Death Drive (Durham, NC: Duke University Press, 2004).

152. Stefano Harney and Frank Moten, *The Undercommons: Fugitive Planning and Black Study*, 118 (Minor Compositions: New York, 2013).

153. Berlant, "Commons" at 395.

154. Rosensteil, "From Syngenta."

A MODERN HISTORY OF
WEST MAUI'S WASTEWATER

Ikaika Hussey

Over the course of three decades, a cavalcade of citizens, scientists,
attorneys and judges forced a reluctant Maui government to change
a bad wastewater management practice for the benefit of West Maui.

A Harsh Sun

The Lahaina coast is rugged and rocky on its southern end but flattens out
on its northward stretch towards Nāpili and Honokōwai. The land is marked
with the contested history of the area. It was once the original seat of the
Kingdom government in Lahaina. Later, plantation flumes diverted water
from kalo fields to acres of sugar now lying below resort towns. Throughout
its history, West Maui's abundance of water resources have been reserved for
the remnants of the island's ruling class.

There, just a few miles from Lahaina town, a series of wells and pipes, a
couple hundred feet beneath the surface, pump partially treated sewage into
the ground along the coastline. Each day, four million gallons of human waste
come into the facility from a sewer system that services forty thousand local
and tourist digestive systems along the West Maui coast. Between half and
one and half million gallons of West Maui's wastewater is tertiary-treated and
disinfected with UV radiation to meet R-1 reuse water standards. It is then
sold to customers like the Kā'anapali Resort for landscape and golf course
irrigation. The rest of the wastewater is disinfected with chlorine to meet
the R-2 standard for treated sewage and forced down one of four Lahaina
injection wells. Across Maui County, there are eighteen injection wells, all of
them near the shoreline: eight in Kahului, four in Lahaina, three in Kīhei and

three on Moloka'i. Depending on the season, about 80 percent of Maui Nui's wastewater is processed through injection wells.

Many recognized from the beginning that this particular strategy for wastewater disposal is a mistake, both in terms of its opportunity costs in the form of valuable water thrown away, as well as in terms of damage to Maui's uniquely interconnected natural ecosystems. Much of this story is about how the county knew from the outset that injecting wastewater into the ground near the shoreline would be an environmental mistake. According to court documents, the original 1973 environmental review by Dr. Michael Chun said that the effluent that was not used for reclamation purposes would be injected into the wells and that these pollutants would then enter the ocean some distance from the shore.

The injected pollutants were noticeable at the nearshore ocean. Ursula and Peter Bennett would migrate on a perennial basis to the area, flocking from their home in the Toronto suburb of Mississauga to Lahaina to swim with marine turtles off the coast of Honokōwai. Peter is a technical writer, and Ursula is a teacher who has taken several oceanography courses offered during the University of Hawaii's summer program. In 1991, they released a videotape contrasting underwater scenes captured in 1989 with footage of the same locations taken in 1991. The video showed dying coral heads and disappeared schools of reef fish—all amid a dense film of green *Cladophora* algae. Farther up the coast, the red alga *Hypnea musciformis*—a species introduced in Kāne'ohe Bay twenty years before—clogged the seas and fouled the beaches. In Kahului Bay, growths of a third type of algae—*Ulva fasciata*, or sea lettuce—were an almost perennial problem.

In 1991, people living along the coast of West Maui began to worry that the algae blooms might not be transient and were causing long-term, dramatic deterioration in the quality of coastal waters. Residents of the area sifted through a U.S. Soil Conservation Service flood control plan for the Lahaina Watershed, connecting dots, analyzing cumulative impacts, and demanding documentation of anticipated impacts of the proposed Honokōwai drainage channel on nearshore water quality. More than two hundred people signed a petition opposing the project, fearing it was a "threat to the coral reef ecosystem." The State of Hawai'i Department of Health established the prosaically named Algae Task Force, whose charge was to look into the possible causes of the algae blooms and recommend remedies.

At one of its earliest meetings in February 1992, the Algae Task Force turned its attention to the injection wells at the Lahaina treatment plant.

Chairman William Magruder, a marine botanist with Bishop Museum, told *The Maui News*, "We really don't know where this stuff's going," referring to the marginally treated human sewage.

The problem was scientific study, or the lack thereof, on the specific hydrology and biology of the injection wells. It would take several environmental advocates and heroes, working in a covalence of common interests, to make the undeniable case that these injection wells damage the public's nearshore waters.

A 1993 study conducted by Tetra Tech identified the Lahaina Wastewater Treatment Facility (LWTF) as one of the three primary nutrient release sources releasing into the Lahaina coastal waters, in addition to sugarcane and pineapple cultivation. That study ranked the LWRF second in annual nitrogen contribution and first in phosphorous contribution to these waters. But since that study, the cultivation of both sugarcane and pineapple has been sharply curtailed, which suggests that the LWRF may now be the primary contributor of nutrients to water in the study area. The West Maui Watershed Owner's Manual (West Maui Watershed Management Advisory Committee, 1997) concluded that the LWRF wastewater injection wells likely contributed about three times the amount of nitrogen, and at least an order of magnitude more phosphorous, to the ocean than did any other source. Improvements in the treatment processing system came in 1995 with the institution of wastewater reclamation based upon the Tetra Tech (1993) study that reduced the quantities of the nitrogen and phosphorus to the LWRF-injected effluent. However, both the concentrations and magnitude appear to remain a significant component of discharge from the submarine springs, as well as from other sources along the West Maui Coast.

This point in history suggesting a clear relationship between the injection wells and the algae blooms was pivotal. If people like the Bennetts and the surfers and shoreline fishers could prove to politicians and judges that this damaging relationship really exists, then they could end it and restore the natural ecosystem of this stretch of coastline. And that's exactly what they did.

There is Cause for Concern

Maui spent much of the territorial period as a sleepy sugar and pineapple plantation economy where different branches of the same missionary-descendant family controlled the political and economic life of the island. However, in an effort to produce economic development and opportunities for the children of sugar and pineapple workers, tourism, and eventually second-home development, woke Maui from that sleep. Population decline reversed and the influx of newcomers resumed.

Among them was Sharyn Matin, a lawyer from Sacramento and the first female state administrative law judge in her region. What started out as an ordinary, holiday escape became home, and later a passion. She and her husband settled down at the Mahana, a condominium overlooking Honokōwai. The "Honokōwai channel" starts in the Honokōwai Valley, way up in the West Maui Mountains, then runs to the sea, finally terminating on the northern edge of the Kāʻanapali Shores Resort. Through her apartment windows Sharyn could see from Black Rock all along North Beach to Honokōwai. One day in 2003, she saw something horrifying—the sea changed color. The amethyst blues gave way to a muddy brown, as far as the eye could see. Only a thin strip of blue remained, crowded out by the newly earthen tones of the ocean.

She formed a new group, the West Maui Preservation Association (WMPA), in 2004, to intervene in the expansion of the Westin Kāʻanapali Ocean Resort Villas, a Starwood timeshare property in the prosaically named Lot 2. The project would add more than eleven acres and 258 units to its growing inventory of timeshare units in West Maui. In addition to concerns about traffic and drainage, WMPA's petition raised concerns about contamination of nearshore waters. WMPA settled with the developer for a series of protections including nearshore water quality testing, dunes preservation program, and other public benefits.

WMPA then intervened in Intrawest's proposal to develop Lot 4— which had originally been owned by Starwood. By 2005, WMPA had reached an agreement with the developer. A special management area permit was granted to allow construction to move forward. However, that permitting process resulted in significant concessions to the public interest through a settlement reached through mediation, including having sewage from the new development redirected towards Nāpili, not to the plant across the street from Mahana, with backflow valves requested for Mahana and the three other condos on that line. With the question of Lots 2 and 4 disposed, WMPA's attention shifted to the discharge and erosion question itself.

To start, WMPA members and supporters tracked West Maui sewage spills—58,000 gallons in March 2004, 18,000 gallons in October 2006, and so on. On March 30, 2006, a twelve-inch sewer line burst on Front Street, spilling 3,125 gallons of sewage. Just six days later, county public works officials begged the Maui County Council Budget Committee for $25.9 million in new sewer projects. "We just can't afford not to replace these things before they break," Wastewater Reclamation Division Chief David Taylor told the committee.

Matin hired Kīhei-based firm Water Quality Consulting, Inc. to analyze the nearshore waters. Called a "synoptic survey"—a look at what Water Quality called a "snapshot in time"—the study contains data collected between Aug. 28 and Oct. 18 of 2006. Water Quality took water samples during wet and dry conditions, from two footbridges that span the channel—one just makai of the Lower Honoapi'ilani Road bridge over the channel, the other just mauka of the shoreline—as well as the sand berm that lies at the mouth of the channel and nearshore waters about one hundred feet north and south of the channel.

The results showed elevated levels of *Enterococcus* bacteria, *Clostridium* and fecal Coliform bacteria—levels she said exceeded state health quality levels—as well as low levels of *E. coli.*

Water Quality's research showed one dimension of the problem, but it didn't explain why it happened. "There are any number of sources," a Water Quality researcher told Anthony Pignataro in a 2007 story for *Maui Time Weekly.* "[But] sewage is a potential source and a likely source, having the sewer lines there, the sewage plant there. There could be leaking sewer lines, septic tanks...There is a cause for concern for recreational users as well as the ecology of nearshore waters."

Permit Opportunity

Since the 1970s, numerous studies have examined the impact of the injection wells. But two studies, one in 2008 and another in 2009, drew a tighter correlation between the algal blooms and the injection wells.

In September 2008, the citizens fighting for the health of Lahaina's ocean had an opportunity to stop it in the form of a permit proceeding. UM-1357 was the county's permission from the state to inject wastewater into the ground. The Lahaina facility needed a permit from the state in order to continue operation. What had become a choreographed routine of renewals and extensions for a harmful injection permit became an opportunity make a lasting significant difference in wastewater management. The Hawai'i Department of Health (DOH) extended the Underground Injection Control (UIC) permit three times for periods of six months each, and four times for periods of one calendar year each.

The U.S. Environmental Protection Agency (EPA) gave the County of

Maui until May 2010 to submit an application for a permit under the Clean Water Act to operate their sewage injection wells. "[The] EPA has determined that the [C]ounty of Maui's operation of the [LWRF] may result in a discharge into navigable waters," explained the EPA's Region 9 Manager for the Ground Water Office. "[The] EPA has reviewed recent studies from the University of Hawai'i (UH) and the United States Geologial Survey (USGS), which strongly suggest that effluent from the facility's injection wells is discharging into the nearshore coastal zone of the Pacific Ocean."

In March 2008, Cheryl Okuma, the county's Environmental Management Department director challenged the EPA's Clean Water Act permit requirement for the sewage injection wells. Okuma admitted to the EPA that the county had "concerns on its ability to respond." She cited the lack of funds allocated for such work and the delays involved in hiring contractors under state procurement laws. Finally, Okuma referred to the 1993 study of effluent fate that failed to "demonstrate that pollutants from the LWRF were being discharged into nearby coastal waters." What's more, she said the nitrogen in the effluent being discharged through the injection wells had been reduced by eighty percent since the time of that earlier study.

The Bennetts' evidence was confirmed years later by eyewitness accounts from other ocean aficionados. In 2008, surfer Wayne Cochran spoke at an EPA hearing. "I started doing stand-up paddle-boarding, where you paddle up and down the coast," he said. "From six feet up, you get a real good view of the reef. The last five years, I've seen the reef just—the live coral disappear right before my eyes. It's just fading so fast. And I've also seen the fish disappear."

In May 2008, Dailer and Darla White, with the State Department of Land and Natural Resources' Division of Aquatic Resources, went back to the Kīhei and Lahaina coasts to take algae samples for the USGS study.

From May 6 to May 28, 2009, researchers Charles Hunt and Sarah Rosa conducted an investigation: wading and kayak trolling with a multiparameter water-quality sonde, marine water column sampling, and collecting of benthic algae samples. Megan Dailer lent her kayak to the effort.

NEW RESEARCH AND THE KĪHEI STRATEGY

The beauty of the scientific method is that it is a long conversation, sometimes over decades, involving scores of peoples who need not work in close collaboration. In 2008, Megan Dailer and Celia Smith from the biology department conducted an isotope study. They found that the nitrogen isotope that is characteristic of human sewage was present where the UH researchers had predicted. Perhaps more importantly, from a management perspective, this work provides a significant nexus between a wastewater source injected into the groundwater and specific surface water quality impacts that prevent the attainment of protected uses, such as the conservation of coral reefs and support of aquatic life.

Dailer and her team studied algae samples from the Kīhei and Lahaina coasts, looking for evidence of land-based nitrogen sources. On both coasts, nitrogen values were found to be elevated in areas corresponding to the presumed sewage plumes. At Kīhei, nitrogen values of fifteen to eighteen parts per thousand were measured across the core of the modeled plume, falling off to values as light as six outside the plume. At Lahaina, the nitrogen values were greater, reaching a maximum of thirty-nine parts per thousand at Kahekili Beach Park in the North Beach subdivision.

The report by Dailer and her coauthors published in 2010 in the *Marine Pollution Bulletin,* calculated that from 1997 to 2008, the county's three sewage treatment plants in Lahaina, Kīhei, and Kahului dumped into the sea fifty-one billion gallons of effluent containing some 3.84 million pounds of nitrogen. This new research focused on Lahaina. But on the south shore of Maui, in Kīhei, another group of community leaders was concerned about the impacts of injection wells on their nearshore waters. This new group, Pūko'a o Kama Alliance, as well as individual Kīhei residents, including Daniel Kanahele, Jimmy Conniff and others filed a lawsuit against the County of Maui and Okuma using Dailer's research. The lawsuit was based on the operation of another injection well wastewater plant down the coast in Kīhei. The plaintiffs, represented by Maui attorney, Lance D. Collins demanded the immediate shutdown of the injection wells. The lawsuit alleged that the plant was in violation of state water quality standards. The plaintiffs also argued that its operation violated the county's public trust duty to assure the integrity of coastal waters, that the plant was a public nuisance and posed a threat to the plaintiffs' health, interfered with the plaintiffs' practice of their traditional and customary rights, and violated the state law that implements the Coastal Zone Management Act.

In the Kīhei case, Pūko'a o Kama Alliance plaintiffs wanted to halt the county's efforts to renew the injection well permit. The old permit was set to expire on August 14, 2010. The county had already applied for a renewal. While there is no provision for public notice in the renewal process itself, the permit's terms allow the public to intervene at any point.

The county sought to have the case dismissed, however, the judge ordered that the issues be remanded to the Department of Health and he stayed the lawsuit. As of this writing, the Pūkoʻa o Kama suit is still stayed. The hearings officer formally dismissed the part of the petition that he felt he could move on and he transferred the rest of it to the state DOH Safe Drinking Water branch. But nothing substantive occurred through this administrative strategy.

WMPA filed a similar administrative proceeding to the one the judge had ordered Pūkoʻa o Kama Alliance to do. The result was the same. The hearings officer refused to rule on anything that potentially could involve the Clean Water Act. Everything involving the Safe Drinking Water Act was sent to the Safe Drinking Water branch for its determination but not through a contested case proceeding.

COMPELLING COMPLIANCE

The new research reports from 2010 proved to be sufficient fuel for new federal action. The reports provided a new complication for the county's environmental management division, which had been renegotiating its own contentious relationship with the state and federal governments. "We're highly regulated by the Department of Health and the EPA," a county environmental manager told the Hawaiʻi local publication *Environment Hawaiʻi* in 2010. Indeed, the county was under a $900,000 consent decree for a decade of major sewage spills from 1989 to 1999. A 1999 EPA press release:

> These spills, ranging from a few gallons up to a million gallons, reached ocean waters in some instances, necessitating the posting of warning signs on public beaches. In other cases, the spills polluted freshwater streams, and in others, raw sewage flowed into public streets, parking lots, homes, and farms.

The causes were manifold—blockage of sewer lines by grease buildup, equipment malfunction and operator error at sewage treatment plants and pump stations, pipe breaks caused by faulty construction work, and corrosion and collapse of aging sewer lines. Under the decree, Maui County was required to increase routine maintenance of sewer lines, implementing a grease-control ordinance to prevent blockages, and evaluate and replace corroded sewer lines and aged treatment facilities.

One aim of the 1999 decree was to "reduce wastewater injection into aquifers, which may cause pollution in adjoining ocean waters." It is against this background of decades-long concern with the injection wells, and the new information provided by the UH and USGS studies, that the local EPA Ground Water chief, David Albright, manager of the EPA Region 9 Ground Water Office, informed the Environmental Management Department's Cheryl Okuma that the county would have to apply for a water quality certification. The certification is required under section 401 of the Clean Water Act before any federal permit can be issued for activities that may result in discharges to navigable waters.

In a letter dated March 10, 1999, the EPA stated it "has determined that the county of Maui's operation of the [LWRF] may result in a discharge into navigable waters." Further, the "EPA has reviewed recent studies from UH and the USGS, which strongly suggest that effluent from the facility's injection wells is discharging into the nearshore coastal." Albright gave the county until May 11, 1999 to submit the application.

Environment Hawai'i reported in 2010 that Okuma challenged the "specific authority under which the EPA is requesting this particular off-site data collection," since most "of the requested sampling would require the county to conduct testing far outside the confines of the LWRF site." Maui lacked the resources and the procurement flexibility to do the work. She also referred to the 1993 study of effluent that failed to "demonstrate that pollutants from the LWRF were being discharged into nearby coastal waters."

Finally, she addressed claims made in a Save Kahului Harbor leaflet about the increasing incidence of staph infections among swimmers and paddlers. Okuma says she spoke with a University of Hawai'i staff member who told her staph cannot survive in a seawater environment. In reference to Okuma's March statement claiming the EPA letter was a "request," Robin Knox, a member of the working group and a water quality scientist with twenty-five years of experience, including regulation and permit writing, insisted that the EPA letter was an enforcement order, not a request. She noted that the EPA had already taken significant steps to address groundwater pollutants, including a mandate to retire large-capacity cesspools.

Environment Hawai'i claimed that as of April, 2010, the DOH had received no application from the county for a water quality certification, nor had the county been in touch with anyone at the Clean Water Branch, which processes such applications. Dave Taylor, then wastewater chief for the county, said he didn't recall the letter specifically. "There's a lot of correspondence that goes on between this office and Dave Albright's group and the Department of Health," he said (Tummons, *Environment Hawai'i*, May, 2010).

THE FIRST HEARING

In November 2008, the EPA convened a hearing on a new proposed UIC permit. The meeting was held at the Lahaina Civic Center, in the social hall meeting area. The transcripts record the comments by many, led off by Wastewater Reclamation Division Chief Dave Taylor, who reminded the crowd that "we don't make pollution. The public makes pollution. The public makes waste." He continued, stating clearly that the injection well water eventually makes its way to the ocean:

> Either we reuse it—and reuse, from the Lahaina treatment plant, about a million gallons day, or about 20 percent of that water. And that's mostly used at Kā'anapali, on the golf courses and for greenways and things like that. So that water that gets reused goes through ultraviolet disinfection, which are ultraviolet lamps that sterilize any pathogens that are in that water. And so about a million gallons of that water every day goes towards reuse. The other water, about four million gallons, maybe a little less, goes down the injection wells. The injection well water is—does not go through the ultraviolet treatment. It goes down these deep pipes into the ground, they go down a couple hundred feet. And that water moves outward through the ground, eventually it comes out into the ocean.

Taylor went on to speak about why it is that the county doesn't reuse more of the wastewater. A questioner asked why only the water headed to the golf course was treated to an R-1 (reuse) standard, to which Taylor responded that they're simply following the rules laid out by the State Department of Health, along with the EPA's federal requirements. The counties argued against the higher levels of government regulation they're expected to follow, claiming they did not have the necessary resources to comply. "And that's not really a choice anymore that we locally have—get to make. We don't get to decide, hmm, is it worth it," Taylor said.

The Pacific Whale Foundation's Brooke Porter spoke against the permit application, raising concerns about the effects to the reefs on algae linked to effluent discharge. The wastewater should be reused, he said. Hannah Bernard spoke on behalf of the Hawai'i Wildlife Fund, the Maui Reef Fund, and the Don't Inject, Redirect Coalition (DIRE). She argued that the permit should be denied based on the public trust doctrine, a gem of Hawaii's public laws which says that the government has a fiduciary obligation to protect the land and natural resources for the benefit of the public. George Lavenson followed Bernard, arguing for the recycling of the wastewater, as well as limiting overdevelopment, which produces the excess waste. Irene Bowie from Maui Tomorrow echoed the concerns.

Russell Sparks, staff member of the state's Division of Aquatic Resources at the Department of Land and Natural Resources addressed the health of the reefs, which his team had been monitoring for more than a decade. "When we stitched together the long-term data set, it was really clear that a lot of reefs are declining quite substantially." He called for the EPA to set a high standard for the proposed permit. Volume should be five million gallons per day and nutrient levels should be capped at seven milligrams per liter. Compared to the previous speakers, Sparks gave a more measured endorsement of reusing wastewater, saying that the permit conditions should lead to a transition to recycling.

In 2010, the County of Maui was reusing approximately twenty seven percent of wastewater processed at its facilities while the rest has been injected. In West Maui, Kā'anapali Resort uses up to 1.3 million gallons per day of R-1 recycled water since the 1990s when the county adopted an ordinance requiring certain commercial water users to use recycled water. Kā'anapali Resort uses recycled water to irrigate parts of two gold courses, landscape features abutting the main highway and median strips within the resort. However, since the ordinance passage and initial development of recycling infrastructure in the mid-1990s, reusing water has not been a county priority and the distribution of the recycled water remains with the Wastewater and Reclamation Division of the Department of Environmental Management and not the Department of Water Supply, which has primarily responsibility over the use of water in Maui County.

EPA REVISES THE PERMIT

In light of the public concerns expressed at the November 2008 meeting, the EPA published a second draft the following May. It proposed to reduce the allowable limit for suspended solids to sixty parts per million (ppm) average and added a nitrate concentration limit of ten ppm. Total nitrogen concentration limits remained at ten ppm. The EPA also proposed new restrictions on overall quantities of nitrogen in the effluent, limiting the total nitrogen mass loading limits to twelve thousand pounds per calendar month and twenty-nine thousand pounds per quarter, with further reductions to be attained over the ten-year lifespan of the new permit. The new draft also required that the county disinfect all wastewater injected into the wells to a standard of no more than one hundred MPN (most probable number) of fecal coliform per one hundred milliliters by December 31, 2011. Lastly, the new draft permit proposed that by December 31, 2011, all wastewater, including the injected effluent, be treated to R-1 standards (a level allowing its use as irrigation water) by ultraviolet disinfection instead of chlorination.

"[The] EPA believes the use of ultraviolet disinfection will allow the county to increase over time the percent of wastewater from this facility that is reclaimed for beneficial use," the EPA wrote in its statement justifying the new draft permit terms. "Moreover, since the LWRF was initially constructed as a reclamation facility, using federal grant money, [the] EPA finds it appropriate to place reasonable conditions in the permit that will shift practices at LWRF from injection to higher levels of reuse."

The EPA held a new hearing in August on the second draft. County staff and citizens assembled for the seventh monthly meeting of the Community Working Group on Wastewater Reuse, established after the EPA conducted an August 2009 hearing to hear testimony regarding West Maui injection wells. "The group was ostensibly organized to incorporate community input about the then-Maui Mayor Charmaine Tavares administration's stated goal of reusing 100 percent of treated wastewater, thereby eliminating the need to inject millions of gallons daily deep into the ground adjacent to coastal waters where the nitrogen-rich content has been linked to excessive algae blooms—and worse," wrote Parson for *Maui Time*. "But some of the twenty-one volunteer members of the working group and members of the ad hoc DIRE Coalition (Don't Inject, Redirect) believe that Tavares and county officials are not doing enough to achieve those goals. Claims of withheld information and obfuscation are clouding the waters and slowing down the process."

Tavares led off the hearing, testifying that the UIC permit should be extended five years. The extension would provide time for her administration to establish a citizens' panel that would formulate a plan. Reuse was a top priority, as it would open the use of algae for bioenergy generation. "Our goal is to use all of the water that's produced by our treatment plants and not put it down any injection wells. That's our goal." That group was to meet the following month. It did, but its members were unable to agree on a course of action.

In a September 21, 2009 letter to the EPA Region 9 Ground Water Office manager David Albright, Department of Environmental Management Director Cheryl Okuma wrote that "the purpose of underground injection programs is to 'prevent underground injection which endangers drinking water sources.'" The EPA statement justifying tighter treatment standards, she continued, "acknowledges that the only nearby public water systems are upgradient and will not be affected." In a document given to the Maui County Council a month earlier, Okuma suggested that the EPA had no scientific data to back up its rationale for the permit changes. When skeptical council members at a September 17 meeting raised questions about her statement, Okuma deferred to deputy corporation counsel Jane Lovell:

> [T]he issuing agency is required by law...to have some scientific connection between the specific parameters that they are imposing on the permit—whether it's the timeline, whether it's limitations on particular chemical components, or anything else.
>
> If the county has concerns about any of the permit conditions...the county would have thirty days within which to appeal any permit conditions to the Environmental Appeals Board in Washington, DC. Given the complexity of the technical issues, the very large amount of money at stake, and a forum in which my office doesn't routinely practice...the corporation counsel may be asking the council at some point for authority to engage outside counsel to assist with any appeal. (Tummons, *Environment Hawai'i*, May, 2010).

Members of the DIRE Coalition objected to the proposed ten-year term of the permit and asked the EPA to require the county to obtain a National Pollutant Discharge Elimination System (NPDES) permit, which is mandatory whenever there are discharges of pollutants from point sources to waters of the US. Most importantly, they demanded that the EPA wait until the DOH gave the county a water quality certification before awarding a new permit, pursuant to Section 401 of the Clean Water Act.

Russell Sparks, who had spoken at the previous year's hearing, testified again on behalf of DLNR's Aquatics Division. "The reefs are collapsing on themselves, and there has been a 50 percent decline in reefs since 1999," he said, "We do not expect the reefs to come back."

Darla White, a University of Hawai'i coral reef researcher and diver who helped Meghan Dailer gather samples for her study, testified that she had contracted MRSA (methicillin-resistant Staphylococcus aureus) seven times because of the pollution in the water from the injection wells. "This is a nasty infection, and many of my fellow researchers are getting sick after being in the ocean," she said.

Lahaina resident and surfer Andrew Lehmann testified about staph infections as well. "My staph infections have been getting worse over the past five years," he told the EPA. "When I went to Australia to surf, I had no staph infections. Within two weeks of returning to surfing in West Maui, I got staph from a little cut on my foot. My whole leg swelled up."

Other testifiers criticized Mayor Tavares' proposal to extend the UIC permit, a proposal that included language about utilizing algae for bioenergy projects.

"Biodiesel from algae is ten years off," Robert Henrikson said in his testimony. "Let Exxon, BP and government consortiums invest $600 million in R&D to take the risks to commercialize this unproven technology. Maui County should not be in this business taking these kinds of risks with tax-payers' money just because algae biofuels have received a lot of publicity and some biofuel company needs a project. Maui has a waste treatment problem to clean up."

According to the *Lahaina News*, Mayor Tavares remained until the end of the meeting and told a small group that she would "meet with US Sen. Daniel Inouye to discuss the county's share of federal economic stimulus money. The county has requested grant money for fifty-two shovel-ready projects, including improvements to the Lahaina, Kihei and Kahului sewage treatment plants." After the meeting, Maui Tomorrow Executive Director Irene Bowie, a member of both the county working group and the DIRE Coalition, expressed her frustration over the situation in Kahului to *Maui Time*: "Why bother with the working group if there's no accurate information," Bowie asked. "Back in December when we heard the 'Wastewater 101' presentation, we were told the eight wells in Kahului were all operational. They never told us they were pursuing an SMA exemption to construct two more. It is clearly a new development in the SMA," insisted Bowie. "It was so wrong for Jeff Hunt to give the exemption" (Parson, *Maui Time*, 2010).

"By fighting this, the county is wasting time and dollars that could be put to solving the problem," Robin Knox told *Maui Time*. Knox was part of a group that took representatives snorkeling to show them where treated wastewater from injection wells was bubbling up near the shores. "In the eleven years between 1997 and 2008, it is estimated that fifty-one billion gallons were injected, much of it with inadequate disinfection. That equates to four million pounds of nitrogen over that time period," Knox reiterated. Knox said the wells should abide by the parameters of the Clean Water Act rather than the less restrictive Safe Drinking Water Act. She had assisted studies and USGS reports that provided a rational nexus whereby a National Pollutant Discharge Elimination System (NPDES) permit should be required. Knox, who runs a water quality consulting business, also questioned Okuma's assertion that saline environments are inhospitable for staph bacteria. "Maui has one of the greatest incidences of staph per one hundred thousand people," she told *Maui Time*.

True to promises she had made at the EPA hearing in August, Mayor Tavares established the Community Working Group (CWG) on Wastewater Reuse, whose members represented a broad cross section of interests and expertise, according to *Environment Hawai'i*. Among them were Irene Bowie, of the planning group Maui Tomorrow, Robin Knox, a water quality expert, and Jeffrey Schwartz, an attorney. All three were DIRE Coalition members. As stated in *Environment Hawai'i*:

> Relations between the mayor's people on the CWG and the DIRE members frayed quickly. The ostensible purpose of the CWG was to develop ideas on how to move forward with the mayor's goal of reusing 100 percent of wastewater effluent and eliminating the need for injection, but the DIRE members came to the conclusion that they would have little input into the CWG's agenda.

Among other things, DIRE members accused the administration of holding back information about plans to drill new injection wells at the Kahului treatment plant. "Although the issue of 'replacement injection wells' came up in the CWG," the alliance stated on its website that the project management team did not disclose to the CWG that new injection wells with a ten to thirty year life were being planned for Kahului, Lahaina and Kīhei. "We learned about it only when the Department of Environmental Management sought an exemption from the planning director so that no environmental assessment and no Special Management Area permit would be required for two new replacement wells in Kahului." Having learned about it, the group moved quickly to try to prevent the action.

However, the county planning director had already determined that the Kahului project was exempt from requirements for public notice or preparation of an environmental assessment, calling it a "minor" action. DIRE and another group, Save Kahului Harbor, appealed the decision to the Maui Planning Commission. In their appeal, the groups argued that the county was violating the Clean Water Act by not having an NPDES permit covering the discharge of pollutants into the ocean. Dailer and her colleagues found strong indicators of wastewater entering the nearshore waters just off the Kahului plant.

"Apart from the legal concerns," they wrote in the appeal, "we believe that important policy, practical, and fiscal concerns make reconsideration or appeal of the [planning director's decision] imperative... We offer one illustrative point about the wisdom of the proposed action. The Kahului plant in question has an uncertain remaining useful life. The seas are rising. The land is sinking. Part of the plant is already falling into the ocean. It is at great risk in case of a substantial tsunami. The plant is approaching forty years old and it is not clear how long the Kahului plant's remaining useful life is. To invest in new replacement injection wells at this time, in the face of this uncertainty, could waste taxpayer money." Dailer and her group concluded that other alternatives should have been (and must be) explored.

Meanwhile, EPA officials met with Mayor Tavares as well as Robin Knox and Earthjustice attorney Paul Achitoff. Knox recalled the EPA's Region 9 Water Division Director cutting short Tavares's spiel on a ten-year plan for algae-to-biofuel production by interjecting, "pardon me Mayor, you have one year." She was referring to the provision of an adequate plan to comply with permit requirements.

The EPA then sent a certified letter to Maui's Department of Environmental Management, ordering "sampling and reporting under Section 308 of the Clean Water Act for the County of Maui's Lahaina Wastewater Reclamation Facility [LWRF]." It called for the county to submit, by April 26, 2010, an effluent and coastal seep sampling and analysis plan, to be followed by a one-year sampling of the wastewater effluent. The EPA cited the previous studies linking the effects on coastal waters to nutrient inputs from the LWRF wells (Parson, Rob, "Wastewater Injection Wells May Be Polluting Our Ocean," *Maui Time*, May 20, 2010). "[The] EPA is investigating the possible discharge of pollutants to the coastal waters of the Pacific Ocean along the Kāʻanapali Coast of Maui," writes the agency. "In 2007 and 2008, the University of Hawaiʻi [study by Meghan Dailer, Robin Knox, et al.] and the US Geological Survey conducted ambient tracer studies, which found substantial evidence that injected effluent from the LWRF is emerging from submarine springs into the coastal water around Kahekili Beach Park along the Kāʻanapali coastline. In order to assess the impact of the LWRF's effluent on the coastal waters and determine compliance with the [Clean Water] Act, [the] EPA is requiring the county to sample the injected effluent, sample the coastal seeps, conduct an introduced tracer study, and submit reports on these activities and findings to EPA."

The May 2010 issue of *Environment Hawaiʻi* contains a 1992 quote from DOH that underscored the problem: it didn't bubble up overnight: "If the algae problem is attributed to the operation of the injection wells, a critical issue will focus over the compliance requirements of the Clean Water Act," reads the quote.

According to *Maui Time*, the county was informed in late January by the EPA about the requirement for studies at the LWRF, but no county budget request was submitted to conduct them. Council members Wayne Nishiki, Sol Kahoʻohalahala and Joe Pontanilla expressed their displeasure over the omission, and inserted last-minute budget provisions to address the need for studies and EPA compliance. "The county is not in a favorable position with the EPA," warned Knox in *Maui Time*. "The county and ratepayers and tax-payers now have a huge liability" (Parson, *Maui Time*, 2010).

Maui Time reported that Director Okuma responded to the EPA letter, which she referred to as a "request," despite the EPA's language: "The Environmental Protection Agency, Region 9 (EPA), hereby requires..." Under what authority, Okuma's letter asked, was the EPA "requesting" off-site data collection. The letter also asked for clarification on the nature of tests and timelines (though both are provided in the EPA letter) and raised the issue of county financial restraints. "The county asks that the deadline for submitting a revised sampling plan be deferred pending resolution of the related issues," Okuma wrote.

Apart from negotiations with the EPA, a rift developed between the DIRE Coalition and the Wastewater Community Working Group. In advance of the primary election, former EPA attorney Jeffrey Schwartz called for a complete reuse plan to be drafted by mid-September. "They told us 'no' to the subcommittees and 'no' to a plan," Schwartz told the newspaper. "So what we're actually doing is only planning to plan, not coming up with a way to implement it." Schwartz further stated that the county has been negligent in providing alternative solutions to injection wells and that 1,900 communities of varying sizes had been able to replace that method of wastewater disposal. The Mayor's spokesperson, Mahina Martin, responded, saying it was "disappointing that DIRE will politicize an important community issue and put their own impatience ahead of everyone else who volunteered to serve on the working group."

The Courts—and New Evidence

The UIC permits issued by the state and federal governments deal with the health of the aquifer. There is a line circumnavigating each island. A wider variety of wells are allowed makai of the line because the underlying aquifer is not considered a drinking water source. The aquifer lying mauka of the line is a source of drinking water. However, the UIC permit doesn't deal with algae blooms or offshore waters. A separate EPA permit, issued under the National Pollutant Discharge Elimination System, manages effluent releases into nearshore waters.

In 2012, the environmental law firm Earthjustice reexamined the potential for a lawsuit. Four plaintiffs emerged—Hawai'i Wildlife Fund, Surfrider Foundation, West Maui Preservation Association, and Sierra Club-Maui Group—and together they filed suit in April to force the county to secure a National Pollutant Discharge Elimination System permit.

The suit was bolstered by a new study by the EPA, the Hawai'i Department of Health, the US Army Engineer Research and Development Center, and researchers at the University of Hawai'i, the results of which were announced in 2013. The Tracer Dye Study on wells 2, 3, and 4 gathered data on the hydrological connections between the injected, treated wastewater effluent and the coastal waters. The study found conclusively that when added to LWRF injection wells 3 and 4, fluorescein tracer dye arrived at coastal submarine spring sites within eighty-four days.

"Any use of the Lahaina facility is illegal"

In May 2015, federal district court Judge Susan Oki Mollway found that the county's unpermitted discharges by wells 3 and 4 were in violation of the Clean Water Act. Half-a-year later, Judge Mollway ruled that the discharges from wells 1 and 2 were illegal as well. The penalty would have been a $100,000 per day fine.

In a public statement, Maui County Council member Mike White called the ruling a first of its kind: "It appears to be an unprecedented ruling to find injection wells are subject to the Clean Water Act, even when they are operating in compliance with permits issued under the Safe Drinking Water Act. The Lahaina wells were constructed with the support of, and operated for, more than forty years with the permission of federal and state regulators. Yet no federal or state agencies are coming to the county's aid in this case or being subjected to the same legal scrutiny or exposure."

Mayor Alan Arakawa said in a statement that the court's ruling had "far-reaching implications, not only for Maui County, but for state and other local governments, which is why the county must appeal this decision." He added that there are more than 5,600 injection wells being used in the State of Hawai'i, and hundreds of thousands more across the country. "This national battle is being fought at the expense of Maui's taxpayers."

Maui County appealed the decision but agreed to pay a $100,000 penalty to the federal treasury. Additionally, the county agreed to spend another $2.5 million on projects designed to divert treated wastewater from its four Lahaina injection wells, and to reuse that water to meet existing water demands in West Maui, should it lose the appeal.

"Today's settlement ensures the lion's share of the penalty for the county's years of violations will be invested to solve problems in West Maui, protecting fragile coral reefs and helping to address chronic water shortages," Earthjustice Mid-Pacific Office attorney David Henkin said in a news release.

"This settlement is a major victory in getting the county to stop using the reef off of Kahekili Beach as its wastewater dumping ground," Lucienne de Naie of Sierra Club-Maui said in a statement. "It requires the county to invest in sensible alternatives to injection, meeting existing demand for precious water in West Maui by constructing infrastructure to get treated wastewater to golf courses, resorts and others." Hanna Bernard, director of the Maui-based Hawai'i Wildlife Fund said, "the devastation to this once pristine coral reef ecosystem is tragic. The county should embrace its role as steward of Maui's natural resources and treat this settlement as a starting point to do all it can to save what's left of this fragile reef, including eventually shutting down the wells for good."

If the county wins its appeal, it will be able to continue operations at the Lahaina facility and avoid all fines. If not, the county will need to abide by the settlement agreement, pay the fines and secure a NPDES permit, which would set limits on the pollutants that can be discharged from the wells. Henkin said Maui residents would be better served if the county, instead of spending thousands more on lawyers' fees, would just spend the money to fix the Lahaina facility's pollution problems. As of this writing, the County of Maui had paid over $4 million to outside attorneys to evaluate their case. Lance D. Collins, speaking for the West Maui Preservation Association, said it was "disappointing that the county chose to fight tooth and nail, wasting taxpayer money on expensive Mainland lawyers rather than trying to protect the reefs at Kahekili Beach." He hoped the settlement agreement would be "a turn in the right direction." Maui County reapplied for a National Pollutant Discharge Elimination System permit but received no comments or approval from the DOH.

Researchers Building on the Lahaina Example

In 2016, researchers at the University of Hawai'i released a new study that linked the quality of coastal groundwater with reef degradation on Maui.[1] The study assessed groundwater quality, coastal water quality and reef health across six different bays on Maui, with various potential sources of pollution. According to *Maui Now*, these scientists stated that the study is the first to show the extent of the impact of wastewater injection wells at Kahului Wastewater Reclamation Facility, Maui's highest-volume sewage treatment plant.[2] In addition to relatively high nutrient levels in Kahului Bay marine surface waters, shallow areas are almost entirely dominated by a thick fleshy mat of colonial zoanthids, a phenomenon not reported anywhere else in the state.[3]

The University of Hawai'i scientists used a combination of field experiments and chemical analysis of water and algae to show that the quality of coastal groundwater plays a major role in determining the health of nearshore ecosystems in Hawai'i. Their study found that coastal waters at Kū'au and Mā'alaea Bays contain nearly one hundred times more nitrogen than less impacted locations, due to fertilizer-enriched submarine groundwater discharge. Reefs adjacent to large areas of sugarcane agriculture are the most impacted of all the sites. A few species of macroalgae dominate intertidal and subtidal surfaces at Kū'au and Mā'alaea Bays. In areas where coastal groundwater nutrient levels are relatively low, researchers observed much greater diversity, and corals were generally present, indicating a healthier, potentially more robust, ecosystem, according to the study.

A concurrent companion study to this work, led by James Bishop at the UH Mānoa Department of Geology and Geophysics, found that water collected from beach sands, which represents coastal groundwater, next to the Kahului Wastewater Reclamation Facility contained up to 75 percent treated wastewater. This finding highlighted the impact of wastewater in this area.[4]

"Our timely study builds on previous research from UH scientists and recent federal court rulings that show that treated wastewater is illegally discharged to the ocean from injection wells at the Lahaina Wastewater Reclamation facility via SGD to Kahekili Beach Park on West Maui," said Daniel Amato, lead author and recent graduate of the UHM College of Natural Sciences. "This is not an isolated or unique occurrence."

According to University of Hawai'i scientists, the study suggests that contaminated groundwater may present a chronic risk to nearshore marine ecosystems throughout the main Hawaiian Islands. "The long-term goal of this research group is to bridge the disciplines of hydrology, geochemistry and marine biology to help answer pressing questions regarding the source and impact of nutrient pollution in Hawaiian coastal waters," wrote Craig Glenn, Henrietta Dulai and Celia Smith, the collaborating principal investigators and coauthors of the Hawai'i Sea Grant project.

CONCLUSION

On February 1, 2018, the Ninth Court issued its opinion in the county's appeal. The Ninth Circuit's 2018 ruling was damning of both the immediate issue of the county's injection wells, and further, of the county's general approach to environmental management. "At bottom," the Ninth Circuit opinion read, "this case is about preventing the county from doing indirectly that which it cannot do directly...The county could not, under the CWA, build an ocean outfall to dispose of pollutants directly into the Pacific Ocean without a (federal pollution discharge) permit. It cannot do so indirectly either to avoid CWA liability. To hold otherwise would make a mockery of the CWA's prohibitions."[5] Whether this ruling will be a harbinger of a new era of responsible environmental stewardship remains to be seen. Under the Trump Administration, the EPA administrator has proposed repeals of safeguards requiring water quality data to be tracked and released. Future efforts to protect Maui's coastal waters may have to rely on other tools, including community advocacy and political pressure on state and local decision makers.

NOTES

1.   Amato DW, Bishop JM, Glenn CR, Dulai H, Smith CM (2016) Impact of Submarine Groundwater Discharge on Marine Water Quality and Reef Biota of Maui. *PLoS ONE* 11(11): e0165825.

2. UH Study First to Show Extent of Injection Well Impact in Kahului, *Mau News* (Nov. 16, 2016) *available at:* http://mauinow.com/2016/11/16/uh-study -first-to-show-extent-of-injection-well-impact-in-kahului/

3. "UH Study First to Show Extent of Injection Well Impact in Kahului," *Maui Now*, November 16, 2016.

4. James M. Bishop, Craig R. Glenn, Daniel W. Amato, and Henrietta Dulai (2015) Effect of land use and groundwater flow path on submarine groundwater discharge nutrient flux. *Journal of Hydrology: Regional Studies*, ISSN 2214-5818.

5. *Hawaii Wildlife Fund v. County of Maui*, 886 F. 3d 737, 752 (2018).

SAVING HONOLUA BAY

Sydney Lehua Iaukea

Saving Honolua Bay from development plans was a journey accompanied by many twists and turns, even as the story of how this place will ultimately be conserved for future generations remains to be written. On a small island space like Maui, the need to conserve and preserve areas stands at the forefront of battles that often position developers against community agendas. This often polarizing engagement, and the coming together of the same parties to resolution, is important in such places where the risk of ruin is a reality. Beautiful and sacred places need protection from overdevelopment, and this often seems to stand at odds with developers' economic agendas. The immediate needs of the communities in these places, and the molding of the various narratives used to express those needs, are complicated because community members, developers, and county council members blend and interchange responsibilities. But ultimately, saving Honolua Bay is important not just for the residents of this area, but also for telling of how to manage the overall wellness of people and special places.

Līpoa Point is named for the brown seaweed that once infiltrated the shoreline. Located at the northwest tip of Maui, the place encompasses cliffs that stretch into Honolua Bay. Beautiful waves make their way from the deep blue seas of the Pailolo Channel and funnel into the bay for some of the best surfing breaks in the world. Rounding the point to Kahakuloa, open vistas are set against sheer cliffs and country roads. It is not obvious at first glance, but the Save Honolua Coalition (SHC), a once small group of community activists, fiercely protects the place. This coalition grew specifically and rapidly to address Maui Land and Pineapple Company's (MLPC) announcement of development plans at Līpoa Point. For decades, acres of pineapple fields made up the backdrop of the point. Development plans here would have altered the terrain and perhaps blocked community access to the shoreline for surfing and fishing. This realization rallied an international community of surfers and ocean enthusiasts, who united with community members and activists for the protection of Līpoa Point in 2007. It also renewed the call for the continued conservation and preservation of the adjoining bays and areas in recognition of the cultural and environmental significance of these places.

Saving Honolua Bay and Līpoa Point from the luxury home development plans of ML&P was nonnegotiable for the people that live, work, and surf in the area. Grassroots activism drew people together from all walks of life. Ultimately, after years of rallying for Honolua Bay, the state of Hawai'i passed Act 214 in 2013 for the preservation of the area. The law allowed the state to purchase the land from ML&P for $19.8 million, to be held for preservation purposes. Specifically, the legislation paid an almost $20 million shortfall that was earmarked for the ML&P pension fund, alongside saving of "one of the most iconic landmarks in Hawai'i."[1] In what seemed to be a public/private agreement, "the department of land and natural resources shall ensure that the seller of the land . . . uses the proceeds of the sale to benefit the pension plan of retirees of the Maui Land and Pineapple Company, Inc." Of course, the bill also stated, "this section shall not be construed or interpreted or deemed to obligate the State for the pension plan liabilities of employees and retirees of the Maui Land and Pineapple Company, Inc."[2] But how else could the agreement be construed?

Some questioned the agenda of bailing out corporate interests as the price tag for saving Līpoa Point and Honolua Bay. ML&P's pension fund had stopped receiving adequate money to cover its employees—the result of years of declining pineapple demand on the worldwide market that began in the late 1980s, alongside increased production competition from Thailand.[3] Even after an upswing in operations by 2000, ML&P eventually closed their pineapple operations in 2009.[4] The title of a *Maui Times* article in 2014 voiced the concerns of merging government monies with corporate interests best: "State of Hawai'i Saves Maui Land and Pineapple Pensions! Also, Līpoa Point."[5] In the article, Anthony Pignataro pointed out that the act was signed into law at the ILWU (International Longshore and Warehouse Workers Union) headquarters on Maui, which is the union for ML&P workers, and not at Honolua Bay with the environmentalists and community members who had fought long and hard for the saving of Līpoa Point. Union interests apparently took precedence over the environmental win.

Even with the payoff to the pension fund, and the wagering of one of the most treasured places on Maui as the site for the battle, the fight itself was a watershed moment on Maui. People were motivated to stop what appeared to be another land development that had more to do with privilege and power than a commitment to a special place. The Save Honolua fight not only raised community voices, it emboldened these same people to run for the county council and other governmental offices, to save this ʻāina and have a voice in future land use and water issues on Maui.

The success story of the Save Honolua Coalition takes its strength from a narrative more closely aligned to local interests—one that recognizes Hawaiian epistemologies and seeks to resurrect these other ways of being on the land and in the ocean, beyond consuming and profiting from both. Stemming from a rising tide of alternative narratives for Maui, this approach places people before profit and pushes for the reassessment of shortsighted development modes and mantras. This approach is also a direct response to the multigenerational, pro-development discourse that has dominated Maui for years. The actual state endeavor to save Līpoa Point is still in the early stages of planning, so how the area will ultimately be managed remains to be seen. Even so, the fight that led to this point offers hope for the thoughtful preservation of places on Maui and elsewhere. Meanwhile, the community looks on to ensure that the conserving, protecting, and managing of this ʻāina are all done properly.

Honolua Bay

Gerry Lopez, well-known and longtime surfing legend, had this to say about Honolua Bay.

> My first experience with Honolua Bay was during high school and it was memorable if only a vicarious one. The best surfer in our class, Jay Clarke had taken a trip to Maui with some other Honolulu guys to catch a swell there. Tim McCullough had captured a brilliant image of Jaybird from the cliff above and it had appeared in Surfing Illustrated magazine along with a story and more of Timmy's photos.
>
> In late 1967, Reno Abellira and I followed Dick Brewer to Lahaina to get boards shaped and I got my first taste of this legendary wave. My surf skills had improved considerably since high school but Honolua still proved to be a formidable challenge, even at only 4'. Before long, I was swimming into the cliff to retrieve my lost and borrowed board. It was a good thing for the friend who loaned it to me that longboards were built strongly. The waves were small and he knew where I would be using his

board for it took a battering. Chasing my board was something I would do there many times in those days before the surf leash was invented. At Honolua, there was the added misfortune of the rocky cliff if the wipeout occurred on the takeoff or initial stages of the ride. A large cave in the cliff often swallowed boards, sometimes not releasing them until they were completely pulverized. The rocky shoreline was the extra cost in surfing this perfect and alluring wave.

In 1970, the Bahá'í Faith Honolua Surf Contest, hosted by John Thurston, came together in some very clean 4'-6' waves. My surfing there had progressed past the point of losing my board into the cave but I still chased after it over the shallow reef inside the Kiddie Bowl during the finals. My trophy was beautifully homemade by John using local koa, monkey pod and seashells gathered from nearby Slaughter House Beach. In my long surfing career, this was, by far, my favorite trophy.

In 1973, I relocated from Honolulu to Upcountry Maui, and my treks to the bay were regular and as numerous as the swells we could see from the slopes of Haleakalā long before the hard-core Honolua locals who lived in Lahaina knew there was surf at their spot. We learned the intricacies and idiosyncrasies of this fine wave. On a north to northeast swell, outside Subs, named after the huge rock in the takeoff zone that looked like a submarine surfacing, could begin a ride that might run for almost a mile, through the next section, known as the Coconut Grove, on into the Point. If one was lucky and skilled, the ride lead into the main cave section in front of the cliff, finishing way inside the bay at the end section, called the Kiddie Bowl. Generally, the best swell direction was north-northwest, and if the swell was enough like Waimea strong on O'ahu, Honolua would light up from Coconuts through the Point and be most focused on the cave.

Honolua is a magical place and not just for its terrific waves. There is an energy about this location that is palpable to anyone sensitive to those sorts of things. The ancient Hawaiians called it mana and the Valley Isle of Maui has an abundance of it. A lot seemed to be focused in and around the dormant Haleakalā volcano. For some reason, the Honolua area seemed also to abound in this psychic energy and perhaps for this reason, it also was the focal point of the best and most beautiful waves to be found on this island. While the world changes, as man builds his things and the population grows, there is a constant, and it is the waves. Somehow, in spite of mankind, the waves at places like Honolua Bay endure and remain unchanged in our ever-changing world and this is a reassurance that all is well. Keep paddling![6]

Lopez's reference to Subs is a reference to Līpoa Point. He traces the mana of this area from the outside point to the inside cliffs. The sense of peace and wonder that he and others find at Honolua Bay marks the importance of the place and highlights the need for preservation.

Honolua Bay is located in the Honolua ahupuaʻa, Kāʻanapali district of Maui. The following is an excerpt about the Kāʻanapali District in my book, *Kekaʻa: The Making and Saving of North Beach West Maui*:

> Up north from Lahaina is Kāʻanapali. Prior to the land divisions that codified contemporary districts, Kāʻanapali was a separate district that stretched from Kekaʻa point and Honokowai to the Ili o Kukuipuka, where Kahakuloa meets Wailuku. Taking in the entire back part of the West Maui Mountains, this area is a large, diverse, and culturally import-ant region for the island of Maui...The northernmost sections of West Maui are still not crossable in places, except via horse and by foot, because they are set against the sheer cliffs and valleys of Kahakuloa. As this area is still one of the least traveled areas on Maui, it contains many intact taro terraces, heiau, and wahi pana (sacred sites).[7]

Besides the wetland taro and numerous and varied heiau and wahi pana, this entire region is also widely known for the zigzag road of Maui (ke alanui kī keʻekeʻe a Maui), petroglyph rocks and prominent stones, battle sites and large burials, and the robust rivers that flow through the various valleys.[8] The summit of the West Maui Mountains, Puʻu Kukui, is home to Mauna ʻEke. This mountain receives around 387 inches of rainfall annually, and once fed the streams of Honokōwai, Kahana, Mailepai, ʻAlaeloa, Honokahua, Hono-lua, and Honokōhau.[9] There is even a hōlua site documented in this area, "which used to cross a hilly part of what is now the West Maui Gold Links at Honolua [Kulaokaʻeʻa—now in pineapples]."[10] Spectacular in breadth and beauty, the trails, cliffs, and streams are written into the moʻolelo about this ʻāina. And so is the ocean, which is an important part of this ahupuaʻa because of its clarity, resources, features, and waves.

Honolua is one of the six bays of Piʻilani.[11] Kanounou is the name of the point, and refers to the pelting of the sea.[12] The importance of the sea and waves at Honolua is recorded in oral tradition and translated documents.

One such moʻolelo recounts how Kihapiʻilani (Aliʻi Nui of Maui and son of Piʻilani) surfed to Molokaʻi from Honolua Bay:

> Many canoes were prepared for the sail to Molokaʻi. On this sailing of the canoes with the chiefs and the commoners for Molokaʻi, the ocean was completely covered with canoes from Kāʻanapali to Waialua on Molokaʻi. As for the chief, Kihapiʻilani, he did not board any canoe but rode a long surfboard from Honolua and the wild surging waves of the Pailolo Sea carried him with no difficulty, a deed by which the famous waves of that deep blue sea were turned into a plaything as well as sport by that chief. And it is proper for you, O Reader, to pronounce these ancient words, "These waves were brushed aside by this steersman." There was also an adornment of lei on the head of the chief as well as on his neck. Not a particle of spray from the waves was seen tossing up over the adornment of lei on this chief, up to the time of his landing on the shore of Waialua on Molokaʻi. And it was a thing of great amazement to the chiefs and men who witnessed this deed of Kihapiʻilani, but he was known as a surfer and perhaps we can recall this chief meanwhile in the incident when the daughter of Hoolaemakua became his at Hauwa at Hāna. This was the very first time for the ruling chief who surfed on the long surf board from Maui to Molokaʻi over the Sea of Pailolo, the sea which dashed to pieces the bodies of men from ancient times until this day. In that way one can compare him with Kaikipaʻananea, the wonderous one who surfed the waves of ʻAlenuihāhā from Hāna on Maui, landing at Puakō on Hawaiʻi.[13]

This moʻolelo shares the imagery and grandness of surfing from one island to another, where "not a particle of spray from the waves was seen tossing up over the adornment of lei on this chief." Aliʻi surfed the longer boards while makaʻāinana (commoners) surfed shorter alaia boards. The skill and talent of Kihapiʻilani, like in other moʻolelo about surfing in Hawaiʻi, are tied to the skill and talent of the person surfing, so that a skillful surfer will probably display ʻike (knowing) and bravery in other areas of life.

Surfing is a cultural heritage that remains rooted in Hawaiian epistemology. In more contemporary history, surfing found its way to the mainstream stage through a relatively small group of surfers from the 1960s and 70s who evolved surfboard design and supported surf cinema to explore and share their love for the ocean. This era of surfing follows the earlier era of the Waikīkī beach boys, first Duke Kahanamoku and then others such as

Rabbit Kekai, who are known as the pioneers of modern surfing. Aliʻi also figured prominently in surf history with Prince Kūhiō and Princess Kaʻiulani regarded as talented surfers.[14] However, following the political upheavals consequent to the overthrow of the Hawaiian Kingdom's monarch and the US Joint Resolution, the act of riding waves was not always viewed favorably in a U.S.-occupied Hawaiʻi, as parts of Hawaiian culture were seemingly erased by the status quo and territorial government.[15] In a *Honolulu Advertiser* article from 1972, John Kelly, a famous Hawaiʻi activist and "a surfer since 1928, said the sport is so sensitive to cultural values that it almost died out around the turn of the century because it doesn't conform to the Western work ethic. 'It was almost stamped out by Westerners because it distracted people from working at the plantations.'"[16]

In this same article, Fred Van Dyke reflects on the elation of being one with the ocean: "my feeling is to become a part of it for a while, to realize that I can only ride along with the wave. That's where the joy is, trying to become a part of it, to accept it on its own terms."[17] Van Dyke also noted the popularity of surfing as people flocked to some of the best waves in Hawaiʻi and around the world in 1972. "Those of us who were first in surfing were outcasts," he remarked about modern surfing. "We were trying to get away from society and we found something in surfing that we couldn't find in an organized world. We became images and now thousands of plastic images are trying to make believe they are finding the same thing."[18] Kelly refers to the crowds at Honolua Bay specifically. "In the old days, you might find four or five surfers there. Now, on an average day, there may be 100."[19] The growth of surfing and the surfing lifestyle led to surf competitions, which were held at Honolua Bay as early as the 1960s.

A standout at the Bay, and other highly acclaimed surf spots in Hawaiʻi and worldwide, is Gerry Lopez. "After a good day in the ocean," he remarked, "I feel good for a couple more days. I don't have a problem when I'm on a wave."[20] In 1970, Gerry Lopez won the World Unity Surfing Meet Men's Open at Honolua Bay.[21] The year before, in 1969, the Honolua Bay surf meet finalists were Vinny Bryan in first, Jock Sutherland in second, and Steve Biglar in third. Sutherland also won a sportsmanship award, alongside Barry Kanaiaupuni and Snake Ah Hee.[22] Sportsmanship was regarded as an important quality at this wave because of the small takeoff area, which limits the number of people actually surfing it on any given day to only the best surfers. A 1966 *Honolulu Star-Bulletin* article emphasized, "contestants will be judged on their best three waves and how they utilize the tight, hollow Honolua surf;

performance in turning, cutbacks, and trimming, along with sportsmanship. The latter will be especially important in this event because Honolua is basically a one-man wave."[23] Today, surf competition at Honolua Bay is on the international stage.

I asked Jock Sutherland about the sportsmanship award he won all those years earlier, and Sutherland recalls winning it because he saved another surfer's board when it was about to wash up on the rocks, as they had no leashes in those days. Sutherland today describes Honolua Bay as a "very beautiful setting, easy to feel a kinship with the ocean and land there because of the remoteness of the place. With Moloka'i in the background and the clean water, it's very satisfying surf if you get it on a good day."[24] Longtime West Maui surfer Geoff Alm also remarked, "Honolua Bay is the main, and most of the time, only good wave in the winter, for the whole island." He adds, "I don't have any vested interest, just a love for the place."[25] This love still propels many to know Honolua on a deeper level. It was ultimately surfers who were among the first to join and lead the Save Honolua Coalition (SHC). Jon Severson, founder of *Surfer Magazine* and longtime West Maui resident, designed the now recognizable single wave logo to save the bay and sparked the call for surfers from everywhere to call for its protection.

Kahakuloa, 1978. Courtesy of Bishop Museum.

Hawea Point, 1950. Courtesy of Bishop Museum.

Kapalua, Roy Okuda Collection. Courtesy of Bishop Museum.

Maui Land and Pineapple Co. (ML&P)

Maui Land and Pineapple (ML&P) gained land ownership and water rights for much of West Maui through land deeds and water leases, beginning in the 1890s with Henry Perrine (HP) Baldwin.[26] Not all of their land consolidation effort has been smooth sailing. ML&P has been regularly challenged over the years regarding its land ownership and water rights. Some of these challenges were provoked by ML&P's pursuit of quiet title cases. Fighting such cases can be a difficult and confusing endeavor because the goal is to simplify ownership of parcels of land that may have many kuleana owners.[27] One recent quiet title case initiated by ML&P occurred within the Honolua Conservation District.[28] A small parcel was sold at public auction in 2012, which former SHC President and county councilmember Elle Cochran and her husband Wayne purchased, perhaps planning to acquire the parcel for SHC conservation purposes.

At the time of the bid, Honolua resident and SHC Secretary John Carter said that "The Cochrans are hardworking people who were forced to spend a lot of money for an important piece. They have always been at the forefront of saving Honolua, and today they really put their money where their mouth is."[29] This quiet title court case was filed in 2006 by ML&P for a 9,471 square-foot parcel, and the Cochrans purchased it for $30,000.[30] The parcel was found to have at least sixty-eight owners; the Cochrans owned 1/28 of a share at the time. With regard to the purchase, Elle Cochran said, "We all felt this was so unfair. None of us wanted to sell—not any of the families, not myself and my husband...They forced the sale on this property, and that's how we ended up here today."[31]

The mass acquisition of land comes with political and social power in Hawai'i. The *Land* in the Maui Land and Pineapple Co. name resulted from adding real estate ventures beginning in the late 1960s, and under the ownership and direction of the Cameron family. The Camerons were descendants of the Baldwins, "who became one of the Big Five families who controlled Hawai'i in the century before World War II, establishing a far-reaching business empire with holdings in agriculture, ranching, coffee, canning, and other activities."[32] *Big Five* refers to the corporations of missionary descendants that generated great fortunes during the sugar plantation era: Alexander and Baldwin, American Factors, Castle and Cooke, C. Brewer, and Theo H. Davies. On Maui, ML&P (an affiliate of Alexander and Baldwin) and Pioneer Mill (owned by American Factors) were the two Big Five entities that wielded power over land and water in West Maui for more than the past 150 years.

Development agendas that would impact entire communities in Hawai'i were determined in the process of merging business interests.

Early history reveals close and interwoven familial ties that consolidated land and power on Maui. The first missionary families were granted tracts of land, often in exchange for their service. Over time, these allowances of land, managed with the political and business acumen of those familiar with Western property laws and customs, became larger and larger tracts of land. Thanks in part to government subsidies and other allowances for capitalist industry, great fortunes were made, and eventually political and social influence was concentrated in the hands of a relatively small number of families and individuals. Determined by these wealthy businessmen and subsidized by government, development placed plantation and hotel workers largely under corporate control.[33] The Big Five decided how land and labor were understood and managed in Hawai'i, and especially for populations across Maui, continue to exert power over the land and people today.

ML&P has asserted that its history provides the justification for its right to make decisions or claim property. In a recent case, "ML&P attorney David Nakamura asserts that ML&P has title derived from a series of sales that began in 1887. In 1930, Baldwin Packers bought the land. ML&P is a successor in interest to Baldwin Packers."[34] Dr. Dwight Baldwin arrived in Hawai'i with the fourth company of American missionaries from New England in 1836. He served as a doctor on Maui for seventeen years. After the completion of his service, he was granted 2,675 acres of land in West Maui to farm and graze cattle.[35] Through careful investments and foresight, his land holdings exceeded 24,500 acres by 1902.[36] First known as Honolua Ranch, then Baldwin Packers, and eventually Maui Land and Pineapple Co. (ML&P) after numerous mergers, Baldwin's initial property therefore ultimately became a source of Big Five power that consolidated land and power in West Maui.

Henry Perrine (HP) Baldwin (son of Dwight Baldwin) partnered with Samuel T. Alexander in 1869. They created the Alexander & Baldwin Company and mass-produced sugar in central and east Maui. HP Baldwin later bought more land in West Maui to begin the Honolua Ranch cattle business, followed by the pineapple plantation. The following business mergers occurred between family members over the next century: the Keahua Ranch Co. was renamed the Haleakalā Pineapple Co., Ltd. in 1929, while ML&P resulted from a merger between Haleakalā Pineapple Co. and Maui Agricultural Company.[37] In 1962, Alexander & Baldwin "merged three of its pineapple operations, Baldwin Packers, Ltd., Maui Pineapple Company, Ltd., and the old Haleakalā Pineapple Company, Ltd., to create what four months later became the Maui Pineapple Company, Ltd."[38]

Following this latest merger, "J. Walter Cameron, Baldwin family member, was named president of the Alexander & Baldwin subsidiary, joined by his son, Colin Campbell Cameron, who was appointed general manager."[39] The result was a powerful family-owned and operated entity, whose "grasp on the Hawaiian economy was comprehensive, maintained by a labyrinthine network of businesses whose development spanned generations of Baldwins."[40] But a split in interests led the Camerons (father and son) to seek business independence, so they purchased Maui Pineapple from the Alexander & Baldwin parent company in 1969 for $20 million.[41] They changed the name to Maui Land and Pineapple Co. to reflect the land ventures now part of their business and it ran under their leadership from the 1970s.[42]

Another famous name in West Maui is David T. (D.T.) Fleming, a horticulturist from Scotland who was hired to cultivate pineapples for HP Baldwin at Grove Ranch in Hāʻiku. In 1909, Keahua Ranch Co. was incorporated to control pineapple operations, and Fleming was hired to grow pineapples at Honolua Ranch in 1910.[43] In 1912, Fleming and Harry Baldwin, son of HP Baldwin, had cattle grazing land redesignated for pineapple production. The name changed from Honolua Ranch to Baldwin Packers in 1924.[44] In the 1940s and 1950s, Fleming also had the foresight to allow company employees to purchase house lots in West Maui, thereby "creating a company policy that continued when Baldwin Packers and Maui Pineapple Company of Hāliʻimaile, merged and became Maui Land and Pineapple Company Inc."[45] This allowed for planation laborers to own parts of the plantation, similar to Pioneer Mill's worker homeowning initiatives on land near Lahainaluna.[46]

The Fleming Journals, a compilation of land deeds and mergers that occurred in the Kāʻanapali moku was prepared between 1905 and 1910 for Alexander & Baldwin. According to the journals, HP Baldwin began acquiring lands from Kekaʻa to Kahakuloa in the 1890s.[47] Edward Austin Jones, or Ed Jones, was "the son of Peter Cushman Jones, a partner in C. Brewer and Company who, in 1893, formed the Bank of Hawaiʻi with James A. King and Charles Montague Cooke."[48] Jones purchased land from Hawaiian families and sold them to either H. P. or Lincoln Baldwin, and "Honolua Ranch also acquired many land parcels from Lincoln's estate when he died."[49] *Lincoln* is Lincoln Mansfield Baldwin, the nephew of H. P. Baldwin. He served as Maui County Treasurer and sheriff of Maui County after working in sugar.[50] Clearly, land and power on Maui were integrated and heavily collaborative.

D. T. Fleming's Beach. Courtesy of Bishop Museum.

Pineapple Hill, Kapalua. Courtesy of Bishop Museum.

Pineapple Hill, Kapalua. Courtesy of Bishop Museum.

Kapalua, 1966. Courtesy of Bishop Museum.

Baldwin Packer Cottage,
Napili Point, 1927. Courtesy
of Bishop Museum.

This consolidation of land and power set the backdrop for the David and
Goliath dynamics characterizing community efforts to save Honolua Bay and
Līpoa Point.

Saving Līpoa Point and Honolua Bay

At Maui County's General Plan Action Committee meeting in January 2007,
ML&P announced plans to develop Honolua Bay and Līpoa Point. The proposal was to build forty luxury homes, a golf course, and other amenities,
on the area overlooking Honolua Bay. The Save Honolua Coalition (SHC)
initiative had already been sparked in late 2006, and gained nonprofit status
with the help of attorney Lance Collins in May 2007.[51] Immediately after the
development plans were announced, multiple layers of local and international
communities, including surfers, ocean users, local residents, and individuals
from near and far who did not want to see the area developed came together
to resist.[52] Elle Cochran, current Maui County councilmember and former
organizer and President of SHC, remembers the early council meetings, and

subsequent community planning meetings to stop development. She calls it the epitome of bringing people from all walks of life together, standing up for a common cause, and gelling around an issue.[53] She recalls John Severson designing the now familiar wave-shaped logo of SHC. They printed T-shirts to raise awareness about Honolua Bay as one of the best waves in the world, and the need to save public access. The coalition was off and running.

On April 20, 2007, after an emotional and vocal antidevelopment public hearing, and after sixteen thousand people had signed petitions, ML&P withdrew its development plans.[54] Cochran recalls that having the children from Sacred Hearts School in Lahaina testify against the development had a big impact on the effort to ensure the development did not occur, since it was an emotional outpouring of keiki voices asking for conservation.[55] The community had banded together to stop yet another expensive luxury development project on prime agricultural lands, and they continued to do so even after the plans were withdrawn. Cochran and Tamara Paltin, successor president of SHC, both recall the input and energy of the community at the early SHC meetings that took place weekly at Wayne Nishiki's Farmer's Market Natural Foods store in Honokōwai. A former Maui County councilmember, Nishiki is a longtime political activist and organic farmer on Maui. We used to buy fruits and vegetables from his food truck in the days when he was running Down to Earth in lower Wailuku. Natural foods then weren't called *organic*. We simply called them food.

Meetings later moved to the Lahaina Civic Center. After seven years the area officially saved by the State of Hawai'i through legislation that became Act 241. In the early months, "Save Honolua members launched a website, hosted meetings, recruited speakers, circulated petitions and lobbied the Maui County Council to acquire the coastal property at Līpoa Point."[56] In 2008, JoAnne Johnson, then Lahaina's councilmember, earmarked $1 million in county funds to save the area. At this time, David Cole, President and CEO of ML&P, had a Save Honolua Coalition sticker on his car. When asked why, he responded, "because I want to save Honolua, too."[57] In the same vein, in 2008 ML&P created a Līpoa Point/Honolua Conservation Compromise. Its first listed goal was to "protect Līpoa and the connecting shoreline areas in perpetuity."[58] The Maui chapter of the Surfrider Foundation and SHC actually formed a partnership with ML&P to protect the Bay, and "Save Honolua initiated monthly, larger quarterly cleanups, native plantings, water quality monitoring and other efforts such as installing day-use mooring buoys and funding two port-a-potties."[59] The community agenda looked promising, and studies that found Honolua Bay to be extremely polluted by runoff and wastewater only strengthened the public call for protection and responsible stewardship.

But in 2012, the Maui County Council removed the protection status of Honolua Bay. Council chair Mike White "made a surprise motion by voting to maintain the agricultural designation of approximately 139 of 270 acres owned by ML&P from Honokōhau Stream to Honolua Stream. This left approximately 131 acres, including all the immediate coastline and the Honolua Bay area, unmodified, effectively removing the area from preservation."[60] The SHC website informed the public that "as of 8/2/12, The Maui County Council voted to remove protection of Līpoa Point at the request of Maui, Land, and Pineapple Company who had used it as collateral to pay pensions."[61] Also noted on the website were the votes of the council—those against preservation were White, Pontanilla, Victorino, Mateo, and Baisa; those in favor of keeping the preservation status on the council were Cochran, Couch, and Carroll.[62]

In 2014, Warren H. Haruki, now ML&P Chairman and CEO, noted that the pension plans remained underfunded after the close of pineapple operations in 2009. This was the reason for the initial development initiative: "to offset some of the debt, the company submitted conceptual plans for a golf course and forty luxury homes at Līpoa Point in 2007."[63] ML&P withdrew the plan after community input but still needed to find a way to increase its funds. Otherwise, ML&P would have to sacrifice seven thousand acres to the Pension Benefits Guaranty Corp. in West Maui that had been offered as security.[64] The agreement struck between the State of Hawai'i and ML&P to save Līpoa Point was therefore also an agreement to save ML&P pensions. Representative Angus McKelvey introduced H.B. 1424, entitled, *Relating to the Acquisition of Resource Value Lands* to the Hawai'i State Legislature.[65]

> Honolua is known worldwide as a premier winter session, big wave surf spot, a sector of the surfing industry that is currently eclipsing the Association of Surfing Professionals World Championship Tour.
>
> The legislature finds, however, that recent contemplation of zoning changes to the area has jeopardized the pension benefits for numerous retirees as the parcel was pledged against a pension fund established by the retirees' former employer in order to make sure that kupuna would continue to receive the benefits that they worked for. If this pension fund should fail, many of the pensioners would have to turn to state services and programs, thereby straining the social safety net, especially in an area where resources are already scarce.

The legislature further finds that acquiring this land for preservation would help protect the area's pristine condition while providing funds to ensure the adequate capitalization of the pension fund. The legislature also finds that the owners of the land have pledged that any revenues derived from the sale of this parcel would be pledged completely against the pension fund, thereby alleviating concerns of the social safety net being stretched even further.[66]

Bill 1424 became Act 241 and Governor Abercrombie "visited Maui and authorized a $20 million appropriation for the purchase of Lipoa Point to preserve the land for future generations."[67] It was presented as beneficial for all: "The land formerly belonged to Maui Land & Pineapple Co., which opposed last year's preservation ideas during county General Plan discussions because of their concerns for the devaluing of the land and subsequent undermining of pension agreement for their workers. This bill, however, includes payment for the pensioners, so lawmakers consider it a win-win."[68] At the time, Councilmember Mike Victorino said, "This wasn't to pay ML&P's debt…This is so future generations will have a place to use, and all our (ML&P) retirees and future retirees—there are a few left—are going to be able to have their retirement."[69] The Department of Land and Natural Resources (DLNR) was designated to guide the transition, and its "Need for Acquisition" statement claims that "In addition to these 'cradle to grave' entitlement issues, the acquisition presents the opportunity to preserve the natural, cultural and recreational resources of the property."[70]

The agreement ensured payment for the pensions of ML&P workers. Depending on who you asked, though, the result was either a reasonable deal for everyone, or a corporate payout. "Today marks the culmination of a unique and extraordinary opportunity to preserve one of Maui's most treasured natural resources, while at the same time securing the hard-earned pensions of our 1,600 retirees," claimed Haruki, Chairman and CEO, adding, "for our shareholders, it resolves one of our most significant legacy commitments and long-term financial obligations."[71] On October 9, 2014, the State of Hawai'i took possession of the area. Acting Governor Shan Tsutsui officially proclaimed the day "Lipoa Point Day"; and in response, Anthony Pignataro, Editor of *Maui Time Weekly* wrote:

For years, Maui Land and Pineapple Co.—a for-profit corporation— loudly and repeatedly told everyone within spitting distance that they would never develop Līpoa Point. Then a couple years, citing sudden and dramatic problems with their employee pensions, they said the point was back on the table. Environmentalists were outraged, and people everywhere commenced much wringing of hands. Which brings us to today—the State of Hawai'i stepping in with a monster $20 million check to *save* Honolua Bay from a company that failed to keep its own financial house in order.[72]

The initial plan was for Honolua to become a state park, managed in collaboration with the Hawaiian Islands Land Trust, Save Honolua Coalition, and the Aha Moku Kā'anapali.[73] But today, though still hopeful, both Paltin and Cochran are somewhat weary of waiting to see how the state will manage the area now that it has been *saved*, since *saved* and *saving* are two very different things. Paltin notes the individuals who were pivotal in the state plan—including John Carty, Glenn Kamaka, State Senator Malama Solomon, and State Representative Angus McKelvey—and helped close the loopholes between the petitioners and the State.[74] Today, the area is under jurisdiction of the State of Hawai'i, DLNR, and ML&P, but the overall management plan and funding for conservation are not yet established, as the state is only beginning the process of requesting funding based on community input and direction.

Over the last number of years, Paltin has written grants for port-a-potties in response to the large amounts of tourists that visit the Bay to snorkel, and for money to pay Les Potts, the caretaker of the area. ML&P pulled all its money out of the area once the State acquired it, except for some funds to help pay Potts. With no real self-sustaining plan in place, funding for primary are needs remains a concern. The current cost for upkeep is basically $1,200 a month to pay Les Potts for caretaking, and $8,000 a year for the port a-potties.[75] More recently, Paltin reports that Makana Aloha Foundation has stepped in to pay Potts for his cleanup and caretaking services. Ultimately, Paltin wants to see the area well maintained, self-sustaining, and connecting back to Hawaiian culture and education for the community, so that the importance of the place can inform a shared narrative.[76]

Conservation of the coastline area actually began years ago. In 1975, Colin Cameron, ML&P President, recommended the protection of the coastal waters off Honolua Bay. The protection model would be Hanauma Bay on O'ahu, the only example of coastline conservation at the time. Cameron "endorsed the Honolua conservation plan recommended by two marine biologists and recommended it to the state board."[77] But the desire to conserve the coastal areas of Honolua Bay was initially fought by some of the local fisherman because of the restrictions it would impose on their ability to provide for their families. In 1977, brokering the conservation of Honolua Bay, along with Mokulēʻia Bay to the south, meant making concessions to akule fishermen for the "infringement on the Hawaiian lifestyle" that conservation would entail.[78] Fisherman Alika Cooper spoke at a community meeting, saying, "it seems strange to me take one of the best akule grounds and make a conservation district out of these grounds,"[79] adding that it was "sad to see only two, three of us part-Hawaiians here; to see all these haoles trying to make laws for us."[80]

The Maui County Fish and Wildlife Advisory Committee held a public meeting for input on writing the conservation regulation.[81] A compromise was reached during this meeting. Fishermen could haul their catch through the conservation district, but "not net the fish in the district" itself.[82] As a result, "a proposed rule to set up a marine life conservation district at Honolua Bay on West Maui has been revised to allow bagging of akule in the bay, Chairman William Thompson of the Board of Land and Natural Resources has announced."[83] The compromise also allowed for a redrawing of the conservation district boundary lines "of the northernmost tip of the bay mauka more than one hundred yards to allow for local net and spear fishing."[84] Finally, Mokulēʻia Bay, the wave also known as Slaughter House, would now be included in the conservation district.[85] In March of 1978, the Honolua-Mokulēʻia Bay Marine Life Conservation District was established, running forty-five miles from Kulaokaʻeʻa Point and Kalaepiha Point to Alaelae Point.[86] On the larger stage, the late 1970s are regarded as the renaissance of Hawaiian culture statewide. Honolua Bay has played a role in this resurgence, both then and today.

Revival of Culture and Conservation, Full Circle

The ocean has mana in this area, and the use of this oceanic space has been important for generations. It was therefore no accident that Hōkūleʻa left for her maiden voyage to Tahiti in 1976 from Honolua Bay, as noted in the book *Kapalua Nui*:

> "Why Honolua?" pondered Herb Kawainui Kāne, a founder of the Polynesian Voyaging Society and the designer and builder of the double-hulled

canoe. "We felt that, from Honolua Bay and up around the north side of the island, we could pick winds that would carry the canoe away from land—clean, clear air without a lot of disruptions caused by the presence of land. Good, straight trade winds: sailing air. The cove from which Hōkūle'a departed offered protection from winds and surf, and after clearing the point, the canoe caught the northeast trade winds and was on its way"[87]

The launch of Hōkūle'a on May 1, 1976 from Honolua Bay, and the return to her first port of call some forty-one years later on July 17, 2017, constituted a full circle moment. Some now legendary members from the first voyage were met by a community beaming with pride and gratitude at the wa'a's return. The bravery and fortitude of these individuals who forged a path across Oceania, as our ancestors had done before them, was celebrated. As the sailing of Hōkūle'a to Tahiti began the cultural renaissance all those years ago by going around the world, it has inspired and redefined a whole generation of people through reconnecting to place, which empowers entire communities in the process.

It was fitting that the first port of call after completing the worldwide voyage would be Honolua Bay, the place where it started, and for many, the place where the reconnection still occurs. On this particular homecoming morning, longtime West Maui waterman and Hōkūle'a crewmember Snake Ah Hee said that while paddling in from Hōkūle'a to the voices of the Kamehameha Schools choir singing on shore, he could feel the emotion—he gestured to his heart.[88] He cried because he didn't know when something like this would come around again. "This is new for Maui," he said, gesturing to the hundreds of people who had shown up for the day, and hiked a mile or so in the rain and light mist after the homecoming, straight up the mountain to a portion overseen by the Pu'u Kukui Watershed Preserve. Part of the ML&P conservation efforts, this place became a protected area through their partnership of DLNR in 1988.

According to the founder of the Hōkūle'a endeavor, Nainoa Thompson, they were there to plant over one thousand koa trees, restore the native rain forest, and make possible the building of future canoes. Overcome with the importance of the moment of the Hōkūle'a homecoming, we could only imagine the genuine joy and sense of accomplishment the original crewmembers must have felt as they returned to Honolua Bay after all these years, and their lifelong experiences in, and around, the ocean. The place where they first set sail because of protection from the wind, now they were back to pay their respects. Ah Hee remembers the day of the departure in 1976, and how Buffalo Keaulana was shuttling people to and from the waʻa, his boat catching three to four-foot waves all day, each time he made his way to shore. Ah Hee says that Honolua always has good waves, because thanks to the bay, there's not much wind.

This day of the Hōkūleʻa homecoming in 2017 was far better attended than the departure forty-one years ago. This time, the community and public officials showed up. At the tree-planting ceremony, Nainoa Thompson recognized the shared efforts to restore the ahupuaʻa from "reef to ridge," and he emotionally insisted, "some places on this earth need to remain sacred." He said they left on the worldwide voyage because "it wasn't an option to stay home," and that our shared kuleana as a people is "to bring love and aloha and to restore our culture." "How does land and culture come together to protect the earth?" he asked. Thompson was recognizing the decades-long efforts that saved Honolua Bay—the hard work of community members and state and government officials, ML&P's preservation efforts—and also the strength of the movement today, which didn't exist in 1976. "We are testament to cultural renaissance" he said, and "when we plant trees, we plant peace, we plant canoes."

Archie Kalepa is a longtime and well-known Maui lifeguard, waterman, Hōkūleʻa crewmember, and community leader. He remarked that Honolua is a "premier wave around the world that everyone loves and shares," and he stressed the importance of the "reawakening cultural value of place and the role it plays in servicing community past and present."[89] For Kalepa, the fight to save Honolua, the return of Hōkūleʻa from the Mālama Honua Worldwide Voyage, and the importance of viewing land and sea as interconnected are all part of the same process: "reconnect(ing) value of mountains to the makai (the sea) and why the rivers need to run and be maintained in all of Hawaiʻi for the people in Hawaiʻi to prosper. Through time we will all become stewards of Hawaiʻi. In terms of the massive accomplishment of the Hōkūleʻa worldwide voyage, Kalepa declares, "the torch was lit and people throwing wood on that fire is a beacon." In reference to the tree planting, Kalepa remarks that "the real work begins now. What are we doing to Mālama Honua should be a question we ask ourselves. By reconnecting streams from the mountain to the sea, aquifers are rejuvenated and streams get saturated again."

"From reef to ridge" is the new directive for taking care of place that Nainoa Thompson issued at the tree planting ceremony. The mountains and

Courtesy of Sydney Iaukea.

Courtesy of Sydney Iaukea.

Courtesy of Sydney Iaukea.

Courtesy of Sydney Iaukea.

Courtesy of Sydney Iaukea.

Courtesy of Sydney Iaukea.

Courtesy of Sydney Iaukea.

Courtesy of Sydney Iaukea.

ocean form the landscape that lies between, just as they inform the people who
live in these places. The ridges of Honolua Bay bracket the valleys in the Puʻu
Kukui Watershed Management Area, the other conservation area now mon-
itored by ML&P within this ahupuaʻa. ML&P began conservation in 1988
with the Puʻu Kukui Watershed Preserve. In 1992, partnership work began
with the State of Hawaiʻi. This public/private partnership is the largest in the
state. It is renewed every six years to continue the allotment of funds, and to
allow for continued planning of the over 8,600 acres of conservation lands, as
noted in the most recent report.[90] The goal of ML&P is to increase the current
conservation area with an additional three thousand acres of land "makai of
the current project area."[91] Nineteen units, including Honolua Valley (unit 12),
Honolua Peak (unit 13), and the Honolua/Honokahua Headwaters (unit 16)
comprise this area. The tree planting ceremony occurred at the Honolua peak.

Geographically, Puʻu Kukui is the second wettest place on earth, after
Mount Waiʻaleʻale on Kauaʻi.

> At the top of Mauna Kahalawai, West Maui Mountains stands the summit
> Puʻu Kukui, reaching 5,788 feet above sea level. Today known as the Puʻu
> Kukui Watershed Preserve, at 8,304 acres "[it is] the largest private pre-
> serve in Hawaiʻi." The rain from Puʻu Kukui flows into the Honokōhau
> stream, and a waterfall measuring 1,700 feet sits at the base of the stream
> at Honokōhau Valley. Many miles ma kai (to the sea) of this area is the
> Honolua-Mokuleʻia Marine Life Conservation District.[92]

Puʻu Kukui is also the realm of wao akua, the place of the gods. The wao
akua is different from the wao kanaka, the elevation where the people worked,
went to gather materials and resources, carried out everyday life. The wao akua
includes the highest mountain peaks in Hawaiʻi. But more than just a physical
space, it is the realm of elevation, and space of being and knowing, that connects Akua, kānaka, and ʻāina in ways that are mostly incomprehensible today.
Those who were permitted to visit there, those specialized kahuna who could
interpret the connections among the kānaka and akua, accessed these high and
lofty spaces with the kuleana, or rights, to enter. These places of material and
spiritual importance were treated with the reverence to which they are entitled.

ML&P has recognized the significance of this area as Wao Akua.

> The bulk of the PKW Preserve was considered a *wao akua* (realm of the
> god) by native Hawaiians and was deemed sacred; with little or no regular

access by the makaʻāinana (commoners) or the aliʻi (chiefs). What little access likely to occur was by certain kahuna (priests), kia manu (those trained to collect native bird feathers for an aliʻi's cloak) or others with specific collection purposes. Therefore; no significant negative impact on cultural resources or historic practices by native Hawaiians is anticipated from the actions delineated in this plan. Additionally, the preservation of habitats and natural communities preserve plant and animal species integral to Hawaiian culture. Many of these species are prevalent in Hawaiian song, chant, and legend, and the protection of these species to be accomplished by this management plan will help to ensure a continuing living culture.[93]

The Honolua/ Honokahua Headwaters, Unit 16, is in the realm of wao akua, and is basically a boardwalk for the top of the world:

At 847 acres, the Honolua/Honokōhau Headwaters unit crosses between Kahana and Honolua streams. Unit 16 centers on an unnamed hill at a 3,540-foot elevation, including the 4,503-foot twin peaks of Nakalalua; some upper sections of forest are in nearly pristine condition. . . . The Puʻu Kukui boardwalk continues through this unit and contains a rain gauge situated along the Puʻu Kukui trail at the base of the upper peak of Nakalalua . . . Unit 16 also includes a rare, remnant ʻOhiʻa Mixed Montane Bog community on an exposed ridge at 3,600 feet.[94]

I·was lucky enough to hike up the Puʻu Kukui Watershed Honolua/ Honokahua Headwaters unit. On a rainy day, a small group of us were permitted to enter the wao akua at Puʻu Kukui (the hill of knowing or enlightenment) with the staff. In the immense quiet, sounds of birds and waterfalls pierced the silence. Besides our chitchat and my incessant questions to Koa, our very knowledgeable and energetic guide and a Field Tech II with the Puʻu Kukui Watershed Preserve, about wildlife, plants, and his own personal perspective on our surrounding, the quiet and calm of the place enveloped our small group.

Rain gear was donned because we would get wet either way, hiking to the highest point in the West Maui Mountains, where the water for the entire west side of Maui begins its flow from the summit. As Pōmaikaʻi Crozier, the Puʻu Kukui Watershed conservation manager told us right before the hike, "you're gonna get wet, it's either a hot wet, or a cold wet." After we were driven in the Polaris ATV from the base camp to the cabin once belonging to D.T. Fleming, we gathered for a short group meeting and pule, or prayer, and then made our way up the mauna. A low-level rainbow greeted us upon arrival, and I knew this hōʻailona, this sign, would mark an incredible journey to the top of the world and to the place inhabited by nā akua. The bog, referred to as the high-level area ʻohiʻa field, is filled with 1,000-year-old ʻohia trees no bigger than a couple of inches from the ground, and with blossoms bigger than the trees. After a very long hike and a short rest before the equally long hike back to the cabin, these miniature trees were our only accompaniment in this place in the clouds. This hike was unbelievable in so many ways. It really was a privilege to enter, and to be, just for a moment, in the Wao Akua.

From ridge to reef and from the ocean to Mount ʻEke, lies in the hands of ML&P and the residents of West Maui today. But as recently as July 2017, Honolua Bay was found to be extremely polluted with enterococci bacteria. The public has been warned to stay out of the water.[95] In November 2017, the State of Hawaiʻi held its first open house at the West Maui Senior Center to plan for management of the area. The state legislature appropriated $500,000 in capital improvement funds in 2016 for the planning and construction of

Courtesy of Sydney Iaukea.

Courtesy of Sydney Iaukea.

Courtesy of Sydney Iaukea.

Courtesy of Sydney Iaukea.

Courtesy of
Sydney Iaukea.

"Violet Lake" and open bog, upper slope of Puu Kukui, about 5000 feet elevation. Courtesy of Sydney Iaukea.

In the rainforest, up the ridge from Nakalalua, elevation about 4600 feet. Courtesy of Sydney Iaukea.

safety measures in the area.[96] Tamara Paltin, President of SHC said it had "been a long road to get to this point. I'm definitely very grateful that it was able to happen."[97] According to John Summers of Planning Consultants Hawaiʻi, the management planning process began in 2016 and will continue until 2019 with community input, along with the completion of an environmental assessment. It should all be done by 2020.[98] What is clear, however, is that Honolua Bay will need continued and careful public monitoring so that responsible stewardship becomes a reality.

Places like Honolua Bay call for care and vigilance to ensure health and continuity not only for the land and ocean, but for the people as well. Archie Kalepa describes this kuleana best. Kalepa says that we need

> Every ahupuaʻa doing our part to take on the challenge to be a part of the restoration, protecting ecosystem versus development. Build with one hundred percent understanding of the system and place, and building around that idea is our gift to the world as living within an ecosystem. Are we leaving kids with beauty or devastation? We need to think long and hard about that and about the future of our place that we call home. Today we're ready. Anything is possible if we put in time and not be afraid to move forward, there's hope. Instead of doing what we want, we do what is right. Fight back out of education, and understanding comes from education and living and doing.[99]

Only then will our most treasured places be truly protected. Only then will the people have the opportunity to reconnect back, so we can continue to move forward.

Notes

1.   Tim T. Esaki, "Maui Land and Pineapple Announces Closing of Lipoa Point Sale," Business Wire, https://www.businesswire.com/news/home/20141009006506/en/Maui-Land-Pineapple-Announces-Closing-Lipoa-Point, October 9, 2014 (cited December 20, 2017) and H.B. 1424, *Relating to the Acquisition of Resource Value Lands*, House of Representatives, Twenty-Seventh Legislature, 2013, State of Hawaiʻi.
2.   H.B. 1424, 2013 House Journal.
3.   "Maui Land and Pineapple Company, Inc. History," Funding Universe, http://wwwfundinguniverse.com/company-histories/maui-land-pineapple-company-inc-history/, p. 3 (cited March 22, 2017).

4. Office of Council Services, "Governor signs preservation of Lipoa Point into law," http://mauicounty.us/state-legislature/governor-signs-preservation-of-lipoa -point-into-law/ June 28, 2013 (cited February 22, 2017).

5. Anthony Pignataro, "State of Hawaii Saves Maui Land & Pine Pensions! Also, Lipoa Point," *Maui Time Weekly*, https://mauitime.com/news/science-and -environment/state-of-hawaii-saves-maui-land-pine-pensions-also-lipoa-point /mauitime.com, October 10, 2014 (cited December 18, 2017).

6. Gerry Lopez interview via email 1/5/2018.

7. Sydney Lehua Iaukea, *Keka'a: The Making and Saving of North Beach West Maui*, Lahaina, Maui, Hawai'i: North Beach-West Maui Benefit Fund Inc., 2014, p. 29–30, referring to Elspeth P. Sterling's *Sites of Maui, A Fornander Collection*. Honolulu: Bishop Museum Press, 1998.

8. Elspeth P. Sterling's *Sites of Maui, A Fornander Collection*. Honolulu: Bishop Museum Press, 1998 (S.M. Kamakau, *Ruling Chiefs of Hawai'i*, Honolulu, Hawai'i: KS Press, 1924, p. 29).

9. Katherine Kama'ema'e Smith, *The Fleming Journals, West Maui Land Records and Family History 1905–1910*. Maui: HK West Maui Community Fund, 2011, XI.

10. Elspeth P. Sterling's *Sites of Maui*, 53 (W.M. Walker, *Archaeology of Maui*, Honolulu: Bishop Museum, 1931, 29).

11. Honolua Bay is one of the six bays that begins with Hono and called Honoapi'ilani, named for the Ali'i nui of Maui, Pi'ilani. The other bays are Honokahua, Honokeana, Honokōhau, Honokōwai, and Hononana. Mary Kawena Pukui, *Place Names of Hawai'i*, Ulukau: The Hawaiian Electronic Library, www.ulukau.org, p. 48 (cited November 16, 2017).

12. Pukui, *Place Names of Hawai'i*, p. 85 & p. 127.

13. Sterling, 53 (Moses Manu, Ka Moolelo o Kihapiilani, *Ka Nupepa Kuokoa*, Aug. 23, 1884. MS SC Sterling 3, 14).

14. John Clark, "Kai Piha; Ka'ahele Ma Waikīkī," HIDOE, Video Production Branch.

15. For Hawai'i as an occupied nation, without a Treaty of Annexation, but only a Joint Resolution, and the resulting socio-political effects, see Sydney Lehua Iaukea, *The Queen and I: A Story of Dispossessions and Reconnections in Hawai'i*. Berkeley: University of California Press, 2012.

16. "Surfers find link with nature in the curl of a wave," *Advertiser*, Tuesday, February 15, 1972, column 1.

17. Ibid. column 2.

18. Ibid. column 3.

19. Ibid. column 3.

20. Ibid. column 4.

21. "Lopez wins Surf meet on Maui," *The Honolulu Advertiser*, January 5, 1970.

22. "Oahu surfers win," *Honolulu Star-Bulletin*, June 15, 1976.

23. *Honolulu Star-Bulletin*, Friday, December 16, 1966.

24. Phone interview with Jock Sutherland, 12/13/17.

25. Interview with Geoff Alm, August 2017.

26. Smith, *The Fleming Journals*, XII.

27. "An "action to quiet title is a lawsuit filed to establish ownership of real property. Quiet titles are legal mechanisms that make it possible to grant a clear title to a single owner when there is the potential for several different claims to ownership." "What is quiet title?," Lawyers Title Insurance Corporation, 2009, http://www.ocltic.com/Uploads/26/99/12699/Gallery/Flyers/Quiet%20Title .pdf (cited December 12, 2017).

28. *Maui Tomorrow*, "Quiet Title—The Scourge of Hawaiian Land Ownership," http://maui-tomorrow.org/quiet-title-the-scourge-of-hawaiian-land-ownership/ February 4, 2012 (cited December 10, 2017).

29. Wendy Oshner, *Maui Now*, "Cochran Hope Auction Bid Will Save Honolua From Development," http://mauinow.com/2012/01/29/cochran-hopes-auction -bid-will-save-honolua-from-development/ January 29, 2012 (cited December 10, 2017).

30. Ilima Loomis, "Honolua land's top bid comes from Cochrans," *The Maui News*, January 29, 2012 (cited December 20, 2017).

31. Ibid, 1.

32. "Maui Land & Pineapple Company, Inc. History," 1.

33. For a discussion of government and industry collusion and the creation of a tourism industry based on Pioneer Mill and Ka'anapali Beach Resort interests, see Sydney Lehua Iaukea, "The Re-Storing of Lahaina" in *Tourism Impacts West Maui*, edited by Lance D. Collins and Bianca Isaki, Lahaina, Maui, Hawai'i: North Beach-West Maui Benefit Fund, 2016.

34. Harry Eagar, "Maui Land & Pineapple Co. has filed a lawsuit to assert legal ownership." http://www.forum.surfer.com (cited December 20, 2017).

35. Peter T. Young, *Ho'okuleana*, Baldwin Packers, June 9, 2013. http://totakeresponsibility.blogspot.com/2013/06/baldwin-packers.html, 1 (cited July 5, 2017).

36. Young, *Ho'okuleana*, 1.

37. "Maui Land and Pineapple Company, Inc.," 1.

38. Ibid. 2.

39. Ibid. 1.

40. Ibid. 1.

41. Ibid. 2.

42. Ibid. 2.

43. Smith, *The Fleming Journals: West Maui Land Records and Family History 1905– 1910*, VIII.

44. Ibid.

45. Ibid.

46. See Iaukea, *Keka'a: The Making and Saving of North Beach West Maui* regarding Pioneer Mill and providing home ownership to their employees.

47. Smith, *The Fleming Journals*, XII.

48. Ibid.

49. Ibid.

50. Ibid.

51. "Kua, Kua'āina ulu 'auamo," Save Honolua Coalition Website, http://kuahawaii .org/partner/save-honolua-coalition/ (cited December 19, 2017).

52. Sky Barnhart, "Saving Honolua: A fragile area on Maui's northwestern shore faces an uncertain future....," http://mauimagazine.net/saving-honolua, 2 (cited November 12, 2017).

53. Interview with Maui Councilmember Elle Cochran, June 2017.

54. Matt Pruett, "Honolua Bay Defenseless? Surf community rallies as famed Maui reef/ pointbreak is removed from preservation," Surfline, http://www.surfline .com/surf-news/honolua-bay-defenseless_76662/ September 27, 2012 (cited December 8, 2017).

55. Interview with Councilmember Cochran.

56. Barnhart, "Saving Honolua," 3.

57. Ibid.

58. "Lipoa Point/Honolua Conservation Compromise August 6, 2008." Maui Land & Pineapple Company, Inc, Maui, Hawai'i, 1.

59. Pruett, "Honolua Bay Defenseless?"

60. Ibid.

61. Save Honolua Coalition website, savehonolua.org, indexscandal.php (cited December 20, 2017).

62. Ibid.

63. "Lipoa Point sale official; 'Confident' we have pensions—retirees," 4mauirealestate .com, October 13, 2014 (cited May 8, 2017).

64. "Lipoa Point sale official; 'Confident' we have pensions—retirees," 4mauirealestate .com, October 13, 2014.

65. H.B. 1424, p.1.

66. Ibid, p.2–3.

67. Maui Real Estate Connection, "West Maui Lipoa Point Preservation," http:// www.mauiluxuryrealestateteam.com/blog/Display/2013/07/West_Maui_Lipoa _Point_Preservation, July 5, 2013 (cited December 8, 2017).

68. Ibid.

69. "Lipoa Point sale official; 'Confident' we have pensions—retirees," 4mauirealestate .com, October 13, 2014.

70. State of Hawai'i, Department of Land and Natural Resources, Land Division, "Approval in Principle for Acquisition of Private Lands situate at Honokōhau and Honolua, Lahaina, Maui, identified as Tax Map Key No.: (2) 4-1—001:010.

71. Esaki, "Maui Land & Pineapple Announces Closing of Lipoa Point Sale."

72. Anthony Pignataro, "State of Hawaii Saves Maui Land & Pine Pensions! Also, Lipoa Point."

73. Save Honolua Coalition, http://www.savehonolua.org.

74. Interview with Tamara Paltin, June 2017.

75. Ibid.

76. Ibid.

77. "Honolua Bay conservation," *Advertiser*, Wednesday, October 15, 1975.

78. "Fisherman cites 'Hawaiian Rights,'" *Honolulu Advertiser*, Friday, December 2, 1977, A-2.

79. Ibid.

80. Ibid.

81. "Two sides agree on Honolua Bay," *Advertiser*, October 6, 1977, A-10.

82. "Fisherman cites 'Hawaiian Rights,'" A-2.

83. "Bay proposal revised to suit akule catchers," *Advertiser*, Friday, January 14, 1978.

84. "Two sides agree on Honolua Bay," A-10.

85. Ibid.

86. "Marine district in effect," *Advertiser*, Saturday, March 18, 1978.

87. Sydney Lehua Iaukea, *Keka'a: The Making and Saving of North Beach West Maui*, 32, quote taken from *Kapalua Nui: Place of Life* by Jocelyn Fujii (Honolulu: Hula Moon Press, 2008).

88. Interview with Snake Ah Hee, July 2017.

89. Interview with Archie Kalepa, June 2017.

90. "Long Range Management Plan for Fiscal Years 2018–2024, Pu'u Kukui Watershed Management Area, Natural Area Partnership Program," Prepared by MLPC for Division of Forestry and Wildlife, Department of Land and Natural Resources, February, 2017, 5.

91. Ibid. 12.

92. Sydney Lehua Iaukea, *Keka'a: The Making and Saving of North Beach West Maui*, 29. This paragraph contains information found in *Kapalua Nui: Place of Life* by Jocelyn Fujii, with the quotation appearing on page 30.

93. "Long Range Management Plan," 11.

94. Ibid. 20.

95. *Maui Now*, "Enterococci Found at Honolua, Maui," July 20, 2017 (cited December 19, 2017).

96. Melissa Tanji, "Community Members offer ideas for state lands in W. Maui," http://www.mauinews.com/news/local-news/2017/11/community-members

-offer-ideas-for-state-lands-in-w-maui/, November 12, 2017 (cited December 20, 2017).
97. Ibid.
98. Ibid.
99. Interview Archie Kalepa.

FAST-TRACKING THE LUXURY HOUSING CRISIS IN WEST MAUI

Lance D. Collins

*It has been explained how [the Hawaiian people] raised plants and how they
caught fish to eat with their poi in order to strengthen themselves and to preserve
life in the body. The third thing necessary for the health of the body was the house.*

—Samuel Kamakau 1976: 95

The present common sense, as reflected in the public statements of legislative statutes, politicians, land developers, media, and community organizers, is that we are in the midst of an affordable housing crisis. Crisis implies
an event over a relatively short period of time and confrontation with a problem that is in danger of not reaching a satisfactory resolution. The expectation
is that the crisis will mark the end of one period and will transform the object
of crisis into a new era. Progress is possible only when crises can be resolved
appropriately and, because it is a crisis, extraordinary measures may be taken
to resolve it.

Crises are a characteristic of the modern global economic system. US
President Obama said in his 2009 inaugural speech, "we are in the midst of
a crisis." Periodically, we have financial crises like the 1997 Asian financial
crisis or the global financial crisis that began in 2008. We are told that Maui
currently has an affordable housing crisis. Such a characterization of the situation is nonetheless worthy of analysis, if not suspicion. What is the duration
of this supposed crisis event? When did the limited availability of housing
become a crisis? Is it properly a crisis at all?

Equally important to engaging effectively with the question of the housing crisis, we must ask what is meant by *housing* in the first place? At its core,
housing is the material condition that satisfies the human need for shelter.

Because it is material, housing also reflects the social and economic relations between humans. In the United States, housing is a commodity and its use value is overshadowed by its exchange value in the market. That is, the value housing has for its use for shelter is eclipsed by the value housing brings when it is bought and sold. For those wealthy enough to own a house, the house becomes the primary store of a family's wealth. Public policy, tax law, and other forces of government encourage most Americans with any savings to store a significant portion of that wealth in the real property value of their home. This process of marketizing housing makes the absence of homeownership into a moral failing on the part of individuals who lack homes, while mystifying the causes of that lack.

Analyzing the value of housing depends on establishing several types of value that the house can be divided into. Housing has a value which reflects the amount of human labor that was put into creating it. Housing has a use value because it satisfies the human need for shelter. When housing is traded it acquires an exchange value. The exchange value is represented monetarily by its price. In a market economy, the supply of housing is determined by the housing's exchange value, not by its labor value or use value. The sale of housing, as a commodity, increases the exchange value which creates profit for the owner of capital, such as the landowner, and therefore increases the value of capital. The price of production of housing is established by the input costs and by the profit margin on the houses that are sold. The price of production also reflects that capital accumulation predominates in the economic system, while at the same time it obscures how the increase in the value of capital in production occurs. In general, when workers produce commodities, they produce by their labor both the value of their wages and the profit claimed by capitalists who control the means of production and the supply of productive capital.

In Hawai'i, like most places plugged into the circuits of the global markets, there is a major shortage of decent housing for working people.[1] We are told that this shortage is a crisis and it is described as a crisis of affordable housing. There are many factors involved in the production and existence of housing. Yet, the prevailing wisdom is that government regulation is a substantial cause of the housing shortage. Louis Rose claimed that government regulations increase "marginal costs... reducing the flow of new housing production" (Rose, 1987: 137). David Callies claims "Hawai'i continues to be the most regulated of all the fifty states" (Callies, 2010: 1). Callies goes on to assert that, "this drives up the price of virtually anything connected with land development" (Id., 2). It is so well understood by the new common sense that government regulation is the problem, it no longer even has to be directly mentioned and never has to be justified. It has acquired mythical status, lacking only in empirical support.

For example, at a community information meeting on the West Maui Community Plan update in late 2017, the County Department of Housing and Human Concerns presented a line graph which plotted the number of affordable housing units for sale between 2005 and 2015. The line graph noted when the county adopted two ordinances: the 2006 workforce housing ordinance requiring 50 percent of new housing units to be affordable, and the 2007 water ordinance requiring land developers to prove there is a sustainable water source for their future development. The line graph shows minimal affordable housing sales between 2008 and 2014, implying some direct link between the passing of these two ordinances and the drop in affordable housing sales. Among the significant factors that were not noted was the collapse of the national housing market and the drying up of credit beginning in 2007, in which the Maui County Council's ordinances had no direct effect. The graph was simplistic, at best, offering a selective understanding of the housing affordability and water availability that benefited those who wanted fewer regulations.

This chapter challenges the common sense explanation that regulation is responsible for the housing situation in Maui, first by challenging the claim that it is in fact a crisis, and second by challenging the explanations that are commonly given to characterize that crisis. Government regulation is not a substantial cause of the shortage of housing. There was an affordable housing shortage on Maui decades before the first land use and building regulation was adopted and implemented. Further, many factors that affect affordability have nothing to do with state and local government regulation of land use and development.

This chapter will first look at the context of housing policy in Hawai'i and the United States. It will then look at the history of government efforts to create affordable housing and the history of state and local government efforts to regulate land use and building of homes. The regulation of land use and home building began in Honolulu fifty years before such regulation appeared on Maui. Therefore, the history and experience of Honolulu in enacting land use and home building regulations provides a good foundation for understanding the development of land use regulation on Maui.

Affordability

There are a number of factors that affect affordability, including the portion of income used to pay housing costs, the market structure, the cost of land, demographic changes, the profitability necessary to incentivize building, and land use controls.

Affordability is affected by the portion of income going to pay housing costs. Housing costs are higher for renters than owners of housing. But the cost of housing in Hawai'i has gone up for both renters and owners over the last forty years, and especially since 2000. Federal housing policy considers paying 30 percent of one's income toward housing costs to be appropriate. People and families that pay more than 30 percent of their income are considered to be burdened. In 1985, 30 percent of renters and 15 percent of homeowners paid more than 35 percent of their income towards housing costs and were considered burdened. In 2009, half of all renters and a quarter of homeowners were considered burdened, with 30 percent of renters spending more than 50 percent of their income on housing costs. Nearly 70 percent of the poor spend more than 50 percent of their household income in housing costs. The lack of affordable housing in Hawai'i has greater, direct implications for those at lower income levels.

The housing situation for those in lower income levels has been exacerbated by wage stagnation. Average wages, adjusted for inflation, have been falling over the last four decades. However, total wages have not fallen or stagnated for all. Wages have risen for the top wage earners. Union membership, however, has declined, as has the real minimum wage. Further, the portion of national income that goes to workers has dropped over the last several decades. This means the owners of the means of production are keeping a larger share of the generated income—technological changes, shifting high intensity production overseas, and other changes in production have all contributed to this change.

Another factor in affordability relates to the market structure. In the typical narrative offered by economists, the functioning of the housing market is described as a quality hierarchy filter that selects for quality and dwelling size. The highest quality houses are typically new houses. These are purchased by the most affluent market participants who typically already own a home. When they buy a new high-quality home, this makes an already built home of a relatively lesser quality available for less affluent market participants who are able to buy their first house, but not necessarily the newly built, high-quality home. This second family gives up their rental home to a family that cannot afford to buy, largely because they cannot obtain financing, but can afford a rental upgrade. This third family then gives up its rental unit to a lower income family, and so on. It is argued that the overall supply of housing is increased by the construction of new housing, and that existing housing moves through the quality hierarchy filter until, in the end, old housing is removed from the supply through destruction or conversion. Theoretically, the larger the housing supply, the lower the overall costs—regardless of what part of the housing market the housing units are constructed in.

While this model offers a compelling story, the historical evidence and present circumstances do not support it, whether in Hawai'i or in the United States. The houses further down the chain do not become cheaper, and the overall impact of new housing is in fact to make houses costlier and more likely to be converted to rentals. Public policy has sought to overcome this failure of the market to produce housing by offering major government subsidies to private developers willing to build affordable housing through low and no interest loans, tax credits, and other supports. Yet, because the problem is not an insufficiency of capital for affordable housing but the commodification of housing, these significant interventions barely touch the problem. The quality hierarchy process is also distorted by banking practices that make it very difficult for low wage workers to obtain a mortgage, even if their monthly payments would be less than their current rent. The hierarchy is also distorted in part by U.S. tax policy, which encourages speculation in housing values. Second-home owners who do not reside in Maui for more than thirty days at a time can deduct the mortgage interest on their houses as if they were their primary residence. House sale prices are exempt from capital gains taxes up to a certain limit, and the capital basis for a purchase can be depreciated, thus sheltering other income from taxes. The filtering system thus does not occur in practice, partly because homeowners who are upgrading do not sell their current houses, and partly because potential first-time buyers do not have the resources to purchase them anyway.

This situation is particularly acute in Hawai'i, where market-rate homes are primarily purchased by nonresidents who do not intend to move to Hawai'i to live full-time. Full-time residents are generally more interested in issues regarding the public good, such as maintaining a clean and healthful environment, and tend to see their house as a home, as opposed to a fungible commodity. As new market and luxury housing units are built, the existing units do not descend down the quality hierarchy. Instead, they continue to circulate in the second-home and speculative-property market of nonresidents or local speculators. Many of these second-home units and speculative properties are held by the hospitality industry, where they serve as short term vacation rentals, propelling a situation that is becoming more extreme with the advent of internet-based, short-term rental systems. Condos, hotels, and timeshare units that are physically forms of housing are being used for commercial purposes.

The movement of housing from residential to nonresidential, short-term uses not only limits the available housing supply, it generates a further need for workers to support the increased number of tourists, which generates a further need for housing. Thus, every time a hotel unit is created, or a housing unit is converted to a short-term rental, the expanded housing generates the need for workers but does not expand the supply of housing through the quality hierarchy. In short, the structure of the market is such that the luxury housing market generates further demand in the affordable housing market, but does not contribute to an increase in supply, which is contrary to what economic theorists had predicted through the so-called quality hierarchy. Rather, new housing construction, subject to these dynamics, makes the housing market increasingly competitive. The production of affordable housing is not the same as the production of luxury housing.

Consider the rate of owner occupancy in affordable projects in Figure 1.

Figure 1.

PROJECTS	OWNER OCCUPIED	YEARS IN EXISTENCE
Single Family Subdivision		
Komohana Hale Subdivision	93%	30 years
Hale Noho	83%	30 years
Lokahi at Kahua	83%	10 years
Napilihau Planned Unit Development	79%	45 years
Honokeana	79%	30 years
Kapua Village	77%	15 years
Wahikuli Terrace	69%	45 years
Apartments		
Villas at Kahana Ridge	48%	10 years
Napilihau Villages I	47%	10 years
Maui Breakers	10%	10 years

Unlike the single-family subdivision projects, which were built to be affordable housing for residents, the apartment projects are part of larger projects with a mix of affordable and market housing. Second apartment units, not single-family homes, are the primary commodity in the housing market in West Maui.

The housing market does not produce housing for the poor because there is relatively little profit in producing housing for low- and moderately low-income families, while there is a fantastic profit to be made from luxury housing. So long as the production of affordable housing is subject to the dictates of the market forces demanding that a commodity create the highest profit at the lowest cost of production, and that the price of the commodity is determined primarily by its exchange value, there will be a lack of affordable housing. In this context, the role of the government has been to mitigate the tendencies of the market towards a highly unequal housing situation, where nonresidents dominate the real estate market that largely excludes local resident participation.

The commodification of housing, however, limits or excludes the government from providing housing because such government participation violates the imperatives of the market. Public provision of housing does not generate a profit and does not accrue wealth to the class of people who own the means of production. Federal, state, and local policies regarding affordable housing start and end with profitability as their object. This is expressed in the structures of government subsidies: tax breaks, supplemental payments to cover rent, low- or no-interest loans or tax-exempt bonds, etc. While it is broadly believed that if the market were free to build affordable houses, affordable housing would be built, that argument is simply unsupported. Rather, when the market does build affordable housing, it does so because taxpayers are paying for the profits of the land developer, directly or indirectly.

Another dynamic found elsewhere in the United States is that affluent areas use zoning and planning laws to limit the building of affordable housing. This occurs where local ordinances require such things as large lot sizes, prohibit multifamily house construction, limit housing density, or prohibit certain generally suitable but less expensive building materials. These strategies have not, thus far, directly been a significant factor in Hawai'i.

In addition to the historical fact that a lack of affordable housing predates government regulation on Maui by decades, another fact eliminates government regulation as a cause of the shortage. As discussed further below, so long as Maui has had building and land use regulations, state law has also exempted affordable housing development from those regulations. Since statutes exist which exempt even entirely private development of affordable housing projects from zoning and planning ordinances, land use regulation cannot be a cause of the shortage of affordable housing in Hawai'i.

Parallel to the use of formal land use controls to limit affordable housing are informal land use controls, such as informal segregation (Brooks and Rose, 2013). Hawaii's housing segregation has been primarily of the economic kind. However, because the sugar plantation economy was organized through the use of racial hierarchies and the promotion of racial antagonisms, housing segregation by class has been coextensive with segregation by race. This organization has also been reproduced in the disconnect between affordable housing markets aimed towards resident workers and luxury housing markets aimed towards affluent nonresidents living in the continental United States and elsewhere in the world. Each of these disconnections are attended with their own variations of racial stratification.

Historically, housing segregation by race occurred both directly and indirectly in Hawai'i. Plantation-controlled housing implemented racial segregation. Milton Murayama, in describing West Maui plantation living, noted that the haole manager lived at the top of the hill, their Spanish, Portuguese and Nisei Japanese lunas lived in nicer looking homes with their own baths and indoor toilets, then below them would be the cookie-cutter wooden frame houses of Japanese camp, and, at the lowest level were the run-down Filipino camps with community bathhouses and communal toilets (Murayama, 28). Murayama noted how even the sewage ditch would start at the managers house and then run down under the houses of the luna, then to the communal toilets of the Japanese camp, then to the communal toilets of the Filipino camp before meeting the concrete irrigation ditch at the lower perimeter of camp. As Murayama stated, "shit too was organized according to the plantation pyramid" (Murayama, 1988: 96).

Even in those areas not under the direct control of the plantations, class was organized around race. Therefore, neighborhoods organized around class were organized around race. The correlation is not perfect; white only neighborhoods admitted some upper-class, part-Hawaiian families as residents. Many of these exceptions had more to do with the political landscape of post-*annexation* politics in the Territory of Hawai'i than with social mobility for working class Hawaiians. Even in the 1950s, which were the declining years of the plantation era, sociologists observed three broad groups that articulated housing segregation in Honolulu: white, Asian/Hawaiian and Filipino (Yamamoto and Sakumoto, 1954: 35–46). At this time, the pan-Asian and Hawaiian working class, local identity did much to eliminate the more invidious forms of racial segregation, but did not specifically address much of the underlying economic segregation. The development of the tourism industry, luxury housing for second homes, and vacation rentals for wealthy North Americans, brought Maui's economic segregation patterns into alignment with U.S. racial segregation patterns. The more recent imposition of affordable housing requirements on market developments in Maui has been effective at perpetuating housing segregation by allowing affordable housing requirements to be entirely unconnected to the building of luxury housing or allowing such building to occur far away from the luxury housing development. There is no community development plan. Rather, there are strategies to build luxury houses with little or no concern for the needs of the local population, or even for the additional needs created by those luxury houses.

Controlling Land Use

The rise of the power and dominance of the sugar plantations in Hawai'i correlates with the integration of Hawai'i into the American economy and into global capitalist relations. As the sugar plantations became dominant in Hawai'i, the availability of housing became increasingly limited. Land, along with water, the most significant factor of production in Hawaii's sugar industry, was taken from Native Hawaiians. This taking occurred in many ways: through changes in foreclosure laws, through questionable uses of quiet title, and through the overthrow of the Hawaiian Kingdom.

In 1874, the Kingdom of Hawai'i passed the Mortgage Act, which created a nonjudicial foreclosure process in Hawai'i. "Capital was available in the Islands, but little if any was being given or lent to the maka'āinana" (Stauffer, 2004: 96). Lenders refused to lend to kuleana owners "because lenders felt foreclosure actions before native juries would not be sustained" (Stauffer, 2004: 96). The 1874 Mortgage Act created a process of foreclosure that did not include the court system at all. This continued until 2012, when foreclosures of owner-occupied houses were required to go through the court system.

As the sugar plantations obtained a monopoly of control over land, the owners of the sugar plantations limited the availability of land for housing. Hawaiians who were able to keep their family lands saw those lands become isolated islands in a sea of sugar plantation-controlled acreage. Urban developments on the margins of the plantation world became areas where shelter could be developed. But these areas at the margins were limited and still indirectly subject to the control of the plantations. These areas were the urban slums of Honolulu, located primarily in areas of poor drainage and lacking in proper sewage disposal. In 1901, the board of health criticized the Bishop Estate for being a landowner that profited from renting land used for slum dwelling (*Honolulu Advertiser,* Feb. 16, 1901). The trustees of the Bishop Estate were all prominent men connected to the sugar industry.

The plantations had no problem with the efficient control of their land and workforce. In addition to shelter, plantation housing was an effective means of controlling workers and reproducing its hierarchies of control. But in areas of Hawai'i where the plantation was not the direct provider of housing to the workers, the plantation was also first to the market. This meant that governance of workers was left to the plantations indirectly. This default mode of governance was much like Bishop Estate whose trustees, all sugar men socially and professionally connected to the plantations, were appointed by the Supreme Court of Hawai'i (Cooper and Daws, 1985: 2–3).

The incorporation of Hawai'i into the United States under the Organic Act democratized the political process from what it had been under the Republic of Hawai'i. Urban Honolulu became the ground for political experimentation with the regulating of building, subdividing of land, land use zoning, and then planning. At the turn of the century, land use in urban Honolulu was described by some as a result of "short-sighted commercial greed and far-sighted civic consideration for the general good" (Johnson, 1991: 293).

But this progressive cause of civic planning for land use and development was not primarily led by the workers that dwelt in the slums. Instead, it was led by civic-minded factions within the economic elite. The orientation of these progressive initiatives was primarily aesthetic—although couched, at times, as concerns over sanitation. Ultimately, appearance, orderliness, and health were inextricably linked. American Progressive Ray Stannard Baker wrote in 1911 that "Honolulu has some of the worst slums in the world—and if poverty in the tropics is picturesque, its gnawings are nonetheless painful. For downright overcrowding and unsanitary conditions, it would be hard to find anything worse than some of the...old tenements which I visited in the city of Honolulu" (*Honolulu Advertiser*, Dec. 2, 2011).

The improvement of roads in urban Honolulu was a major focus of civic planning. Road improvements led to the planning and development of parks. This led to legislation that allowed the creation of improvement districts, which would then permit the assessment of a frontage tax. That meant properties adjacent to roads could be taxed for their paving and upkeep. The implementation of these laws at the county level (in Honolulu) turned out to be more complicated than anticipated. The Democratic Party, which was the minority party at that time, felt that taxing the wealth of the Territory could support improvements being paid out of general government revenues.

Honolulu then created a planning commission. Its stated purpose was "to provide for and regulate the future growth, development and beautification of the City and County of Honolulu, in its public and private buildings, streets, parks, grounds and vacant lots, and to provide plans, consistent with the future growth and development [of] Honolulu and its inhabitants, sanitation, services of all public utilities and harbor, shipping and transportation facilities." The planning commission, however, was purely advisory. It was also called to address "the need of beautifying the city along artistic lines."

There were relatively few rules regarding building standards. However, following the Progressive political movements in the United States, local Honolulu elites pushed for comprehensive government regulation of building standards. The movement gained steam in 1910 as serious negotiations began. The *Honolulu Advertiser* noted, "the minute the rain stops there will be a hundred hammers at work around the tenements being rushed to completion in a race with the promised new building ordinance. The ordinance is a promise, the tenements are actualities." (*Honolulu Advertiser*, Jan. 17, 1910: 5) At that time, building standards ordinances were passed and included construction materials standards, setback requirements, structural requirements, density limitations, as well as sanitary and plumping requirements. The two interest groups most vociferously opposed to these ordinances were the owners of tenements and the sugar plantations. These ordinances were not adopted on Maui at this time.

Honolulu adopted an ordinance to regulate subdivisions of land. But the lack of meaningful standards and the influence of politics in the decision-making led to the repeal of the ordinance in the following year.

As urban Honolulu expanded, significant monies were devoted to reorganizing the use of land in Waikīkī with a canal, sanitary sewers, and improved roads that were designed in a grid. When the first canal system successfully diverted the floodwaters from the early 1923 rains, more money was allocated to expand what is now the Ala Wai Canal. Within four years, the Royal Hawaiian Hotel opened.

On the other side of Honolulu, government officials sought to replicate their Waikīkī successes in Kapālama. The difference was that Kapālama was full of people. Instead of draining wetlands and taro patches in Waikīkī, improvement of Kapālama required moving people. The *Honolulu Star-Bulletin* reported an extreme example: one large building had over four hundred people living on one floor and all sharing one bathroom (*Honolulu Star-Bulletin,* Jan. 2, 1920). In other words, there was an affordable housing shortage.

The landowners and tenement building owners joined together to oppose any regulation. There was no profit to be made in upgrading urban housing. The profit lay in the shortage of affordable, sanitary housing, and that shortage also allowed the sugar plantations to indirectly control labor off of the plantation. Progressive forces obtained building inspector orders that, by 1921, had three hundred tenements torn down and another forty-three remodeled. Nevertheless, the tenement problem persisted. As Frank Midkiff explained, "with the capital investment long since written off and with improvements of very low value, nevertheless, these shacks are terribly overcrowded with families paying relatively high rents. Due to this, our slum properties pay high dividends and there is strong inclination not to disturb the situation and to discount the overall city costs accruing to the general taxpayer" (Johnson, 1991: 317–318).

In 1921, Honolulu's planning commission proposed a zoning ordinance that established fire, industrial, business, and residential districts within urban Honolulu. It gave enforcement powers to city inspectors over construction and repair work on private property within those districts. Supervisor Manuel Pacheco opposed the ordinance, saying he favored high standards but opposed housing shortages and high rents, and that standards would create shortages and drive up rents. Jonah Kumalae claimed that a zoning ordinance would hurt the working class and opposed it. Many landowners and tenement owners in Kalihi and Kapālama opposed the ordinance. The city council passed a weakened version but the prolific requests for variances from the ordinance were anyway approved through political channels. The owners of the sugar plantations, which were the large landowners and controlled other large landholdings, opposed zoning regulation. The opposition to zoning was not because it would hurt working people, but rather because it would limit absolute control over land use—and subordinating the use of land to the policy choices of the electorate—and thereby limiting the range of choices to profit from control of land. Any potential harm to the working and lower-classes was incidental.

Housing Policy

A coordinated US federal housing policy began during World War I as a means of providing housing to defense workers through the use of loans to land developers and appropriations for additional housing. After the war, these housing units were sold to private owners.

One of the provisions of the Organic Act in 1900 prohibited any person or corporation from owning more than one thousand acres of land. It also had a provision that allowed lands to be withdrawn from the public lands trust for homesteading at the petition of twenty-five citizens. Although this did not stop the sugar plantation elite from controlling seemingly unlimited amounts of land, it did require adherence to burdensome and time-consuming formalities, and the petitioning provision threatened vast tracts of land being leased to sugar plantations.

In 1920, the Hawaiian Homes Commission Act was passed to *rehabilitate* Hawaiians. In exchange, the formal limitation on land ownership in Hawai'i was removed and the commission was allowed to shelter lands under its control from the homesteader petitioning provisions. The Hawaiian Homes Commission Act set aside lands in remote locations with poor soils and areas that were rough, rocky, and dry. Some fifty-five thousand acres were simply barren lava and another eight thousand acres were steep parts of mountains, described by Territorial Representative James Jarrett as "lands that a goat couldn't live on. The whole thing is absolutely a joke! The real purpose of this bill is to cut out homesteading. If you want to cut out homesteading, then pass this bill!" (*Honolulu Star Bulletin*, April 23, 1921). The Hawaiian Homes Commission Act made more land available to the sugar plantations, even while it was purportedly an act designed to rehabilitate Hawaiians by making lands available to individual Hawaiians for homesteading. The sheltering provision enabled the commission to be perpetually funded by a 30 percent share of highly cultivatable, prime agricultural land leased to the sugar plantations.

One result of this legislation was that the Hawaiian Homelands program excluded public lands leased to sugar plantations from the homesteading provisions of the Organic Act. Also, the limitation on landownership was eliminated. Other than the Hawaiian Homes Commission Act and the homesteading provisions in the Organic Act, there were no other significant housing laws enacted until the Great Depression era.

When the Depression began, U.S. President Herbert Hoover created a commission that endorsed "family home ownership as a long-term strategic response to Depression era economic instability." (Isaki, 2008: 88) This vision was codified into law when Congress passed the Emergency Relief and Construction Act of 1932, as well as the Federal Home Loan Bank Act. The Emergency Relief and Construction Act ended in failure. Only two loans were made and its failure was attributed to its sole reliance on private investment to provide housing to low income families and for reconstruction of slum areas. But the idea of motivating people who could not afford to own a home to instead take out massive debt in the form of a mortgage secured by that home had taken root.

After the 1932 election, Congress passed the National Industrial Recovery Act. On the federal level, housing development was transferred from the Reconstruction Finance Corporation to the Public Works Administration— from supporting private industry with loan assistance to publicly led development. The Public Works Administration built 21,600 units in fifty low-rent public housing projects, and another fifteen thousand units in resettlement projects. The Public Works Administration hit a wall when the Supreme Court ruled that it lacked the power of eminent domain. Housing development that required land acquisition shifted the Public Works Administration to funding of state development. However, the new construction under this procedure was priced beyond the reach of low income families.

In 1934, Congress passed the National Housing Act, which established the Federal Housing Administration (FHA). The FHA was designed to regulate private housing mortgages through an insurance program as well as by stimulating construction. Its stated purpose was to "encourage improvement in housing standards and conditions, to provide a system of mutual mortgage insurance, and for other purposes." What was most urgently needed at that time was a major expansion of low-rent housing, but Congress instead focused on increasing employment in the building construction industry. Hawaii's Territorial delegate encouraged the Territorial legislature to adopt several pieces of legislation to coordinate Territorial law with the changes in federal law to qualify for federal support for housing projects. One of those pieces of legislation was Act 190, which created the Hawai'i Housing Authority. According to its finding and declaration of necessity:

> It is hereby declared that unsanitary or unsafe dwelling accommodations exist in various areas of the Territory of Hawaii and that many inhabitants thereof of low income are forced to reside in unsanitary or unsafe dwelling accommodations available to all the inhabitants of the Territory

and that consequently many persons of low income are forced to occupy overcrowded and congested dwelling accommodations; that these conditions cause an increase in and spread of disease and crime and constitute a menace to the health, safety, morals and welfare of the inhabitants of the Territory and impair economic values; that these conditions cannot be remedied by the ordinary operations of private enterprises; that the clearance, replanning and reconstruction of the areas in which unsanitary or unsafe housing conditions exist and the providing of safe and sanitary dwelling accommodations for persons of low income are public uses and purposes for which public money may be spent and private property acquired; that it is in the public interest that work on such projects be instituted as soon as possible in order to relieve unemployment which now constitutes an emergency.

Hawai'i Housing Authority development projects were required to comply with "the planning, zoning, sanitary and building laws, ordinances and regulations applicable to the locality in which the housing project is situated."

The federal housing program, which was administered between the Federal Housing Authority and the earlier Public Works Administration, was made permanent by amendments in 1937 under the Wagner-Steagall Housing Act of 1937. The land development, building construction, and real estate industries strongly opposed the program. In a compromise, Congress required that housing built through the federal program be built as cheaply as possible, restricted it to the poorest households, and prohibited new units from being built except in relation to each unit destroyed in slum clearance. The determination of where to locate housing projects was delegated to local governments which, by and large, protected land developers from having to compete with publicly funded housing and landlords from having to compete by lowering rents. Housing was only one of the aims of the Wagner-Steagall Act. The act noted its purpose was to "to alleviate present and recurring unemployment and to remedy the unsafe and unsanitary housing conditions and the acute shortage of decent, safe, and sanitary dwellings for families of low income."

In summary, federal housing policy during the Depression was aimed at returning the unemployed to work through stimulating the private construction industry. Improving the housing situation for working people was a secondary goal used to draw popular support for these laws and expenditures.

Public housing policy in the United States during World War II moved further away from the aim of providing housing to low income families. Congress passed the National Defense Housing Act of 1940, which limited federally assisted defense housing construction to areas where private industry had entirely failed. Representative Fritz Lanham, the Act's main sponsor and vocal opponent of low-income public housing, was able to secure an amendment to the act which prohibited the conversion of defense housing to low-income public housing without congressional approval. Hawaii's two projects that resulted from this legislation were the Kalihi War Homes (where Kūhiō Park Terraces is now located) and Mānoa Housing (Mānoa Marketplace, Mānoa Innovation Center and Noelani School).

On December 7, 1941, the governor of the Territory of Hawai'i handed over power to the US military, who declared martial law in Hawai'i. Prices, rents, and wages were frozen. Workers were not permitted to leave their jobs without military approval. Aspects of martial law, such as price controls, were codified by Congress to apply nationally in the Emergency Price Control Act of 1942.

In 1944, Congress passed the GI Bill of Rights, which authorized the Veterans Administration (VA) to guarantee loans to veterans for home purchase, building, and improving. While veterans cut across economic class, this housing program was not directed toward, and did not assist, the working poor, who were otherwise ineligible for the liberalized requirements of VA and FHA loans.

Although President Truman encouraged Congress to reauthorize prewar housing policy in 1945, a bipartisan bill stalled after significant opposition from the private housing industry. The Housing Act of 1947 temporarily prevented evictions of low-income tenants in public housing if such an eviction would cause undue hardship. This concern over hardship lessened in light of the federal government's construction of middle-income housing. Eviction protection was short-lived, as the protection was repealed by the Housing Act of 1948, which liberalized mortgage eligibility requirements but did not reauthorize public housing and urban renewal provisions.

In 1949, the Territorial legislature amended the Hawai'i Housing Authority statute by passing Act 338 to broaden the agency's powers to build and operate permanent housing projects. The legislature found the following:

> [t]here is an acute shortage of housing within many areas of the Territory; that with a greatly increased and growing population and severe limitation upon land use in such areas, many persons are unable to obtain hous-

ing; that there is such an emergency condition in the Territory that public improvement projects must be carried out with a view to the consequences in terms of housing which might be destroyed and the clearance
of unhealthful, unsanitary residential areas cannot be carried on without
the provision of new housing for persons displaced by such clearance;
that emergency temporary housing constructed during the last world
war is rapidly deteriorating and will soon have to be replaced because
of its condition as well as because of the terms of federal laws relating
to a substantial part thereof; that while a number of individual homes
have been constructed in the past two years, private enterprise has failed
to construct the large number of housing units necessary to remedy the
above-mentioned conditions; and that the provisions hereinafter enacted
are necessary to assure the availability of housing which otherwise would
not be provided at this time or in the immediate future.

The House amended the Senate's bill to expressly require that proposed projects "shall conform to the master plan for the City and County of Honolulu."
(Hawai'i House Journal, 1949: 2273) The conformity requirement had no
discernible effect limiting or restricting the development of housing.

Meanwhile, Congress further amended federal housing policy to address
a postwar crunch in low-income housing by authorizing the construction
of nearly one million units of public housing through the Housing Act of
1949. Congress sought to maximize private industries' participation in housing construction and focused on slum clearance. Subsequent to congressional
authorization, the federal government did not fund the one million housing units goal. Half a million low-rent units were destroyed and replaced by
one hundred thousand units of luxury housing. Federally funded highway
projects, which supported higher income suburban housing developments,
destroyed another 330,000 housing units under 1955 amendments. Congress
here protected private industry by requiring the local housing authority to
certify that there was at least a 20 percent gap between the rent to be charged
by the proposed low-income housing project and the lowest rent charged by
the private sector for standard housing.

Regulating Land Use on Maui

As the powers of plantations were successfully contested by organized labor,
and the external control over life shifted from plantation board rooms to
government agencies, the power to regulate the use of land was confirmed

and taken up by the counties. Maui first adopted a building code in 1950 and hired a plumbing and sanitary sewer inspector that same year. Amendments and additions followed, however, a house building code was not adopted until 1967.

In order to get a handle on the unregulated proliferation of subdivisions, Maui County passed a subdivision ordinance in 1951. Until then, a landowner could subdivide the land simply by having a surveyor call out the portion of the parcel to be divided off. Land was also subdivided through partition actions in court. The subdivision ordinance was expanded. Since 1972, however, all subdividing of lands requires approval from the county.

In the late 1950s, the legislature empowered the counties to engage in comprehensive zoning. Maui County adopted an interim zoning ordinance. By 1971, Maui County had adopted a comprehensive zoning ordinance which zoned a portion of the county and left the remainder in interim zoning. This zoning ordinance was the original form of land use planning in Maui County. Later, a general plan was developed, as well as community plans, to guide how land use development was to progress or unfold. Comprehensive zoning is considered one way of implementing the general and community plans. Land use decisions must be consistent with zoning and the general and community plans.

In 1961, the legislature created the Land Use Commission, which sought to provide a statewide system of planned land development by classifying all lands within the state into one of four districts. The purpose of the commission was to prevent uncoordinated development by ensuring that development occurred in a way that maximized the delivery of public services and conserved prime agricultural lands from urban sprawl and scattered residential development. While for many years the commission was resented by longtime local communities as seemingly being a rubber stamp for land developers, by the 1990s the tide turned. Now, the land use commission is seen by developers as an obstacle to land development.

County officials and representatives of American Factors (Amfac) worked together in the late 1950s to establish Lahaina town as a historic district. As noted by Sydney Iaukea, the district and its standards took little from Lahaina's long history as the capitol of the kingdom and earlier chiefdoms and instead focused on the decadelong history of whaling in the nineteenth century. Since this short period had little to no impact on the architectural history of Lahaina, county officials and Amfac executives established architectural regulations from Nantucket, Massachusetts. In 1976, the legislature created a comprehensive program for historic preservation along the lines of the 1966 National Historic Preservation Act.

In 1965, the board of supervisors adopted a zoning ordinance, at the request of the Napili Kai Beach Club and other area landowners, which designated the area around Nāpili Bay as a special zoning district called the Napili Bay Civic Improvement District. It was created to "encourage, secure, and maintain the orderly and harmonious appearance and esthetic development of land and structures." (Ordinance No. 371, Sec. 1) The ordinance imposed height restrictions on floor area to lot area ratio, building materials must have been new, and new buildings were to be built in the architectural style of the existing buildings. These were restrictions designed to maintain high-class housing, and neighborhoods, for wealthy owners. An advisory committee was appointed to review all plans and their recommendation would be forwarded to the Maui Traffic and Planning Commission, whose decision on permits could be overridden by the board of supervisors. Land continued to be added to the district.

After twenty years of attempts, in 1967 the legislature passed a leasehold-conversion law called the Land Reform Act which was intended to broaden the base of landowners. It met a series of obstacles to implementation. For many outside the sugar plantation power structure, the presence of a few large landowners limited the supply of land for housing, which drove up the price of housing. Land reform was intended to broaden the base of landowners by making the land of large landowners available to working and middle-class families. However, instead of focusing on the lands of the sugar plantations and their related businesses, the law was aimed at Kamehameha Schools-Bishop Estate, who, unlike the plantations, had made vast tracts of trust land available for residential development on a long-term, leasehold basis, starting in the 1940s. To be eligible for FHA lending, most leases were fifty-five years long. Many families benefited from this arrangement, as the initial ground rent ended up being well below market rate. Twenty or thirty years later, ground rents began to reset to then-current market rates, which were significantly higher. The middle class, who had become wealthy by this arrangement, revolted and pressured the state to fix the problem and allow leasehold-conversion to occur. The large landholdings of the sugar plantations and their related businesses were basically exempt from land reform, while Kamehameha Schools-Bishop Estate—a charitable trust established by the Hawaiian chiefs to provide educational benefits to Hawaiian children—became the primary target, and only because the trustees had opened their landholdings to affordable residential development decades earlier. Meanwhile, the sugar plantation and related business lands were being developed for resort development and luxury housing.

In 1972, Congress passed the Coastal Zone Management Act to assist coastal states in developing and managing their coastal resources. In Hawai‘i, the coastal zone constitutes the entirety of the state. But for purposes of regulating development, a much smaller area of land along the shoreline called a Special Management Area (SMA) is subject to special regulatory control under the act. No development is allowed to occur within the SMA unless the county's permit-granting authority approves a permit. In Maui County, that authority is vested in the planning commission. For West Maui, this meant, amongst other things, the power and influence of the Napili Bay Civic Improvement District's advisory committee waned as the SMA regulatory framework was fully implemented. The advisory committee was abolished in 2004.

In 1970, the legislature adopted Act 132, which created the Office of Environmental Quality Control. The following year, Governor Burns issued an executive order requiring state and county agencies using state or county lands to prepare environmental impact statements for major actions. Then, in 1974, the legislature adopted a new statute, "Environmental Impact Statements," codified at Chapter 343, Hawaii Revised Statutes. Actions involving the use of state or county lands or state or county funds, use of land within the conservation district, use of lands within the shoreline, use of any historic site designated in the National or Hawai‘i Register, any use of land within Waikīkī, or any amendments to existing county general plans trigger environmental review document preparation requirements. An assessment is first prepared and if there is a finding of no significant impact, then the process ends. If there are significant environmental impacts, an environmental impact statement is to be prepared. The overall purpose of these assessments and statements is to ensure that government decision makers have all the relevant facts regarding environmental impacts when it makes decisions on covered actions.

The state's historic preservation program was broadened in 1989 after Native Hawaiians across the state protested Maui Land and Pineapple Company's Ritz-Carlton Kapalua project in Honokahua, where a massive number of burials had been uncovered. The protection of Hawaiian burial sites became a significant focus of the historic preservation program.

Housing Policy After Statehood

In 1961, the federal government began to move away from government construction and the operation of low- and moderate-income housing with public moneys. Instead, the federal policy shifted to providing subsidies, such as
tax incentives and below-market-rate financing to private investors to encourage housing development. In 1962, Congress passed the Senior Citizen Housing Act, which sought to address housing problems for senior citizens who
could not benefit from the liberalized, long-term mortgages made available
through the federal home mortgage programs, among other issues. The act
authorized $100 million to provide below-market-rate-interest loans to non-
profit organizations that built rental and cooperative housing for low income
persons over sixty-two years old.

In 1964, the Hawai'i legislature adopted Act 22, which included a *down
payment reserve plan* that allowed tenants in nonsubsidized housing to have
the portion of their rent beyond the per-unit operating costs of the housing
authority credited to a down payment reserve, which would be paid to the
seller of a suitable low-cost home. Act 52 of 1964 authorized the Hawai'i
Housing Authority to issue revenue bonds for a series of low-income housing
projects, including the eighteen-unit Lahaina low-income housing project,
now called David Malo Circle. The Hawai'i Public Housing Authority built
Pi'ilani Homes in Lahaina town.

Congress established the Department of Housing and Urban Development in 1965, encouraging the privatization of public housing although sought
as a goal, socially and economically integrated housing. This integrated housing was to be accomplished through privatizing low-income housing through
leases and through rent subsidies. Rent subsidies were established for lower
income families that included elderly or disabled members, or persons displaced from their homes by government action or natural disaster.

In 1968, Congress passed the Civil Rights Act of 1968, which included
Title VIII, known as the Fair Housing Act. The Fair Housing Act made it illegal to discriminate in selling, renting, or financing housing on the basis race,
color, religion, sex, or national origin. The act included prohibitions against
advertising discriminatory preferences or intimidating or interfering with a
person's enjoyment of housing for discriminatory reasons. In 1988, the act was
amended to include persons with disabilities and families with children. For
Hawai'i, this meant that common forms of race and sex-based discrimination
in housing transactions were no longer broadcast in newspaper ads.

Congress also passed an updated Housing and Urban Development Act in 1968. The goal of this act was to build or rehabilitate twenty-six million housing units, including six million for low- and middle-income families. This was to be accomplished by providing subsidies to land developers. The result, however, was President Richard Nixon declaring a moratorium on federally subsidized housing in 1973 because of widespread fraud by land developers in obtaining subsidies. As has often been the case, efforts to create housing for low-income people was ultimately dominated by the designed profit, whether legal or not. Nevertheless, this law included the so-called Section 235 home ownership program for low-income families. In 1970, the state legislature passed Act 105, which was supposed to address the existence of a "critical shortage of housing units for lower and middle income residents" in Hawai'i. The legislature pronounced that the problem of the critical shortage was the high cost of housing. The causes of this high cost were said to be "the cost and availability of land, the cost of development, the cost and availability of financing, the cost added by government regulation, the cost and availability of labor and materials, the inflationary state of the economy that makes high cost housing more profitable to produce and more attractive to 'risk' capital."

Act 105 greatly expanded the powers of the Hawai'i Housing Authority by allowing it to directly develop housing and to adopt rules for "health, safety, building, planning, zoning and land use which relate to development, subdivision and construction of dwelling units in projects" that would "supersede, for all projects... [,] all other inconsistent laws, ordinances and rules and regulations relating to the use, zoning, planning and development of land, and the construction of dwelling units[,]" except safety standards or tariffs approved by the Public Utilities Commission. Land development activities in the agricultural or conservation district required the approval of the land use commission. Maui Mayor Elmer Cravalho wasted no time. In partnership with Hale Mahaolu, the county developed Wahikuli Terraces as a federal Section 235 and a state Act 105 housing project in West Maui. Hale Mahaolu partnered with the Hawai'i Housing Authority to develop Lahaina Surf in 1972. Mayor Cravalho persuaded the county to contribute $50,000 and obtained financing of $1 million. Also, under both Section 235 and Act 105, the Hawai'i Housing Authority partnered with the Maui Land and Pineapple Co. to develop the Napilihau Planned Unit Development. The timing for the Napilihau development could not have been better because Maui Land & Pine had been ordered by the Department of Health to close Honolua camp because of raw sewage entering Oneloa Bay. After the Department of Health

Wahikuli Terrace,
County of Maui File
Plan No. 1208.

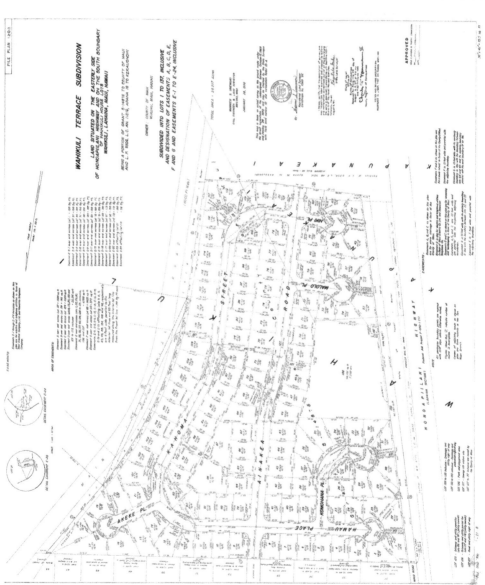

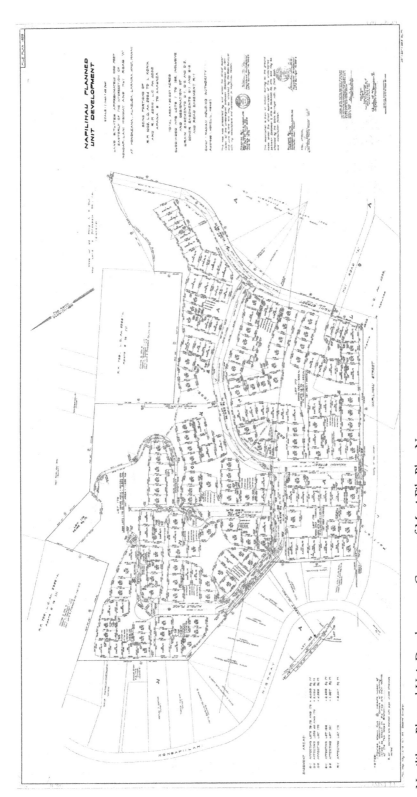

Napilihau Planned Unit Development, County of Maui File Plan No. 1392.

ordered Honolua camp closed, Maui Land & Pine had an immediate need to find housing for the residents of Honolua camp.

Congress passed the Housing Act of 1974, which made permanent the shift from direct production of housing to merely subsidizing housing rent and development, and to shift decision-making to state and local housing agencies. Section 8 rent subsidies are perhaps the most well-known. The program was significantly modified and turned into the present voucher system. Section 8 rent subsidies are one of the primary means of providing affordable housing in the U.S. To date, Maui County has received nearly $500 million in Section 8 subsidies, and last year received over $20 million. The subsidies are meant to address the short-term problem of working and low-income renters by facilitating their access to safe and decent housing. In the long-term, however, the subsidies are actually subsidies to landlords. Instead of tax monies being used to develop affordable housing, or infrastructure for affordable housing, or both, the subsidies transfer wealth to private landowners through rents, which are often inflated.

Another aspect of the Section 8 program was the "supply-side," which provided subsidies for housing unit development designated for low-income renters. The federal government subsidized 75 percent of the market rent for each unit. Section 8 housing owners also were given access to below-market financing and tax deductions. This part of Section 8 housing was terminated in 1983 by President Reagan; nevertheless, it spurred the creation of nearly a million housing units designated as affordable.

The Housing Act of 1974 also established the Community Development Block Grant program which provided federal funding for affordable housing, social services, and economic development. Block grants can be used for housing-related programs, but new housing construction is limited to so-called "last resort" housing carried out by nonprofit organizations. Much of Maui's social services infrastructure was built with block grants.

Mayor Cravalho used a patchwork of federal funds and financing, including block grants, to develop the Luana Gardens project. Luana Gardens in Kahului, is one of the few examples where the County built a housing project and then became a landlord receiving Section 8 subsidies, thus harnessing federal funding to build and expand affordable housing in the County.

In 1976, the state legislature amended Act 105 by establishing the basic framework for fast-track housing developments. The legislature found that "the shortage of housing affordable by residents of low and moderate income remains one of Hawaii's major social problems." It also found that the housing development program adopted in Act 105 should continue, and be "the primary form of public intervention in this problem[.]" It did so by creating the so-called 'fast-track' process whereby the Hawaiʻi Housing Authority would partner with private housing developers and fast-track housing projects. It expanded the exemption from land use, zoning, planning, and development laws to these private housing developments, provided that more than half of the dwelling units built were designated affordable.

The legislature also passed Act 108, which allowed counties to engage in experimental and demonstration housing projects that proposed to "reduce the cost of housing in the State." These projects, which required county council approval, would be "exempt from all statutes, ordinances, charter provisions, and rules or regulations of any governmental agency or public utility relating to planning, zoning, construction standards for subdivisions, development and improvement of land, and the construction and sale of homes[.]" The Hale Noho subdivision in Nāpili in 1986, the Honokeana subdivision just mauka in 1990, and the Komohana Hale subdivision next to the Lahaina Recreation Center in 1988 were all West Maui experimental housing projects approved under this process. Kapua Villages, built in 2002, was done to satisfy Maui Land & Pine's obligations in the development of the Honokeana subdivision. In 2004, the county council allowed Maui Land & Pine to use the development of Hale Noho and Honokeana subdivisions to satisfy their affordable housing obligations consequent to the development of the Ritz-Carlton Kapalua (County Council Resolution No. 04-77). The Lahaina Affordable Apartments, now called the Weinberg Court Apartments, were also developed under this process in the mid-1990s.

Since 1976, few changes have been made to the so-called "fast-track" exemption process. Generally, the county council and/or the Hawaiʻi State Land Use Commission have forty-five days to approve or disapprove a proposed project. The process outlined then is substantially the same as it is now. The powers of the Hawaiʻi Housing Authority regarding fast track housing projects is now vested in the Hawaiʻi Housing Finance and Development Corporation, and it continues to be empowered to "exempt from all statutes, ordinances, charter provisions, and rules of any government agency relating to planning, zoning, construction standards for subdivisions, development and improvement of land, and the construction of dwelling units thereon." HRS §201H-38. It can also accept and approve housing projects with similar exemptions that are "independently initiated by private developers." HRS § 201H-41.

Hale Noho, County of Maui File Plan No. 1830.

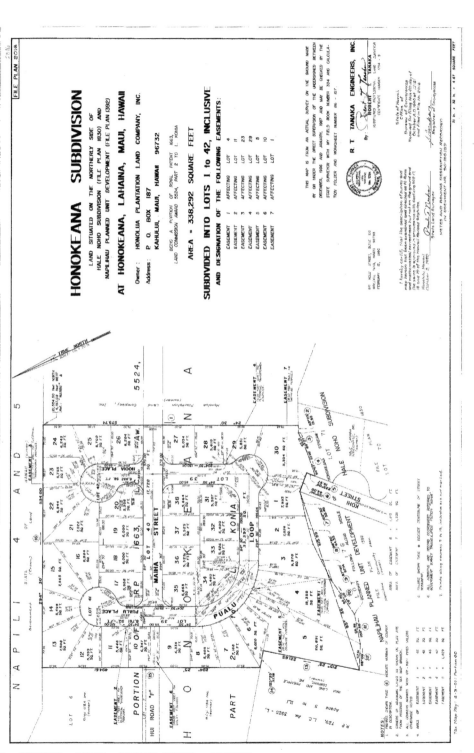

Honokeana, County of Maui File Plan No. 2016.

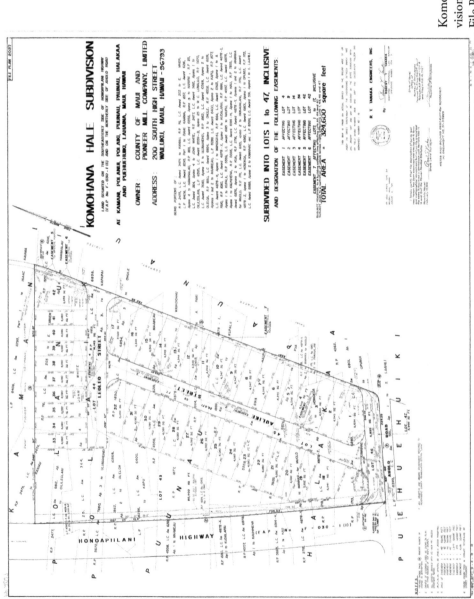

Komohana Hale Subdivision, County of Maui File Plan No. 2027.

Kapua Village, County of
Maui File Plan No. 2332.

FILE PLAN 2332

KAPUA VILLAGE SUBDIVISION

LAND SITUATED ON THE WESTERLY
SIDE OF HONOAPIILANI HIGHWAY
[F.A.P. No. RF-030-1(5)]

AT KAHANA, LAHAINA, MAUI, HAWAII

OWNER: HONOLUA PLANTATION LAND COMPANY, INC.

ADDRESS: P. O. BOX 187
KAHULUI, MAUI, HAWAII 96732

Being a Portion of Grant 1166 to D. Baldwin,
J. F. Pogue and S. E. Bishop

SUBDIVIDED INTO LOTS 1 TO 50, INCLUSIVE
AND DESIGNATION OF EASEMENTS 1 TO 14, INCLUSIVE

EASEMENT 1 AFFECTING LOT 12
EASEMENT 2 AFFECTING LOT 30
EASEMENT 3 AFFECTING LOT 35
EASEMENT 4 AFFECTING LOT 43
EASEMENT 5 AFFECTING LOT 45
EASEMENT 6 OVER AND ACROSS LOTS 1 AND 47
EASEMENT 7 OVER AND ACROSS LOTS 7, 8, 9, 24, 25, 26 AND 27
EASEMENT 8 OVER AND ACROSS LOTS 28, 29, 31, 32, INCLUSIVE
EASEMENT 9 OVER AND ACROSS LOT 2
EASEMENT 10 OVER AND ACROSS LOTS 10 AND 23
EASEMENT 11 OVER AND ACROSS LOT 47
EASEMENT 12 AFFECTING LOT 48
EASEMENTS 13 AND 14 AFFECTING LOT 48

DESIGNATION OF RESTRICTION OF VEHICULAR ACCESS
RIGHTS AFFECTING LOTS 1, 3, 14, 45 AND 47

SUBJECT, HOWEVER, TO EXISTING RESTRICTION OF VEHICULAR
ACCESS RIGHTS AFFECTING LOTS 27 TO 37, INCLUSIVE, AND LOT 48

SUBJECT, ALSO, TO PORTION OF EXISTING UTILITY EASEMENT
AFFECTING LOT 48, EXISTING SEWER PUMP STATION EASEMENT
AFFECTING LOT 48 AND PORTION OF EXISTING DRAINLINE
EASEMENT AFFECTING LOTS 46, 47 AND 48

AREA = 477,865 Square Feet

R. T. TANAKA ENGINEERS, INCORPORATED

By: _____
KIRK T. TANAKA   DATE

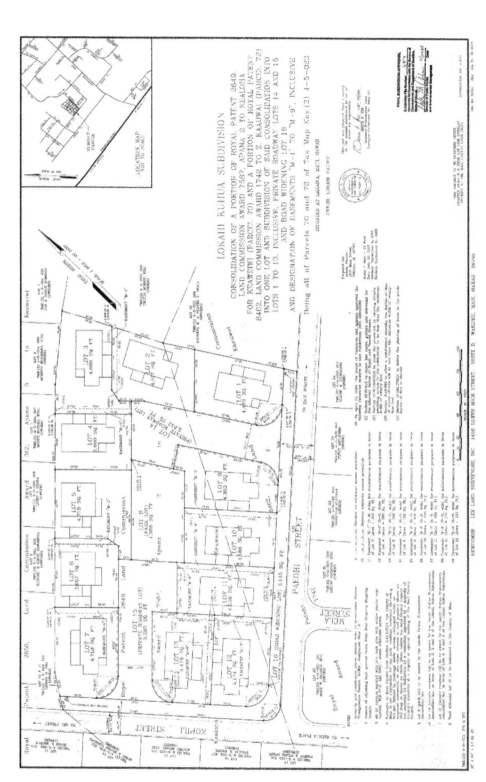

Lokahi at Kahua, County of Maui File Plan No. 4.873.

In 1986, Congress adjusted the tax code by adopting the Low-Income Housing Tax Credit. This credit provided substantial subsidies to land developers who built and operated low-income housing. The calculation of the credit is complex, determined on a per project basis, and granted on a competitive basis. Private developers are also able to obtain other subsidies in the form of tax credits and incentives. Since 1986, the Low-Income Housing Tax Credit has been the main generator of low-income housing construction in the United States. Honokōwai Villa, which was the recipient of Farmers Home Administration financing, eventually also obtained the Low-Income Housing Tax Credit. Both the Lahaina Affordables (Weinberg Court) and Front Street Apartments have also obtained the benefits of the Low-Income Housing Tax Credit.

Front Street Apartments obtained a fast-track exemption to build 142 affordable rentals in Lahaina town that would be kept at affordable rates for fifty-one years. The developer obtained financing in part from the state Housing and Community Development Corporation of Hawai'i. It also obtained $15.6 million in the form of the federal Low-Income Housing Tax Credit and state tax credits (*Honolulu Advertiser*, Jun. 19, 2001: B6; *Honolulu Advertiser*, Jul. 6, 1999: B1). However, shortly after the ten-year period in which the tax credits were distributed, the developer announced that it had sought approval from the Hawai'i Housing Finance & Development Corporation to end the affordability requirement of the project, and has announced that its rents will be raised to market rate in 2019. Community members have challenged the developer's contention that it can exit the fifty-one-year affordability requirement in court, but to date, neither the state nor the county has been willing to actively challenge it. The legislature and county have recently passed legislation to buy the developer's interest to keep housing units affordable. However, the market value of properties like Front Street Apartments, which is across the street from the shoreline, is substantially more than the market value with decades of affordability requirement restrictions in place.

In the early 1990s, the Napilihau Villages project also obtained $10 million from the Low-Income Housing Tax Credit, and other financing from the state, in exchange for a promise to keep apartments affordable for low-income renters for thirty years (*Honolulu Star-Bulletin*, Aug. 29, 1997: B-4). The development was approved through a conditional zoning ordinance in 1994, although concerns were raised in 1996, which delayed construction because a condition of zoning was that the apartments would be sold, not rented (*Honolulu Advertiser*, Oct. 18, 1996: B1).

The Hawai'i Finance and Development Corporation partnered with private developers to build Honokowai Kauhale and Honokowai Villa. They also proposed and obtained Land Use Commission approval for the Villages of Leali'i, which was to be a mixed luxury and affordable housing development. The Villages of Leali'i project was never developed due to controversies concerning the state's authority to dispose of the crown lands that composed the lands underlying the proposed project. After two decades of litigation, the makai phase was transferred to the Department of Hawaiian Home Lands for use in its housing program.

In 1990, Congress also created a separate block grant program for low-income and very low-income households called the HOME Investment Partnerships Program. This program allows funding to be used for down payments for the purchase of a housing unit from a bank, building or rehabilitating housing for rent or ownership, or funding to community housing nonprofit organizations that provide housing to low-income households.

In 1991, Maui County adopted Ordinance No. 2093, which was its affordable housing policy for hotel-related developments. It stated, "The council finds that there is a critical shortage of affordable housing in the County. The current shortage is largely attributable to the growth of the visitor industry in recent years and the inability to develop a supply of housing to keep pace with demand." The policy required hotel developers to construct one affordable housing unit for every four hotel units constructed.

Much of the 1990s in federal housing policy consisted in the expansion of Section 8 subsidies and deregulating aspects of government-insured mortgages, including in the 1995 Appropriations Act, which allowed Ginnie Mae mortgage-backed securities to be eligible as collateral for multi-class securities that it guarantees. Unlike Fannie Mae and Freddie Mac, Ginnie Mae mortgages are exclusively government issued. The Fair Housing Act was amended to eliminate the requirement of providing significant facilities and services for older persons from the definition of "housing for older persons."

The American Homeownership and Economic Opportunity Act of 2000 authorized local housing officials to allow Section 8 recipients to aggregate up to a year's worth of subsidies to use towards purchasing a home.

MORTGAGES

The mortgage has been the mainstay of American policy regarding housing for the last century. Most Americans who purchase a home are able to do so because they purchase it with significant long-term debt. The home mortgage interest deduction is by far the largest tax break in housing in the United States. Until the 1930s, very few Americans purchased their homes with debt. Financing a home purchase with a mortgage was an activity of the rich. During the Great Depression, President Roosevelt established the Home Owners Loan Corporation, and then later the Federal Housing Administration, to insure mortgages designed for the ordinary American worker: the thirty-year loan. The Home Owners Loan Corporation refinanced over a million homes that were at threat of foreclosure.

After the Second World War, the Veterans Administration assisted veteran families to obtain mortgages on homes. The program, established by the FHA, institutionalized the standard thirty-year mortgage. For decades, for those not covered by the FHA or VA, this debt was issued by a local bank that would then service the debt, which was insured by the federal government. However, today, the companies that lend money to homebuyers sell the debt to another company which creates securities that are backed by many mortgages, like stocks or bonds. The securitization of mortgage debt marked the full integration of American homeownership into global financial markets.

The most recent housing crisis occurred because of changes in investor demands made to the housing financing system. The demand for mortgage-backed securities in the context of deregulated financial markets encouraged lenders to dramatically increase the number of mortgages to an increasing number of persons with greater risk of defaulting. The widening of the pool of potential borrowers also increased the use of the more exotic forms of mortgages on terms that were entirely inappropriate to the people who were borrowing. Because mortgage lenders simply resold the mortgages once they were made, there was nothing reinforcing the obligation to ensure that borrowers could afford their mortgages. In many cases, lenders and brokers simply lied about borrowers' incomes or encouraged borrowers to lie. Housing prices skyrocketed as the number of families purchasing homes with debt rose to unprecedented levels.

This strategy of providing easy credit to generate homeownership worked until the Federal Reserve raised the federal fund rate, and interest rates on adjustable rate mortgages shot up. Adjustable rate mortgages are an exotic form of debt that is entirely inappropriate to ordinary homeowners with regular incomes, but were anyway pushed on many nontraditional borrowers because of the attractive, initial low payments. These payments remained low while interest rates were low. When interest rates went up, payments adjusted upward, causing widespread defaulting. Prior to this widespread default, demand for housing caused an asset bubble that overpriced houses. Mortgage debt was issued to pay for these overpriced houses. When the bubble burst and housing prices came down, a financial crisis was born. Because of the widespread investment in mortgage-backed securities, the risk of defaulting was spread across the globe. Families lost their homes and the economic activities predicated on profits from the risky mortgage-backed securities caused a major crisis in the global economy, and the worst economic recession since the Great Depression of the 1930s.

As mentioned above, the county adopted a workforce housing ordinance in 2006 which broadened the range of development required to provide affordable housing from the hotel development policy. The council found "there is a critical shortage of affordable housing, making home acquisition by the majority of county resident workers extremely difficult, and creating a shortage of affordable rental units." The object of the 2006 ordinance was to require "any development, including the subdivision of land and/or construction of single-family dwelling units" to provide 50 percent or more of its dwelling units to be sold or rented to Maui residents within income-qualified groups established by the policy.

In 2008, the Economic Stimulus Act raised the statutory limits on how much home mortgage debt could be purchased by Fannie Mae and Freddie Mac, as well as increased the loan limit for FHA-insured mortgages. Congress also passed the Housing and Economic Recovery Act, which established three programs. The Neighborhood Stabilization Program authorized funding to every state to address the rapid rise of foreclosures. The HOPE for Homeowners Program was supposed to help distressed homeowners keep their homes out of foreclosure with mortgage modifications. The third program authorized the Department of Housing and Urban Development to oversee each of the fifty states to establish uniform licensing requirements for mortgage brokers.

The Economic Stimulus Act was followed shortly by the Emergency Economic Stabilization Act which established the Troubled Assets Relief Program, or TARP. TARP permitted the Treasury Secretary to purchase and insure troubled assets in order to prevent disruption of the US economy and financial system. Fannie Mae and Freddie Mac received $187 billion. Private institutions such insurance company AIG received near $68 billion, Bank of America and Citigroup received $45 billion each (as well as other government aid), and JP Morgan Chase and Wells Fargo received $25 billion.

Goldman Sachs and Morgan Stanley each received $10 billion. In Hawai'i, Central Pacific Bank received the lion's share of TARP funds, at $135 million (of $136 million to Hawai'i-based institutions). Most of the subsequent legislation implicating housing in the past ten years has sought to clarify and change how home mortgages are regulated.

Fast-Tracking Affordable Housing Projects

Starting in the 1990s, housing projects began to seek approval through Hawaii's fast-track approval statute. The fast-track exemption process allows any development to seek exemption from land use regulations, as long as half of the development is affordable. Said another way: Land use regulations are not an obstacle to the development of affordable housing because the statute allows the County Council to exempt a project from most land use regulations.

Hale Mahaolu obtained fast-track approval for its senior housing rental project along Lahainaluna Road (County Council Resolution No. 95-53). Front Street Apartments, which also received the Low-Income Housing Tax Credit, obtained fast-track approval for the rental project makai of the state's Pi'ilani Homes project near Kahoma (County Council Resolution No. 99-158). The county developed an emergency housing project called Na Hale o Waine'e just mauka of the Lahaina Recreational Center, also called the West Maui Resource Center, through the fast-track process (County Council Resolution No. 00-29). The developers of the Villages at Kahana Ridge obtained fast-track approval in 2002 (County Council Resolution No. 02-87).

Lōkahi Pacific and West Maui Land obtained two fast-tracked approvals from the county council for the Kahoma Residential project built along the south side of Kahoma Stream (County Council Resolutions Nos. 09-42 and 11-126). The Council also approved another Lōkahi Pacific fast-tracked project called Honokowai Project, which has not been developed (County Council Resolution No. 09-43). Stanford Carr obtained council approval for his Kahoma Villages project makai of Honoapi'ilani Highway along Kahoma Stream (County Council Resolution No. 14-14). In 2004, however, Kent Smith's Pu'unoa subdivision was voted down twice by the county council, primarily over concerns related to traffic.

Makila Kai obtained a fast-track approval from the Council in 2017 (County Council Resolution No. 17-108). Makila Kai represents the overall trend on Maui regarding fast track approvals. Private developers build half affordable and half "market" rate housing. The exemptions from government regulation are then applied to the entire project. In the case of Mākila Kai, the council conditioned actual development on the developer obtaining a district boundary amendment for portions of the land that needed to be rezoned within six months. While there was a disagreement regarding whether the land use commission or the council was the appropriate authority to grant a district boundary amendment, the developer sought an amendment from the council which did not approve it by the deadline.

CONCLUSION

Hawai'i has suffered a shortage of clean and decent housing for working people for as long as the sugar plantations took and consolidated control over the available land in Hawai'i. Yet, since the 1970s, we have been told that government regulations are the cause of the shortage of affordable, descent housing—a costly obstacle to the production of housing for working people. But historically, most government regulations regarding the production of housing on Maui were enacted at the same time that state laws were adopted to exempt affordable housing production from those government regulations. Further, the housing shortage has existed for more than a hundred years, yet the regulations and the exemptions for housing development have existed only for fifty years.

Even with the fast-track exemption process, the shortage continues. There have been few studies to determine how much luxury housing development generates an additional need for affordable housing. A fast-track exemption process which allows a one-to-one ratio for luxury to affordable houses may actually be increasing the affordable housing shortage, while allowing luxury housing to be developed that otherwise would be illegal.

The Hawai'i Housing Finance & Development Corporation recently sent out to bid the process to privatize other properties it holds and manages, including the Honokowai Kauhale project in West Maui. (*Honolulu Star Advertiser*, Sep. 17, 2017: F2) It has claimed that privatization is necessary to generate revenue to pay off current debt and to generate funds for new affordable housing development, primarily by allowing the successful bidder to raise rents after five years. In other words, in order to generate revenue to produce new affordable housing, it will have to convert present affordable housing supply to market housing.

The most successful housing developments, measured in terms of the percentage of homes remaining owner-occupied, are developments where all units start as affordable and are not convertible from the affordable working family market to the luxury nonresident market.

There is no evidence to support the contention that government regulations are obstacles to the production of affordable housing in Hawaiʻi. Yet, David Callies and others repeat two simple, and theoretically elegant, syllogisms: Regulation raises transactional costs; transactional costs increase the price of houses. Therefore, regulation increases the price of houses. Affordable house pricing is subject to the same market forces which regulate market houses. Regulation increases the prices of houses. Therefore, regulation increases the price of affordable houses. The problem with this simple and elegant theory is that it is not supported by historical or contemporaneous evidence.

This is particularly true on Maui, where the shortage of affordable housing predates county laws regulating building and land use by decades. And when these regulations came into existence, state law specifically exempted affordable housing projects from those county laws. Rather, the long monopoly of control over land by the sugar plantations has been reproduced by their successors, the developers and speculators who presently control the plantations' former lands and restrict its availability for use by the workers to satisfy their housing needs.

The simple truth is that the building of housing for the luxury housing market generates a further need for housing for workers. When housing developments are proposed for fast-track development—which are a mix of luxury and worker housing—that development likewise generates a further need for worker housing beyond the part satisfaction of the preexisting need. In other words, fast-tracking developments that are less than 100 percent affordable produces an increased, rather than decreased, need for housing for workers.

Note

1. Much of the theoretical work of this chapter came from David Madden and Peter Marcuse's *In Defense of Housing: The Politics of Crisis* as well as Emily Molina's *Housing America: Issues and Debates*.

Works Cited

Richard R.W. Brooks and Carol M. Rose. *Saving the Neighborhood: Racially Restrictive Covenants, Law and Social Norms.* Cambridge, MA: Harvard University Press, 2013.

David L. Callies. *Regulating Paradise: Land Use Controls in Hawai'i*. Honolulu: University of Hawai'i Press, 2010.

Lance D. Collins and Bianca Isaki. *Tourism Impacts West Maui*. Lahaina: North Beach West Maui Benefit Fund, 2016.

George Cooper and Gavan Daws. *Land and Power in Hawai'i*. Honolulu: University of Hawai'i Press, 1985.

Daly & Associates. *Housing for Hawai'i's People*. Honolulu: Hawai'i Housing Authority, 1977.

Victor Geminiani and Madison DeLuca. *Hawai'i Vacation Rentals: Impacts on Housing & Hawai'i's Economy*. Honolulu: Hawai'i Appleseed Center for Law and Economic Justice, 2018.

Ulla Hasager and Marion Kelly. "Public Policy of Land and Homesteading in Hawai'i" in 40 *Social Process in Hawai'i*, 2001.

Stuart Hodkinson. "The Return of the Housing Question" in 12(4) *Ephemera* 423–444 (2012).

Tim Iglesias and Rochelle E. Lento. Eds. *The Legal Guide to Affordable Housing Development*. Chicago: American Bar Association Publishing, 2005.

Bianca K. Isaki. *A Decolonial Archive: the Historical Space of Asian Settler Politics in a time of Hawaiian Nationhood*. Honolulu: Ph.D. Dissertation, 2008.

Susan E. Jaworowski. *Ohana Zoning: A Five-Year Review*. Honolulu: Legislative Reference Bureau, 1988.

Donald Johnson. *The City and County of Honolulu: A Governmental Chronicle*. Honolulu: University of Hawai'i Press, 1991.

Samuel Kamakau. *The Works of the People of Old*. Honolulu: Bishop Museum Press, 1976.

Noel Kent. *Hawai'i Under the Influence*. University of Hawai'i Press, 1993.

Henri Lefebvre. *Spatial Politics, Everyday Life and the Right to the City*. London: Routledge, 2014.

David Madden and Peter Marcuse. *In Defense of Housing: The Politics of Crisis*. London: Verso, 2016.

Jack, Margaret and Dorothy Millar. *The Unbeatable Dream: The First 25 Years of the Nāpili Kai Beach Club*. Wailuku: Richard Wirtz, 1985.

Emily T. Molina. *Housing America: Issues and Debates*. New York: Routledge, 2017.

Milton Murayama. *All I asking for Is My Body*. University of Hawai'i Press, 1988.

Milton Murayama. *Plantation Boy*. University of Hawai'i Press, 1998.

Milton Murayama. *Dying in a Strange Land*. University of Hawai'i Press, 2008.

Pacific Urban Studies and Planning Program. *Perspectives on Housing in Hawai'i*. Honolulu: University of Hawai'i, 1974.

Louis Rose. "Impact Fees and Housing Exactions Programs: An Economic Analysis" in Dan Davidson & Ann Usagawa (eds) *Paying for Growth in Hawai'i: An Analysis of Impact Fees and Housing Exactions Programs*. Honolulu: Land Use Research Foundation of Hawai'i, 1988.

Patrick A. Stanley and Dewa, Roger Y. *Public Housing in Hawai'i: The Evolution of Housing Policy*. Honolulu: Legislative Reference Bureau, 1967.

Robert Stauffer. *Kahana: How the Land Was Lost.* University of Hawai'i Press, 2004.

Alexander Vasudevan. *The Autonomous City: A History of Urban Squatting.* London: Verso, 2017.

Douglas Yamamura and Raymond Sakumoto. "Residential Segregation in Honolulu" in 18 *Social Process in Hawai'i* 35–46 (1954).

THE HONOKAHUA BURIAL
SITE CONTROVERSY*

Tomone K. T. Hanada

I. Introduction and Overview of Honokahua Burial Site Controversy

In the early 1960s, late Maui Land and Pineapple Company (MLP) Chief Executive Officer Colin Cameron had envisioned a high-quality resort development in Kapalua, Maui. Honokahua, the location slated for the Ritz-Carlton Kapalua Hotel development, was known to contain an ancient Hawaiian burial site. This fact was well documented throughout public hearings leading to the granting of a special management area permit (SMA) for the hotel project. However, as archaeological disinterment work began in 1987 and continued through 1988, it became obvious that the magnitude of the burials was severely underestimated. Media coverage of the disinterment activity infuriated Native Hawaiian activist groups, whose collective consciousness was quickly evolving, and they demanded that the disinterment cease.

This controversy highlights the basic conflict between the value system of Native Hawaiians and the business world's interpretation of value in a profit-oriented, monetary sense. The fundamental differences in belief systems between the management of MLP and Native Hawaiians are reflected in their divergent interests and their generalizations about each other. Initially, these generalizations precluded active listening and meaningful communication, the keys to discovering interests, creating value, and movement away from a zero-sum mindset towards a non-zero-sum mindset. In the end, despite an initial distributive, zero-sum scenario, the Honokahua burial site conflict was resolved with the help of third parties who facilitated a creative, integrative, non-zero-sum solution.

---

* This chapter was researched and written in 1995 in partial fulfillment of the requirements for a Master's degree in Business Administration at the University of Hawai'i.

The purpose of this paper is to examine and analyze the initial conflict, the dispute resolution negotiations, the role of intervenors and agents, and the solution arrived at between the MLP, the Native Hawaiian activist groups, and the State of Hawaiʻi. The analysis will proceed based on the chronology of events (a detailed timeline of events is contained in Table 1, Appendix A).

II. The Stakeholders and Their Conflicting Interests
A. Maui Land and Pineapple Company

MLP is a Hawaiʻi corporation consisting of a parent corporation, MLP, and two major subsidiaries, Maui Pineapple Company and Kapalua Land Company. The Cameron family (descendants of Henry Perrine Baldwin, cofounder of Alexander and Baldwin, Incorporated, one of Hawaii's Big Five corporations) maintains a controlling interest in MLP.

MLP's three business segments are pineapple, resort development, and commercial property management.[1] MLP, as referred to herein, is a reference to the Kapalua Land Company subsidiary.

Pineapple, although profitable in the late 1970s, showed a substantial decline in sales and fluctuating profits in the 1980s. MLP survived the 1960s and the 1970s, while Libby, Dole, and Del Monte failed, by concentrating on packing premium private labels for mainland supermarket chains, a decision made by Colin Cameron and his father, J. Walter Cameron, in the 1950s.[2]

In the early 1960s, when pineapple was MLP's sole focus, Colin Cameron and his father J. Walter Cameron, pursued financial stability for MLP through diversification and envisioned the development of the Kapalua resort as a means to diversify the company and protect it from the cyclical profitability of pineapple cultivation. In 1974, the Camerons commissioned a master plan for Kapalua, focusing on quality over size, identifying only two resort hotel sites: the Kapalua Bay Hotel and the Ritz-Carlton Kapalua Hotel (RCKH) (earlier identified as the Kapalua Village Hotel).[3,4] The master plan also identified a burial site within the thirteen-acre Honokahua site identified for the RCKH.[5] The Bishop Museum archaeologist overseeing the archaeological survey portion of the environmental assessment recommended that the remains be removed and reinterred before development commenced, according to then current practices.[6] However, a key factor in the controversy—the number of burials at the Honokahua site, which exceeded one thousand—never became evident throughout the RCKH development approvals process.

The Kapalua Bay Hotel, the first hotel developed by Colin Cameron, nearly sank the company due to the operating losses it incurred. For years the hotel lost more than gained since it opened in 1978.[7] Since MLP was a relatively small company and profits from pineapple operations were marginal, MLP had difficulties paying off $52 million in debt in 1984, twice the small company's net worth.[8] In 1985, Colin Cameron made the decision to sell the Kapalua Bay Hotel for $26 million, which improved MLP's financial position and allowed MLP to purchase what is now the premium commercial retail property in the county of Maui, the Ka'ahumanu Shopping Center.[9] Cameron then focused his efforts on the development of the second and final hotel in the Kapalua Resort Area, the Ritz-Carlton Kapalua Hotel, through a general partnership, called Kaptel Associates.[10] The general partners along with MLP were the Ritz-Carlton Hotel Company and Nissho-Iwai Corporation. MLP was to lease prime beachfront Kapalua land, Kaptel, Ritz-Carlton was to provide hotel operations expertise, and Nissho-Iwai Trading Company was to provide $20 million in cash to qualify the partnership for external financing of the RCKH development.

Cameron's next objective beyond formation of the partnership was to seek special management area (SMA) permit approval from the Maui Planning Commission (MPC) as a prerequisite to obtaining a building permit. The SMA permit was required by section 205-A, Hawai'i Revised Statutes and sections 20.12.640 and 20.12.650 of the Maui County Code.

B. Hui Alanui O Mākena

On December 19, 1986, attorney Isaac Hall and his wife Dana Naone Hall were in attendance at a regularly scheduled MPC meeting. Isaac and Dana are spokespersons for Hui Alanui O Mākena, a Native Hawaiian activist group whose primary interest prior to the development of the Honokahua controversy was preserving the great Alaloa, a round-the-island road built by ancient Hawaiian kings which circumscribes the island of Maui.[11] Many local Native Hawaiians ascribed great cultural significance and importance to the Alaloa and the hui sought to preserve the Alaloa.[12]

Native Hawaiians maintain an oral tradition of cultural descendancy. In contrast to western tradition, there are very few written documents which record their history and culture. One of the few means by which their culture can be preserved is to preserve those artifacts which currently exist.[13] Isaac and Dana's purpose at the December 19th MPC meeting was to prevent Seibu Corporation's Maui Prince Hotel development from destroying or preventing access to the Alaloa, the ancient "king's trail," which ran through

Seibu's property in Mākena. Also on the MPC agenda for the evening was SMA permit approval for the RCKH might also contain part of the Alaloa trail. When the RCKH SMA permit came before the MPC for approval, Isaan went on record requesting the Alaloa to be preserved where it was on the Honokahua site. The MPC voted to approve the RCKH SMA permit at the same meeting.[14] At the close of the MPC meeting, Isaac requested that all findings of fact and conclusions of law regarding the RCKH SMA permit approval to be served on Hui Alanui O Mākena. Only later, after reading the archaeological report made available by the MPC, did the Halls and other members of Hui Alanui Mākena learn that the Honokahua site also contained an ancient burial ground. The hui then formally requested, through filing of a motion for reconsideration with the MPC, the reopening of the hearing on the RCKH-SMA permit.

C. The Basic Conflicting Interests: The Viability of the Kapalua Development and the Preservation of a Burial Site Significant to Native Hawaiians

At the heart of this conflict and the controversy that surrounded it was the basic need for MLP to maintain its economic well-being and viability as a *going concern* through its desire to develop Kapalua as a small, first-class resort destination. Specifically, this meant building the RCKH on the only remaining beach-front location MLP had left. Colin Cameron clearly stated, "the Kapalua resort community needs this vital [RCKH] element to succeed," and implied the economic success of the hotel was directly tied to a beach-front location.[15] In 1998, at the height of the Honokahua burial site controversy, Maui Land and Pineapple had suffered its worst revenue loss to date, $6.4 million, largely due to its pineapple cultivation activities.[16] Continued development of the Kapalua resort was necessary to buffer the pineapple segment's losses.

Diametrically opposed to MLP's interests were the interests of Native Hawaiians which center around a sense of belonging and ethnic connectedness based on recent cultural revival. In recent years, Native Hawaiians have experienced a cultural resurgence and emerging solidarity as a group. They considered disinterment activity a desecration of their burial sites.[17]

Hawaiians did not mark their burial sites, in contrast to western tradition, since they believed mana (spiritual power) was contained in the iwi (skeletal remains). Any disturbance of the iwi by persons other than family members was an evil act, since maintenance of the iwi was conducted only by trusted family members and friends. Hence the bones of the aliʻi (royalty) were often hidden in caves whose locations were kept secret, since the ene-

Photo of protestors at the Honokahua burial site. (Photo by Ed Tanji, *Honolulu Advertiser*, Sun. Dec. 11, 1988) Courtesy of the Hawai'i State Archives.

Photo of members of the Hui Alanui o Makena. (Photo by Ed Tanji, *Honolulu Advertiser*, Sun. Dec. 11, 1988) Courtesy of the Hawai'i State Archives.

mies of the aliʻi would often want to steal their adversaries' iwi to capture their mana. Sand dunes were also favored burial sites by the ancient Hawaiians because these areas were not used for food cultivation and the burial sites could be easily disguised.[18]

Cultural and lineal descendancy was perpetuated through the mana in the iwi.[19] Thus, sanctity of Hawaiian burial sites is of very high importance to many Native Hawaiians, and the concept of respectful disinterment was a paradox.[20]

III. Analysis of Negotiations Prior to Maui Planning Commission Decision and Order Granting SMA Permit on February 26, 1987

A. The Issue

Prior to MLP's request to extend its RCKH SMA permit in November 1988 was met by public outcry by Native Hawaiians across the state. Hui Alanui O Mākena's objection to MLP's SMA permit approval was articulated through legal motions filed with the MPC. Communications between parties were in the form of written procedural motions cast in the adversarial framework created by the SMA permit approval process. The motions filed revolved around a single distributive, fixed-pie, win-lose issue: whether MLP should be granted an SMA permit for the RCKH development. If either party won, it meant the other would lose something: MLP would lose its chance to develop RCKH or the Native Hawaiians would lose a burial site of significant cultural importance.

B. MLP Agreement, Risks and Constraints, Position on the Issue, Strategy, and Use of Agents

At this point in time, MLP's Best Alternative to Negotiated Agreement (BATNA) with the hui was to continue to defend its SMA permit approval before the MPC.[21] There was a high probability MLP could defend its SMA permit approval through all levels of the legal system, since MLP met all the legal requirements set forth by the SMA permit approvals process. As discussed earlier, without the RCKH development, the financial stability of the Kapalua resort and MLP, in general, was at risk. In addition, the stability of Cameron's Kaptel partnership was also at risk if partners were to withdraw based on failure to obtain an SMA permit. These risks, in the absence of any creative alternatives, constrained the MLP in terms of viable alternatives.

Being relatively risk adverse, MLP's dominant strategy was to sue its agents, using attorneys from the firm of Carlsmith, Wichman, Case, Mukai, and Ichiki, to defend MLP's SMA permit. The position taken by MLP on the SMA permit issue was to argue before the MPC that MLP properly followed all of the required rules for an SMA permit, including disclosures through public notices. MLP further argued that a reversal of the MPC's decision to grant MLP the SMA permit would represent *extreme prejudice* against MLP and unfairly penalize MLP.[22]

C. Hui Alanui O Mākena Agreement, Risks and Constraints, Position on the Issue

The Hui's BATNA with MLP was to continue to pursue an appeal for reconsideration of the SMA permit before the MPC or higher-level court. According to Dana Hall, hui members had visited the burial site in January 1987 and the visitation was a "psychologically galvanizing event."[23] Isaac and Dana Hall, as hui representatives, had conducted legal research on unmarked, precontact burials and found no precedents. Although they realized they had probably no legal recourse, their BATNA was strengthened by their belief system and the knowledge that they had practically nothing to lose and everything to gain (i.e., minimal risk, low switching costs), which committed the hui to staying involved and continuing to challenge the granting of the SMA permit. According to Dana, they "had to stay involved because who else was going to look after the kūpuna?"[24]

D. Analysis of Negotiations

The MPC is an administrative third party, a local decision-making entity, with respect to the granting of SMAs, and hence wielded a tremendous amount of procedural power based on the legal authority vested in the MPC by Maui County Code. The MPC attempted to obtain objective standards and further clarification from the State Historic Preservation Office (SHPO) on the significance and proper treatment of burial sites. However, the responses from SHPO were noncommittal.[25,26]

To address the motions filed by Hui Alanui O Mākena, the MPC held a special meeting on February 20, 1987, regarding MLP's request for a RCKH SMA permit. The adversarial process of coming before an administrative entity, such as the MPC, set a competitive negotiating tone, focused the parties on value claiming, limited the perception of the zone of agreement to outcomes associated with a distributive issue, and precluded the creation of value—there was no opportunity to expand the negotiation to include jointly developed, value-creating possibilities. The MPC was a poor conduit for communication between the parties.

Missing from the SMA permit process were opportunities for representatives from MLP and the hui to establish rapport and clear communication, engage in dialogue, share information, cultivate common interests, and seek additional help in pursuing a jointly negotiated solution. The MPC failed to facilitate or mediate a constructive agreement that met the hui's basic interests. Was there not a way to preserve the archaeological sites, pursue development, and share in the economic gains? Was there anyone else with the skill and talent to harmonize each party's interests and find or add value—perhaps a mediator?

Hui Alanui O Mākena involved the Office of Hawaiian Affairs (OHA) as a tactic to provide legitimacy to their concerns, and to expand options before the MPC.[27] OHA Trustee Manu Kahaialii delivered testimony at the hearing explaining the cultural and historical significance of burial sites.

> Hawaiian attitudes towards burial sites and human bones is generally one of respect, awe, or fear. Contemporary Hawaiians continue to revere and regard burial sites and human bones with a protective attitude. Much of this attitude stems from traditional practices of 'unihipili (ritual feeding and caring for bones of a deceased relative), the deification of a chief's bones, and the protection of bones from vandalism and desecration (for example, human bones were sometimes used as fishhooks or as support posts for kahili). Although these practices are not common today, the belief system that supported them is still a part of Hawaiian culture today.
>
> [....] For Hawaiians, the best answer would be to leave the graves totally undisturbed. I know that this is not possible. The graves have already been damaged by sand mining, the weather, and visitors to the area. However, the alternative of moving the hotel away from the graves and preserving them was not discussed in the archaeological report. This is an alternative which should be considered.[28]

Although OHA Trustee Kahaialii presents the idea of moving the hotel, and more information is made available about the basic motivation of the Native Hawaiians, the MPC, MLP, and the hui are still focused on positions rather than interests at this juncture of the negotiations. Each party had yet to achieve a clear understanding of the other party's interests behind their positions, an understanding which was a prerequisite to jointly inventing options and generating action ideas to support implementing those options. In hindsight, the movement of the hotel site was the eventual outcome. If that option had been pursued at this juncture, both parties would have saved themselves significant effort and expense.

E. The Outcome

The appeal by Hui Alanui O Mākena to the MPC regarding reconsideration of the RCKH SMA permit approval resulted in a decision and order dated February 27, 1987, amending the RCKH SMA permit conditions. The MPC denied all requests contained in the motions filed by the hui but amended the SMA permit conditions to add two additional requirements of MLP.

> That the applicant shall develop a program for reinterment of human remains, in consultation with the Office of Hawaiian Affairs and the State Historic Preservation Office, and that said program shall include but not be limited to procedures for public input and site selection subject to final review and approval by the Maui Planning Commission.
>
> That the applicant shall develop a procedure for removal and reconstruction of the trail (Site T-4) on-site or at a nearby location in consultation with the Office of Hawaiian Affairs and the State Historic Preservation Office for purposes of interpretation, public display and data recovery and that said procedure shall be subject to final review and approval by the Maui Planning Commission.[29]

The hui's tactic of involving OHA was successful in that it resulted in MLP and the hui negotiating directly with each other to create value, and both parties claimed the resulting value. The hui received the promise of respect and care of the iwi at MLP's expense during the disinterment process, and MLP preserved the validity of its SMA permit. The distribution of power between MLP preserved the validity of its SMA permit. The distribution of power between MLP and the hui improved in favor of the hui because of the additional information provided. Both parties did better than their BATNAs. However, the issues dealt with were still distributive in nature—upholding the SMA meant MLP won the right to continue to desecrate a burial site of paramount importance to the Native Hawaiians.

Based on precedents set by the negotiation of memorandum of agreements between OHA and other developers in similar situations, Paul H. Rosendahl, the lead archaeologist for the disinterment work and other developers in similar situations and negotiation agent for MLP, and Hui Alanui O Mākena representatives embarked on a series of meetings held over approximately four months at the law offices of Isaac Hall in Wailuku, Maui, which resulted in an memorandum of agreement (MOA) approved by MLP, Hui Alanui O Mākena, OHA, and SHPO, on July 25, 1987 (see Appendix B for a copy of the MOA). The MOA was subsequently accepted by the MPC on September 1, 1987.

The strength of the MOA was its obvious sensitivity to the concerns of Native Hawaiians by calling for respectful and dignified treatment of the iwi; the MOA made cultural preservation an issue for all parties to the agreement. However, there were two weaknesses with respect to the durability of the MOA: it failed to include a clause for dispute resolution, such as ritual Hawaiian Hoʻoponopono or other forms of mediation, and it was silent on the potential for temporal and financing constraints.[30] Time, in the form of permit and construction delays, was of significant value to MLP throughout this controversy, and this constraint was later exploited by the hui and OHA. The exclusion of a timeline and dispute resolution clause may have been to MLP's short run advantage, in terms of expediency, especially since the actual magnitude of the burials was unknown at the time. The MOA certainly put MLP at a disadvantage since the costs related to implementing the MOA, which was amounted to $2 million by the time the SMA extension was requested, were to be borne solely by MLP, and there were no limits set on disinterment costs. However, for the short run, MLP's interest in developing the RCKH on a beach-front location was protected.

Fisher and Ury state that prevention works best.[31] Had the relationship between MLP and the hui evolved beyond arm's length transactions in which they and OHA cultivated anon-zero-sum, positive, and ongoing working relationship, some of the costly delays incurred later by MLP might have been avoided. MLP's tactic of using Rosendahl as an agent precluded MLP management from understanding the seriousness and the emotional nature of the burial site preservation issue.

IV. Analysis of Negotiations Resulting From Maui Land and Pineapple Company Request for Extension of SMA Permit

A. Overview of Events Occurring Between SMA Approval on February 27, 1987 and Final Resolution of the Controversy on April 18, 1989

In August 1987, Paul Rosendahl began excavation work on the burial site. He estimated that the job would cost $800,000 and be completed five months later, in January of 1988.[32] It soon became obvious that the site was a major Hawaiian burial ground which had been used between 700 AD and 1700 AD, and contained more than seven hundred burials.[33] In the summer of 1988, when Cameron learned of the magnitude of the discoveries, he called a meeting with members of the hui and OHA to ask if the disinterment process could be accelerated by recording less data, but hui and OHA representatives refused.[34] The leadership of the hui and OHA sensed anxiety on the part of Cameron when he later requested approval from the hui and OHA to build a fence dividing the burial site into two sections, a lower tier and a higher tier, before the SMA permit expired.[35] That request was also denied by the hui and OHA.

A standard constraint imposed by SMA permits on developers is the requirement that construction begin within two years of issuance of the permit and in the RCKH case, that meant construction had to start by February 27, 1989. Although the MOA called for limited and controlled access to the enclosed burial site, information leaked to the press about the disinterment work. To quell rumors and avoid media publicity, Cameron held a press conference in early November 1988 to attempt to tell the truth but "people got even more upset and said what we were doing was terrible."[36] The media coverage of the disinterment activities infuriated Native Hawaiian activist groups on the other islands like the Protect Kahoʻolawe ʻOhana. On December 11, 1988, a group of protestors, including members of the Hui Alanui O Mākena and the Protect Kahoʻolawe ʻOhana held protests at the burial site regarding the disinterment of over 950 sets of human remains. On December 20, Governor John Waiheʻe intervened, expressing his concern over the magnitude of the burials at the Honokahua site. Governor Waiheʻe appointed a task force consisting of state Planning Director Harold Masumoto and the state Department of Land and Natural Resources Director Libert Landgraf to review the Honokahua situation. Governor Waiheʻe also asked Maui County Mayor Hannibal Tavares to review the situation.

State Planning Director Matsumoto acknowledged that MLP had properly obtained all the necessary permits and probably could not be ordered to stop disinterment.[37] On December 22, Native Hawaiian activist groups held a twenty-four-hour vigil outside the governor's residence, and circulated petitions calling on Waiheʻe to protect the burial site. On December 23, Waiheʻe stated the disinterment was a moral issue and "as far as the disinterment goes, there is no compromise... it must stop."[38] Colin Cameron *went to the balcony*, as defined by William Ury in *Getting Past No*, by not instinctively reacting and instead agreeing to have MLP suspend archaeological excavation until January 4, 1988:

> The next day, after speaking with the governor and reading news reports of the demonstration at Washington place, Cameron agreed to stop further excavation. "I absolutely knew it was the only thing that could be done," he says... Colin had a legal right to proceed. But the question was really a moral one and whether he could live with himself if he continued. He did what he thought was right—to stop.[39]

Although MLP was legally permitted to continue the excavation, Cameron ordered the suspension to give all parties time to explore solutions. The local community's consciousness regarding the disinterment controversy was rising given the media coverage of Native Hawaiian activist groups' protest activities. To have continued disinterment would have further fueled the emotional outrage felt by the activists and delayed joint problem solving.

On December 23, Mayor Tavares called Cameron into his Wailuku office for a meeting.[40] Tavares pulled out a large map of the Honokahua site and a picture he had drawn of the planned hotel set back about 200 feet behind the burial site. The mayor then told Cameron the bones should be reburied exactly where they had been found and the area landscaped and retained as a cemetery. Tavares also agreed to work with the MPC and the county council to cut red tape so construction on the relocated RCKH could proceed as soon as possible. Cameron studied the proposal and agreed it had merit but he told Tavares he would first need to meet with this architect, engineers, and his RCKH partners to discuss the proposal. Later that week, Cameron and his associates met at the Honokahua site and walked the area. Cameron stated, "We realized that the new site would be even be better because it was twenty feet higher than the original one, which would allow better views and more rooms than the 450 we had planned."[41]

After obtaining expert information from his consultants regarding the value of relocating the hotel, Cameron then talked of offering the state a permanent easement over the burial site to protect the site into perpetuity while MLP retained the underlying fee title. Negotiations among Cameron, Mayor Tavares, and the state task force continued through mid-April 1989 to explore how to *make Cameron whole* with respect to the issue of sunk design and excavation costs if MLP moved the hotel site.[42]

On February 21, 1989, Colin Cameron announced at the RCKH SMA permit extension hearing that MLP had agreed to move the hotel away from the burial site. Members of Hui Alanui O Mākena and OHA were pleased Cameron changed his mind about moving the hotel. Dana Hall stated, "I don't know why he (Cameron) changed his mind about relocating the hotel, but I'm glad he did…That is the largest burial site next to Mokapu on Oahu…That makes me wonder if Cameron was well served by his archaeologists."[43]

The MPC proceeded to grant MLP its requested SMA permit extension on February 21, 1989.

On April 18, 1989, Governor Waiheʻe announced the state had reached a tentative agreement with MLP to pay its subsidiary Kapalua Land Company $5.5 million to purchase a preservation easement over the burial site, and $0.5 million to reinter the excavated human remains.

B. *The Issues*

Because of the intervention of third parties, the issues had expanded in number and in nature, from a purely distributive issue to issues which could be categorized as integrative, depending on whether the solutions implemented to address each issue created value. Due to the intervention of Governor Waiheʻe, the state task force members and Mayor Tavares played the dual roles of agents of the Native Hawaiians and informal mediators facilitating the development of solutions to the issues. The procedural power and control over state and county resources these third parties brought to the negotiation was key to the quality of the negotiated outcome, since the Native Hawaiian activist groups did not have the knowledge or power to suggest and implement solutions which added value to the negotiations. The issues under negotiation expanded, resulting in the following:

1. RCKH SMA permit extension and MLP's legal right to retain SMA permit approval and to continue hotel development
2. Restoration and preservation of the Honokahua burial site
3. Relocation of the RCKH to another site
4. *Making MLP whole* on its sunk costs if the RCKH was relocated

C. *The Role of Intervenors, Informal Mediators, and Their Tactics*

Governor Waiheʻeʻs role of intervenor changed the tone of the negotiation from an adversarial process to one of a reframing, joint problem-solving endeavor. The introduction of Mayor Tavares and the state task force added value, broadened the zone of agreement by virtue of increasing the number of negotiable issues, and assisted in creating solutions to the issues which created value and movement toward the Pareto Frontier.[44]

Colin Cameron and Mayor Tavares were already good friends who trusted each other. Their relationship set forth a tone of agreement. Informal mediation and facilitation provided by Mayor Tavares and the State Task Force encouraged Cameron to brainstorm, transform a zero-sum mindset to a non-zero-sum mindset, resulting in the formulation of a potential solution: to relocate the hotel for a better view and higher capacity, put an easement over the burial site, and take the proceeds from the granting of the easement to offset sunk costs. Cameron stated:

> I had no idea what we were going to do...Most problems can be solved if you know what you want to achieve and who to talk to. But with this, I had no good answers and had no idea who to turn to...I wasn't looking for lawyer answers...I didn't want to sue anybody or have the land condemned and get a $30 million check. I want a nice hotel there...But we didn't have another (oceanfront) spot.

Tavares and the state task force members were then able to take the proposed solution—payment for the easement and additional development approvals—and develop action ideas for implementing the solutions to resolve the issues.

Since the logistics of effective mediation require decision makers with full authority to be present during negotiations, it was a boon that Tavares, who could cut the County of Maui red tape, and the State Task force, who could lobby for legislative support and funding for the solutions, serve as informal mediators and facilitators. Cameron depended on the power held by Governor Waihe'e and Mayor Tavares—they were in a position to maximize Cameron's dependence, based on their ability to let Cameron claim the additional value the solutions would generate: cash payments to offset over $7 million in sunk costs, an easement instead of condemnation of MLP land, and preferential and expeditious treatment of MLP matters within the state and county bureaucracies.[45]

In addition, Mayor Tavares used the tactic of politely threatening Cameron to get him to think hard about Tavares's solution for relocating the hotel. "Up until now, I've been on your side," Tavares told his longtime friend. "But if you don't accept this, I'll have to be against you.[46]

Given the friendship and trust between the men, Cameron must have sensed that Tavares meant what he said, and that he would support the Native Hawaiian activists if a compromise was not reached.

D. MLP BATNA, Risks and Constraints, Positions on Issues, Strategy

MLP's BATNA with the hui and state was to continue to defend its SMA permit approval through all levels of the legal system. There continued to be a high probability that MLP could defend its SMA permit approval through all levels of the legal system, since MLP met all the legal requirements set forth by the SMA permit approvals process. As discussed earlier, the financial stability of MLP and the stability of Cameron's Kaptel partnership was also at risk if the partners were to withdraw based on failure to obtain an SMA permit extension. To continue to protect tis BATNA, MLP continued to file legal motions with the MPC counter to those filed by the hui and OHA.

However, the game had changed with the media exposure and intervention of Governor Waiheʻe and Mayor Tavares. MLP's interests expanded to include consideration of the long-run impact of the protests on the company's reputation and standing in the community. Colin Cameron's moral and ethical values, and his patient, long-run perspective began to surface as MLP interests through his direct involvement in MLP negotiations. In discussing the potential for a perpetual easement over the burial site, Cameron stated the following.

The easement would protect the site in perpetuity while Kapalua retained the underlying fee title... that would give us the obligation to maintain the area... Why do we want that? Because Kapalua will be around a lot longer than the state legislators and other officials who might forget its importance. It must be done properly."[47]

Instead of concentrating on things that divided the parties, Cameron reflected on his long-term vision for Kapalua. Through the strength of his character and his integrity, Cameron avoided a weakness of many negotiators, which is to lose sight of the possible long-range benefits.[48] The intangible gains, such as the good will generated by the decision to relocate the hotel, were of significant undeterminable value to MLP.

MLP's strategy was to maintain a cooperative negotiating posture with Mayor Tavares and the state task force. Mayor Tavares spoke in praise of Cameron, "Colin is the key to making this work. If he were a hardheaded guy and said the hell with it, we would have had a major confrontation. But Colin is a man of great compassion."[49]

The position of MLP on each of the issues was to support the integrative solution set of relocating the hotel and obtaining a perpetual easement.

E. Hui Alanui Mākena BATNA, Risks and Constraints, Positions on Issues, Strategy and Tactics

The hui's BATNA wth MLP was to continue to pursue an appeal for contested case before the MPC of higher level court. The hui faced minimal risks, since it still had practically nothing to lose by losing. However, they faced a temporal constraint in that if they failed to prevent continued disinterment, the burial site would totally be desecrated, given MLP had an SMA permit.

The hui, OHA, and other activist groups planned a strategy of raising the public's consciousness to build support for their concerns. The blockage tactics (protests, petitions, media coverage) utilized by the Native Hawaiian activist groups of protesting and asking Governor Waihe'e, a Native Hawaiian, to intervene were very successful. It ultimately increased MLP's dependence on state and county officials.

F. Evaluation of the Final Outcome

The introduction of informal mediators produce a solution with value for both parties (i.e., expansion of the pie), which adversarial problem-solving through attorneys and the MPC could not have created. The adversarial system did not bridge cultural differences and impeded successful joint problem-solving processes.

The outcome of the Honokahua burial site negotiations was documented in a restoration agreement. The parties to the agreement were the State of Hawai'i, through its department of land and natural resources, and MLP. The agreement clearly states its purpose was to settle the controversy stemming from the discovery of ancient Hawaiian burials at Honokahua on property owned in fee by MLP intended for the RCKH. The terms and conditions of the written agreement are summarized as follows.

State receives from MLP:
1. Preservation and conservation easement covering entire 13.6-acre site.
2. MLP is obligated to rebury skeletal remains uncovered in easement area.
3. MLP is obligated to landscape easement area (including the erection of appropriate signage, walkways, fencing, etc.).
4. MLP is obligated, in perpetuity, to maintain easement area as historical/cultural preserve.

5. MLP is obligated, in perpetuity, to provide security for the easement area.
6. MLP will provide to the State of Hawai'i a written release from MLP and Ritz-Carlton Hotels.

MLP receives from State of Hawai'i:

1. $5,500,000 in cash for easement.
2. $500,000 in cash for reburial and restoration work.
3. Written release from the state.

Requirements for a Reburial and Restoration Plan:

1. MLP must submit to the state a reburial and restoration plan within 30 days of department of land and natural resources approval of the burial site restoration agreement.
2. The state will establish a procedure for approval or rejection of the plan.
3. Mayor Tavares' special Maui task force will assist the state in reaching consensus or agreement on the plan with parties.
4. The existing MOA may require cancellation or amendment.

This durable agreement reflects a balance of interests and a basic fairness to all parties. The parties have remained satisfied to date. In affirmation of the negotiated outcome, Dana Hall stated the following:

> Mr. Cameron's decision reflects well on him as someone who grew up on Maui and has several generations here behind him...This is really what has to happen in the future: developers have to work closely with the community and have to be very sensitive to their concerns...In the past, whenever there was a protest, it was labeled antidevelopment or anti-tourism. But in this case, we are seeking to protect the things that are uniquely Hawaiian and, at the same time, accommodate the growth we need. That kind of balancing benefits everybody in the state.

This negotiation process, specifically the SMA permit approval portion, should include mediation to improve the management of these types of conflicts. It is clear the introduction of a mediator sooner in this negotiation to facilitate face-to-face communication would have resulted in a solution much earlier, saving all parties a significant amount of emotional and financial stress.

Appendix A: A Timeline of Events

DATE	PARTY (OR PARTIES)	ACTION
1976		
January 25	Maui Land and Pineapple Company (through subsidiary Kapalua Land Company)	Files for special management area (SMA) permit for Ritz-Carlton Kapalua Hotel (RCKH) development with Maui Planning Commission (MPC)
1986		
August 7	Maui Land and Pineapple Company	Files environmental assessment (EA) with MPC as prerequisite to receiving SMA approval
December 9	Maui Planning Commission	SMA permit approved for RCKH
	Hui Alanui O Mākena	At MPC meeting, Isaac Hall voices objection over potential destruction of alanui trail if RCKH development were to proceed
1987		
January 16	Hui Alanui O Mākena	Files with MPC motions for reconsideration; to reopen the docket and take further evidence; to vacate order for lack of adequate notice; to intervene; to require environmental assessment and environmental impact statement; and to waive rules
January 21	Maui Planning Commission	Sends January 16 motions to Hawai'i State Department of Land and Natural Resources State Historic Preservation Office (SHPO) for review and clarification regarding archaeological significance of Honokahua site and required mitigation measures
February 3	State Historic Preservation Office	Letter to MPC in response to request of January 21; states SHPO practice over the last 2 years is to point out to developers in early planning stages that burials are sensitive sites and to consider public input prior to determining whether preservation in-place or respectful reinterment is the more viable alternative.
February 13	Maui Land and Pineapple Company	Files with MPC memorandum in opposition to motions on January 16
February 19	Maui Land and Pineapple Company	Files with MPC supplemental memorandum in support of motions filed on January 16
	State Historic Preservation Office	Additional letter to MPC clarifying letter of February 3 stating minimum recommended level for mitigation of burial site excavation is archaeological data recovery and respectful reinterment or archiving of skeletal material
February 20	Maui Planning Commission	Special hearing regarding request to reconsider granting of RCKH SMA permit
	Office of Hawaiian Affairs	Trustee Manu Kahaialii delivers testimony at MPC hearing and requests consideration of the alternative of moving hotel away from burial site

(*continued*)

DATE	PARTY (OR PARTIES)	ACTION
February 27	Maui Planning Commission	Decision and order approving RCKH SMA permit with additional conditions requiring Maui Land and Pineapple Company to: 1. Develop a program of reinterment of human remains which will include procedures for public input in consultation with the Office of Hawaiian Affairs (OHA) and SHPO, and 2. Develop a procedure for removal and reconstruction of the trail onsite or at a nearby location in consultation with OHA and SHPO.
July 25	Maui Land and Pineapple Company, State Historic Preservation Office, Hui Alanui o Mākena, Office of Hawaiian Affairs	All parties enter into a memorandum of agreement (MOA) regarding respectful disinterment and reinterment of remains and preservation of archaeological features of Honokahua site
September 1	Maui Planning Commission	Accepts MOA between OHA, Hui Alanui O Mākena, SHPO, and Maui Land and Pineapple Company (MLP)
	Maui Land and Pineapple Company	Begins disinterment work at Honokahua burial site
1988		
November 17	Maui Land and Pineapple Company	Applies to MPC for one-year extension of RCKH SMA permit
December 11	Native Hawaiian activist groups (Protect Kahoʻolawe ʻOhana, Hui Alanui O Mākena, and others)	Hold protests at Honokahua excavation site regarding disinterment of over 950 sets of human remains
December 20	Governor John Waiheʻe	Appoints task force consisting of state Planning Director Harold Matsumoto and state Department of Land and Natural Resources Deputy Director Libert Landgraf to review whether Honokahua should be used as a resort site; asks Mayor Hannibal Tavares to also review situation
December 22	Native Hawaiian Activist Groups	Held 24 hour vigil outside Washington Place, the governor's residence; circulated petitions calling on Waiheʻe to protect burial site
December 23	Governor John Waiheʻe	Meets with Native Hawaiian groups and states, "as far as the disinterment goes, there is no compromise. It must stop."
	ILWU Local 142	Representing 4500 hotel workers on Maui, went on public record stating SMA permit should be reconsidered.

DATE	PARTY (OR PARTIES)	ACTION
	Maui Land and Pineapple Company	Agrees to suspend archaeological excavation at Honokahua site until January 4, 1989
	State Task Force	Meets with MLP CEO Colin Cameron
December 26	Native Hawaiian Activist Groups	Held press conference at Pukulani Square to state "all diggings at the site must stop and not resume; the bones should be returned to their original resting place; and the site shoud be honored and preserved."
December 27	Hui Alanui O Mākena	Files motion with MPC to reopen and review issuance of SMA permit
1989		
January 4	Maui Land and Pineapple Company	Colin Cameron announces disinterment will not resume provided compromise negotiations between himself, Mayor Tavares, and state task force continue
January 13	Hui Alanui O Mākena	Files petition to intervene and for a contested case with MPC
January 18	Mayor Hannibal Tavares	Announces, "I feel I have a workable solution to the problem. But there are many details still to be worked out."
January 24	Maui Land and Pineapple Company	Files memorandum in opposition to petition to intervene and for a contested case with MPC
January 27	Maui Land and Pineapple Company	Files memorandum in opposition to petition to intervene and for a contested case with MPC
January 31	Office of Hawaiian Affairs	Files petition to intervene and joinder in petition to intervene with MPC
	Maui Planning Commission	Hears arguments on pending motions and votes to defer action until February 21, 1989 meeting
February 7	Maui Land and Pineapple Company	Files memorandum in opposition to OHA's petition to intervene and joinder with MPC
February 17	Office of Hawaiian Affairs	Files reply memorandum in opposition to OHA's petition to intervene and joinder with MPC
	Maui Land and Pineapple Company	Colin Cameron states at SMA's hearing that MLP has agreed to move hotel away from burial site
	Maui Planning Commission	Extends RCKH SMA permit for a period of one year
February 25	Maui Land and Pineapple Company	Colin Cameron asks the Hawai'i Senate Ways and Means Committee to buy easement to protect burial site
February 27	Maui Land and Pineapple Company	RCKH SMA expiration date
March 14	Governor John Waihe'e and Mayor Hannibal Tavares	Meet in Maui to discuss compensation plan for Maui Land and Pineapple Company

(*continued*)

DATE	PARTY (OR PARTIES)	ACTION
March 18	Maui Land and Pineapple Company	Colin Cameron submits written proposal for compensation to Mayor Hannibal Tavares
April 18	Governor John Waiheʻe	Announces tentative agreement reached calling for the state to pay Kapalua Land Company $5.5 million to purchase preservation easement over the burial site and $0.5 million to reinter remains
May 27	Board of Land and Natural Resources	Approves $0.6 million settlement between state and Maui Land and Pineapple Company
September 7		Parties sign reinterment agreement in the office of Mayor Hannibal Tavares
1990		
May 6	Hui Alanui O Mākena, Office of Hawaiian Affairs, and Maui Land and Pineapple Company	All entities participate in a formal reburial ceremony at the Honokahua burial site

Note: This timeline was compiled from newspaper articles and special management are permit-related documents that are referenced in the Bibliography.

Appendix B: Memorandum of Agreement

Memorandum of Agreement
He Palapala ʻAelike

Regarding Disinterment and Reinterment Standards
And Conditions Related to the
Honokahua Sand Dune Burial Area
No nā kulana o ka hana ʻeli iwi a kanu paʻa hou
a me nā ʻano no ka wahi kanu paʻa i ka
Puʻeone ʻO Honokahua

General Conditions: Nā Kulana Laula

1. Any and all costs associated with the terms of this Agreement shall be borne by the Kapalua Land Company, Ltd.

Na Kapalua Land Company, Ltd. e uku i nā mea e pili ʻana I kēia palapala ʻaelike.

2. Prior to formal disinterment activities the site area will be fenced to prevent desecration or denigration of the Honokahua sand dune; surface-lying human remains will be gathered for safe-keeping; and the Project Archaeologist will contact Alu Like, Inc. to assist in the hiring of Hawaiians as members of disinterment teams; and

Ma mua o nā hana ʻeli iwi kūpono, e pā ʻia ai ka puʻeone Honokahua no ka hoʻino ʻole; e hoʻili ʻili i na iwi kupuna i kaulaʻi ʻia no ka mālama pono ʻana; a pono ka Project Archaeologist e kahea aku ai i Alu Like, Inc. i kokua a paʻa i na poʻe kanaka kokua no kēia hana.

3. Before formal disinterment begins, a blessing will be conducted at the Honokahua site. This ceremony will not be publicized. Additional blessings before reburial begins and a closing ceremony will be conducted at the reinterment grounds.

Ma mua o ka ʻeli iwi ʻana hoʻolaʻa ʻia kahi Honokahua. Aʻole e hoʻolaulaha ʻia kēia hana. E hoʻolaʻa hou ka hana mua a ka hana pani ma kahi kanu paʻa hou.

DISINTERMENT: Ka Mālama Iwi ʻAna

1. Archaeological teams will adhere to the highest standards of professional conduct, displaying respect and sensitivity to the removal and curation of human remains;

Na nā kime o nā mea ʻike hana lima o ke au I hala e oihana kupono, ka mālama pono a hoʻihi a ke aloha kūpuna i kēia hana.

2. Community access to the site during disinterment will be allowed if on-site safety permits and only after notification to and permission from the Kapalua Land Company regarding time and number of visitors;

Hiki i nā kamaʻaina o nēia ʻaina ke holo i wāho inā lākou e mālama ai i ke kino me ka haʻi a ʻae ʻana ʻo Kapalua Land Company. Pono nō lākou e hoʻike ka manawa a nā helu kanaka i kipa mai.

3. Community representative Leslie Kuloloio will be retained by Kapalua Land Company. The OHA Archaeologist will conduct periodic site reviews and, in consultation with the Project Archaeologist and Mr. Kuloloio, will submit progress reports to OHA;

Na Leslie Kuloloio i hana i Kapalua Land Company. Nānā ka luna makaʻaianana. E nānā pinepine aku ke kanaka ʻike hana lima o ke au i hala o OHA i ka wahi. Nānā i kuka me ka Project Archaeologist a me Kuloloio kane, a haʻawi aku ai i na palapala ia OHA.

4. Removal will retain individual integrity, and any associated burial artifacts will be retained and reburied with the individual;

I ka manawa I hemo I nā iwi, e pono e hemo pakahi ai i ke kanaka piha, a kanu hou pu kona mau mea kuleana.

5. An archaeological data recovery plan has been reviewed by the Office of Hawaiian Affairs, the Hui Alanui O Makena, and the community. This plan, as approved by the State Historic Preservation Office, will be conducted by Project Archaeologists Paul H. Rosendahl, Inc. to meet the needs of a reasonable scientific study, and a recognition of traditional Native Hawaiian beliefs and respect for ancestral bones (ATTACHMENT 1). The fireld photographs of human skeletal remains will be restricted to articulated skeletons, or as approved by community representative Mr. Kuloloio.

Ua hoʻomaʻamaʻa ʻia kekahi papahana hōʻimi hou i na naʻauao e ka Office of Hawaiian Affairs, ka Hui Alanui O Makena a me ka poʻe ʻo Maui. Ua ʻae ka State Historic Preservation Office I keia papahana, na ka Project Archaeologists ʻo Paul H. Rosendahl, Inc. e hoʻoponopono i kēia papahana i paʻa i ka makemake no ka lawa pono a hoʻopaʻa haʻawina ʻike noʻeau kaulike a me ka hoʻomaopopo ʻana o ka manaʻo mana o nā kupuna i hala a kū hoʻihi ʻana o na iwi kupono. Hiki ke paʻikiʻi ma ka papahana i nā iwi no ke kino piha aiʻole i ka ʻae ʻana o Kuloloio kāne (KA MEA I PAʻA ʻIA HELU 1).

6. All necessary curation prior to reburial will be in reasonable proximity to the site, and adequate security will be provided;

E hana ana I kēia mau mea kokoke pono i kahi kanu a paʻa i ke kiaʻi.

7. The use of any heavy machinery will be confined to sand removal identified as containing no remains.

Aia no nā mekini kaumaha i ke one ma nā iwi ʻole.

8. Ten copies of the final written report required by the approved mitigation plan will be transmitted to the Office of Hawaiian Affairs. All photographs and negatives of human skeletal remains will be archived at the offices of Maui Land and Pineapple Company, with the understanding that access is restricted. Requests for access will require the approval of KLC, OHA, SHPO, and the Hui Alanui O Makena, or their successors.

Hoʻouna ʻia ʻumi mau palapala sila akakuʻu i ka Office of Hawaiian Affairs. Aia nā kiʻi o na iwi kino i ka waihona i ke keʻena o Maui Land and Pineapple Company. Ua maopopo ʻia ʻaʻole hiki ke lawe aku kela mau kiʻi me ka ʻae ʻole mai KLC, OHA, SHPO, a me ka Hui aʻohe aiʻole ko lākou mau hoʻilina.

REINTERMENT: Ke Kanu Hou

1. Subject to permit approvals, the reburial site will be at a parcel near the project area identified on the accompanying map (ATTACHMENT 2);

I palapala ʻae, aia kahi kanu hou i ka māhele kokoke o kahi papahana I ka palapala ʻaina me kēia palapala (KA MEA I PAʻA ʻIA HELU 2).

2. Reburial will be of individuals, wrapped in kapa and placed in baskets with any associated burial artifacts. The kapa and baskets will be provided through a contract arranged by Mr. Kuloloio;

E kanu hou i kēia mau iwi I ke kapa I loko o na ʻeke me nā mea i kanu ai. Loaʻa kēia mau kapa a ʻeke me nā mea I kanu ai. Loaʻa kēia mau kapa a ʻeke mai Kuloloio kāne.

3. Individuals will then be reburied underground. An earth mound and encircling of plants will designate the reburial area. The association and arrangement of the burials within the reinterment site will approximate their original associations. A map will be made to show the location of each individual in the plot.

Ua kanu hou kēia mau ʻeke iwi ma lalo o ka ʻaina. Ke ahu lepo a me kekahi po'ai kī na ho'āilona o kēia wahi kanu hou. Ua kanu hou i kēia wahi kanu hou. Ua kanu hou i kēia mau iwi I ka 'ano wahi e like me ka manawa i wehe 'ia. E kākau 'ia kekahi palapala 'āina e hō'ike 'ia ka wahi e kanu 'ia ai nā iwi kino pākahi.

4. An appropriate marker wil l be installed outside the enclosure, and the inscription will be provided OHA in consultation with the community, Hui Alanui o Mākena, SHPO and Kapalua Land Company;

Aia kekahi maka ma waho o kēia wahi me kekahi mau 'ōlelo mai OHA me ka mana'o o nā po'e o Maui, a me ka Hui Alanui o Mākena.

5. Title to the reburial area will be transferred to the Office of Hawaiian Affairs after reinterment is complete. Maintenance of the site will be the responsibility of Kapalua Land Company; and

Ha'awi 'ia ka palapala ho'onā i ka Office of Hawaiian Affairs ma hope o ke kanu hou 'ana. Na Kapalua Land Company e mālama mau i kēia wahi.

6. Designation of the reburial site as a "cemetery" or registered site will be pursued with the State Historic Preservation Office.

E 'imi ana ka palapala kuhikuhina i kahi kanu ai'ole kahi kakau ho'opa'a me ka State Historic Preservation Office.

Trail Restoration and Display Standards
Affecting the Removal and Reconstruction of the
Kapalua Paved Trail
Ka Hoʻihoʻi hou a ke kūlana mua ʻana o ke ala a nā kulana
hoʻike o ka hemo a kukulu hou o
Ke Ala Hele Kapalua

PRESERVATION OF TRAIL: Ka Mālama Mau ʻAna o Ke Ala Hele

1. An existing portion of trail located in the lower West portion of the project site nearest to what is now the fourth fairway of the adjacent Bay Golf Course will be preserved;

E mālama mau i kekahi māhele o ke ala hele i kahi komohana lālo o kahi o kēia papahana, aia hoʻi kahi kokoke ka fairway ʻeha o Bay Gold Course.

2. Planned hotel construction will be adjusted to allow preservation and reconsruction of this trail portion at its present location;

Hoʻololi ʻia ke kukulu ʻana o ka hōkele hou i mālama a kukulu hou i kēia māhele o ke ala hele.

3. This section of trail will be augmented by the incorporation of other trail segments within the project to reconstruct a trail/walk on the grounds of the project;

E hui ʻia kēia māhele o ke ala hele me kekahi mau ala i loko o kēia papahana e kukulu kekahi ala hele no kēia hana.

4. Interpretative signs will mark and describe the significance of the trail. Kapalua Land Company shall submit the text for these signs to the SHPO and OHA for review and approval to ensure accuracy. This review shall be done in cooperation with the Hui Alanui o Mākena and the community, as this site is considered to potentially be culturally significant;

E hōʻike ʻia ka moʻolelo o kēia ala hele me kekahi mau papa hōʻike. E haʻawi aku ʻo Kapalua Land Company ke moʻolelo no kēia mau papa hōʻike i SHPO a me OHA no ko lākou ʻaelike a ka manaʻo pololei. Hoʻomaʻamaʻa i kēia mau moʻolelo me nā poʻe o Maui, a me ka Hui Alanui o Mākena no ka mea, no lākou kamaʻaina.

5. The SHPO and OHA will verify the successful completion of the trail restoration and interpretation.

Na SHPO a OHA e hoʻoiaʻiʻo ka pau ʻana o ka hoʻihoʻi hou a ke kulana mua ʻana a moʻolelo o ke alahele.

This Memorandum of Agreement (MOA) is concluded in fulfillment of two Shoreline Management Application (SMA) permit conditions adopted by the Maui County Planning Commission on the 20th of February 1987.

(a). That the applicant (Kapalua Land Company) shall develop a program for the reinterment of human remains, in consultation with the Office of Hawaiian Affairs and the State Historic Preservation Office, and that said program shall include but not be limited to procedures for public input and site selection subject to final review and approval by the Maui Planning Commission.

(b) That the applicant shall develop a procedure for removal and reconstruction of the trail (T-4) onsite or at a nearby location in consultation with the Office of Hawaiian Affairs and the State Historic Preservation Office for purposes of interpretation, public display and data recovery and that said procedure shall be subject to final review and approval by the Maui Planning Commission."

Nā wai e hoʻala i na iwi? Nā mākou.
Who will care for the bones? We will.

Nā wai e mālama i ke ala hele? Nā mākou.
Who will care for the trail? We will.

Signed by:

Moses K. Keale, Sr.
Chairperson, Board of Trustees
Office of Hawaiian Affairs

William W. Paty
State Historic Preservation Officer

Richard Cameron
Vice President
Kapalua Land Company

Dana Naone Hall
Hui Alanui o Makena

Appendix C: Reference Material Related to Colin Cameron and Maui Land and Pineapple Company

Kapalua Master Plan.

Honokahua burial ground in undeveloped form. Courtesy of Richard M. Knowles.

Architectural rendering of Ritz-Carleton Kapalua hotel with burial site in foreground. Courtesy of Richard M. Knowles.

KAPALUA LAND COMPANY, LTD.
ACCOUNTING OFFICE
800 VILLAGE ROAD
KAPALUA, MAUI, HAWAII 96761
(808) 669-7733

DATE: 11-16-95 —   TIME: 8:30 AM

FAX NO: 244-0862

TO: KAREN MURAOKA
DIRECTOR OF ADMINISTRATION
MAUI COMMUNITY COLLEGE

FROM: RICK KNOWLES
RECORDS ADMINISTRATION
KAPALUA LAND CO., LTD.

MESSAGE: AS WE DISCUSSED
COLIN CAMERON'S SPEECH
THAT WAS DELIVERED AT THE
PUBLIC HEARING FOR THE
SMA PERMIT EXTENSION

.vE ARE SENDING __6__ PAGES INCLUDING THIS COVER SHEET BY CANNON FAX MACHINE
MODEL L775. IF PROBLEMS OCCUR, PLEASE CALL ___Rick___ AT (808) 669-7733.
FAX NUMBER: (808) 669-7734

Kapalua

Muraoka records request to Kapalua Land Company.

Maui Land & Pineapple Company, Inc.
PO Box 187, Kahului, Maui, Hawaii
96732-0187 / (808) 877-3351

January 31, 1989

Chairman & Members of the Maui Planning Commission
Ladies & Gentlemen:

In coming before you today to request a twelve-month extension of our SMA permit, I want to address two separate but interrelated issues.

The first is our legal right to ask for this extension; the second is our moral right and obligation to remove the remaining bones from this burial site and later reinter them with the up to 85% of the burials which have been already carefully removed according to the terms of the Memorandum of Agreement. This was signed in August of 1987 by Kapalua Land Company, the Office of Hawaiian Affairs, the Hui Alanui O Makena, and the State Historic Preservation Office.

As to the first issue, we should be granted this extension. Existing precedent provides for such extension if the applicant has diligently pursued completing the requirements of the permit. Certainly we have done this, as the over $2 million we have spent and the 75 archaeological workers employed to date shows. We have followed the Agreement carefully and respectfully; none of the parties involved (the Office of Hawaiian Affairs, the Hui Alanui O Makena, or the State Historic Preservation Office) have said otherwise. I have a memorandum from the Department of Land & Natural Resources stating this as well. The Hui Alanui O Makena has had a representative, Leslie Kuloloio, paid by Kapalua under the Agreement, who has been on site the full time to ensure this and to report to OHA.

The only legal argument advanced by the parties was Isaac Hall's statement that there have been changed conditions which should lead you to not extend the permit, these changed conditions which should lead you to not extend permit, these changed conditions being the approximately 925 burials found to date. I must disagree with Isaac as to his statement that conditions had changed. From the beginning, the burial site was known to be a major site. Two months before work started, the official newsletter of OHA, dated June of 1987, said this site was comparable to the Mokapu site on Oahu, where, as it stated in the article, over 1,100 burials had been found. This figure is larger than the number of burials found here. The article, by the way, went on to praise Kapalus for "demonstrating the common care and love for Hawaii best described by 'kamaaina'."

By reason of Leslie's daily presence, the Hui knew of the number of burials found each day and each week. At a meeting we had with the Hui last fall, when there had been some 700 burials found, I proposed that we might reduce the amount of repetitious scientific data recorded for each subsequent burial. At that time the Hui did not comment on nor express concern about the number of burials but they did state that they felt the information was extremely valuable in learning more about the early Hawaiians and that they did not want us to reduce the amount of data retrieved.

The Office of Hawaiian Affairs also received the weekly reports. I do not doubt the sincerity of the Trustees' recent statement that they were surprised at the number of burials found since they have many other matters to consider, but the information was sent weekly to their office and their staff did visit the burial site regularly.

This being the case, there were no "changed circumstances." This was known to be a major burial site, which is the reason the carefully worked out Agreement was adopted in the first place. The Agreement, by the way, took the parties six months to work out. Because work could not commence until the Agreement was signed, the delay from February to August of 1987 is one of the reasons the extension is necessary. The work also took longer than anticipated because of the extremely meticulous procedures necessary in uncovering each burial.

Leslie, Charlie Maxwell, and many others have stated correctly that the information found is extremely valuable. I would point out that if we had not done the archaeological work this would never have been known.

Kapalua has lived up to the conditions of the permit and the Agreement in total good faith and we have spent a lot of money in doing so. We do not think it would be fair and proper to deny us this extension. We need the additional time to complete the work we agreed to do and are obligated to complete under the Agreement. The extension will also permit us needed time to try and work out with the interested parties how best to address the serious concerns of many people and groups.

If the permit extension is denied, everything will be in limbo; if it is granted, we are committed to resolve the situation. Accordingly, I ask you to extend the permit for one year.

This brings me to the second issue. Should we continue? Do we have a moral right and obligation to? Obviously, I am not Hawaiian, except in the sense of being born in Maui, growing up here, raising a family here, burying my wife here, and loving my children, my granddaughters, and my neighbors. My ancestors also lived here for many generations. So although my feelings may not be the same as some who are ethnic Hawaiian, my love of and commitment to Maui is no less.

I have long thought long and hard about this situation and prayed, too, and spent sleepless nights as well. I have talked to many people—religious leaders, government officials, friends, and associates, Hawaiians and others. Some have said the bones already removed should go back. Some have said this is impossible, but no more should be taken out. Some have said that proper and respectful preservation of all the bones is the most important thing. Some have pointed out that the site was previously untended and desecrated by the uninformed public, and that the disinterment and reinterment elsewhere is an improvement of this condition. Some have said we owe the living a responsibility too.

We have considered all the alternatives we could think of. The site cannot be reconstructed as it was. If the remaining burials are left in the sand, either as they are or with the bones already removed being replaced on the site, they will someday wash away. Not in ten years, maybe not in fifty, but it is a sand dune and this will happen someday. We originally knew it was a burial site because bones were already being exposed by the weather as long as forty years ago.

Also of concern to us is the extensive publicity, through media coverage and demonstrations, that the site has drawn. We fear that the curiosity of some who may not maintain the proper respect could cause harm to the remains.

In the Agreement a site on a hill behind the beach was selected for the reburial. This site would be turned over to OHA for preservation and protection in perpetuity. We would be willing to consider other sites as well.

The burial site stretches across two-thirds of the hotel site. The hotel, which is fully designed and on which three million dollars have been spent, is ready to go to the building department for a building permit. It is deliberately planned to be low and unobtrusive, like the existing Kapalua Bay Hotel. To accomplish this it spreads across a large part of the parcel, including a location on a significant part of the burial site itself. Moving the hotel slightly, which could be done, would still leave the same situation.

We have not other location for this hotel; even if we were to start over, toss out the plans, and very probably lose our partners and financing commitments, there is no other location at Kapalua for a beach front hotel—and beach frontage is necessary for a successful resort hotel. Our other two beach front sites are committed—one to the Kapalua Bay Hotel, and the other to residential use. Honokahua Beach, the one in front of the hotel, also has a four-acre public park, D. T. Fleming Beach Park. We need this hotel to provide long-term stability and strength to the resort and to ensure its continued health. We are a small development. By comparison, for example, Kaanapali how has over 3,700 hotel rooms, and Wailea will soon have over 2,500 hotel rooms. Kapalua is and will remain a smaller community. With this second and last beach front hotel. Kapalua will still be only a fourth the size of Wailea and a sixth the size of Kaanapali. The Kapalui resort community needs this vital element to succeed.

We have been talking and will continue to talk with the Governor's task force and with other respected leaders and mediators. We believe that with goodwill and aloha on all sides that we can resolve this situation.

Men and women lived in this area for over a thousand years. They left many signs behind—walls, house platforms, at least two beautiful heiaus—and of course the burials. We believe that the most respectful and proper way to treat and preserve the bones of the people who lived here is to complete the disinterment and to rebury them along with the others already removed in a location and in a manner that OHA and others may want. If they are to be reburied near the ocean, then this should be done in a manner which will protect them from the ravages of time.

To conclude, we must have the extension on this SMA. Without it, no one wins.

The bones already removed would be reinterred at this site. The site would remain in its current partially excavated condition, subject to further erosion and possible desecration.

The question of future reinterment would remain unanswered—where and when and at whose expense? No one knows. We do know that the legal questions raised, coupled with the moral and religious issues, will create the kind of contentious environment which can only hurt rather than support all of our and others' efforts to create a harmonious community.

If the SMA extension is granted, we can proceed to resolve the remaining issues with the Governor's task force, OHA, and others with the care and dignity it deserves.

We promise not to start the excavation again until we and the other interested parties have seriously sat down to talk in order to resolve this. We both need time—but as an earlier speaker said—the pressure has to be on both sides. I do not know exactly how much time is needed, but we will have to set a deadline, after which we would start work again.

Sincerely,
(signed)
Colin Cameron
Chairman
Kapalua Land Company, Ltd.

Colin Cameron 1927–1992

"The farther backward you can look, the farther forward you are likely to see."
—Winston Churchill

Colin Cameron was a stunning continuation of the Baldwin dynasty. He was cast in the mold of his great grandfather, HP Baldwin, a planter, a grower, a visionary. Each was sustained by an unshakeable optimism.

On Novemeber 12, 1869, Samuel Alexander and Henry Perrine Baldwin purchased 11.94 acres in the Makawao area and began to grow sugar cane. From this beginning, Alexander & Baldwin was established.

Alexander was the designer, the drafter of plans. Baldwin was the partner in the front lines getting the job done. The former traveled extensively, the latter's contemporaries called him a "Maui boy." His interests and his vision were focused on his island. The Haiku ditch was designed by Alexander to carry water from the rainy slopes of Haleakala to their burgeoning plantation. Baldwin built it, and to this day the project is called the most dramatic water story in Hawaiian history.

The 25-mile ditch was a challenge; spanning Maliko gulch was Herculean. The workers refused to lower themselves over the cliff into the ravine 300 feet below. Balwin, clutching a rope with his legs and his one arm (he had lost the other in a mill accident), swung into the gulch. He repeated this feat day after day until the job was completed. After the first day his men followed him!

These pioneers came up against formidable competitors. Borrowed money, on occasion, kept their dream alive. They held fast to their vision and they prevailed. This is the heritage which Colin carried with him all through the years.

When Colin's grandfather, Harry Baldwin, and his father, J. Walter Cameron, formed Maui Pineapple Company in the early '30s they held the same affinity for the land. The two possessed the prerequisite faith that farmers must nurture which calls for a bumper crop to follow a failed one.

In 1953, Colin joined the company where he was taught to take a long view. He learned by example that a successful enterprise is most often a collective endeavor. When he assumed management responsibilities in 1962, respect for his fellow employees was one of the basic principles on which he operated. This never changed over the succeeding 30 years.

For a brief period following the merger with Baldwin Packers, the family lost control of the company to A&B. This eventually led to Colin's resignation in 1967. Engaging in a hard-fought proxy fight, in which loyalties were tested and sometimes found wanting, he won a seat on the A&B board. From this vantage point he felt better able to fight the proposed plans for Maui Pineapple Company, which did not coincide with his own.

In 1969 Colin faced his own Maliko gulch, but he had scope carefully the dimensions of the challenge he faced. With their support, he plced the family's fortunes on the line. A $16 million loan was negotiated with Bank of America; the entree based on friendship, the loan predicated on full faith in the Cameron family and the company's potential. The family purchased a portion of the Maui Pine stock owned by the A&B and obtained the remainder in exchange for A&B stock held by the family. Thus was born Maui Land & Pineapple Company Inc.—a minor name change but a significant one.

Having prevailed with A&B, Colin was not about to be derailed years later by Harry Weinberg. This formidable adversary mounted two campaigns to win a seat on the ML&P board. Harry held very strong convictions on which directions the company should be led as did Colin. With wise guidance and creative strategies, once again Colin won the day. Colin enjoyed a fair fight, but personal animosity was never a driving force.

Colin called Kapalua a "special place with a special mystique." Developing the 750 acres at Honolua into a well-planned, luxury destination resort and community became his special dream. It began in 1970 and from step one "quality" was the watchword. Planning, permits and financing all placed strictures on the pace of development. The golf courses, the hotel, the condominiums, shops, restaurants, all came on line in studied increments. The Kapalua Bay Hotel, crown jewel of the complex, had to be sold to settle pressing financial demands.

A second hotel had been an important part of the original resort plans. When ground was broken in 1989 for the $200 million Ritz-Carlton Kapalua, it was a dream come true. Nobody imagined that the site selected contained at least a thousand Hawaiian graves and artifacts of significant historical importance.

Working with state and county governments, with the Hui Alanui O Makena and the Office of Hawaiian Affairs as well as individual Hawaiian activists, a solution was found. It was a compassionate but multi-million dollar resolution, and lends credence to OHA's earlier statement that Kapalua Land Company was "demonstrating the common care and love for Hawaii best described by kama'aina."

The graves were restored with great respect and the area in questioned designated a cemetery. A new location was selected for the hotel and planners went back to the drawing board. Colin summed up his decision this way: "Our continued success also rests with the feelings our employees have about us and the kind of company we are."

He did not live to see the Ritz-Carlton Kapalua Hotel completed, but it stands there today in some way an embodiment of his spirit. His vision, his tenacity, his compassion and integrity are encompassed in that structure, all a part of the mystique of Kapalua which he respected.

Maui was always more than a "sun and fun" place to Colin and he frequently expressed concern about the island's growing dependence on tourism. In the very early '80s, at the behest of Mayor Hannibal Tavares, he headed a group which established the Maui Economic Development Board. Under the leadership of Don Malcolm, and with each board member sharing the challenge, the Maui Research and Technological Park opened in May of 1992—a major first step in accommodating high tech tech industry on Maui.

At the first annual Conference on Business and the Environment, which he helped organize, Colin set forth a strong position on the topic. "I believe passionately that good business practices and environmental concerns are inextricably linekd together, locally, nationally, and globally," he said.

Colin looked on community involvement not so much a duty but as an opportunity to make a difference. Through his work with The Nature Conservancy of Hawaii, the Maui Community Arts & Cultural Center, the Lahaina Restoration Foundation, the J. Walter Cameron Center, and many other organizations, he did make a measurable difference.

He had his own articulated management philosophy: "Quality over size. This all ahs to be fun, interesting. People have to feel rewarded for what they are doing, recognized, respected. We have been trying very hard to do this."

A writer for the *"Mauian"* magazine captured him in a reflective mood in a 1986 interview. "This is a good company. The family is very much involved in it. We have been here for a number of generations and Maui has been very good to us. I have been raised as a child here and I want to put back what we have taken out. I can do this by running the company in the best way I can. I can't speak for three generations ahead, but I can speak for the family now. We are very close knit. We all love Maui."

A reporter once asked Colin if he enjoyed his work, did he like, "being in the driver's seat?" His candid response was "That's a silly question. I love it."

Loving what he did was never, ever, the least of his capacities. This knowledge afforded a measure of comfort to his family and friends when he died on Friday morning, June 12, 1992.

In 1911, when Henry Pierre Baldwin died, the Alexander & Baldwin board of directors drafted a resolution which cited "his unfailing courtesy to those with whom he was associated and his consideration for their welfare, which endeared him to their hearts." It noted his "legacy of inspiration not only in commercial and industrial affairs, but in the furtherance of education, religious, and philanthropic work." He was, they stated, "a power of good in the community of these islands." These words could have been written, with determinate truth, about his great grandson these 81 years later.

At the funeral service conducted for Colin on Tuesday, June 16, at Makawao Cemetery, his brother-in-law Richard Hartley spoke of the friendship they shared over a 40-year span. Dick shared with the hundreds of those present his personal insight of Colin's love for his family and his community. He reflected on his genuine and discerning appreciation of music, art, and poetry. His recollections included the heart-wrenching grief Colin experienced at the loss of Margaret and how family and friends rejoiced in his new found happiness with Pam. Throughout his talk, Dick's deep respect and love for Colin were reflected and shared by so many listening to his words. He noted finally, as others had, that Colin was first and last a "Maui boy."

Each year Colin presented in this publication his observations of the preceding year. Invaribaly his offering closed in amanner which speaks volumes about the man. The 1987 example could have been presented today. "...Finally, a special note of appreciation to everyone who works here. I know I've said this before, but that does not make it any less true: without your loyalty the Company and to each other there wouldn't be a Company. Mahalo nui loa, Colin C. Cameron."

Written by: Nora I. Cooper, Editor Emeritus, *The Maui News*

MAUI COUNTY COUNCIL
BOY SCOUTS OF AMERICA
DISTINGUISHED CITIZEN DINNER

HONORING
COLIN C. CAMERON
JUNE 17, 1988
MAUI MARRIOTT, KAANAPALI

Written by Colin Cameron
Edited by Effie Cameron

...suggested that he gain experience by working for a year before by working for a year before reapplying. He took Harvard's advice to heart and ended up in San Francisco, where he met a lovely Hilo girl studying for her teaching degree at San Francisco State. They met on a blind date; actually, he met her roommate on a blind date, but it was the girl in the living room, dressed in her pajamas, who blinded him. He knew at that first meeting that he was going to marry Margaret Hartley. A year later they did marry, on August 25, 1951.

The next year, Harvard Business School relented and the young couple moved east to live in Cambridge for two years. He graduated as a Baker Scholar in 1953 and, weary of the cold weather, moved back to Maui with Margaret and their infant son Douglas. Colin went to work at Maui Pineapple Company in the Corn Mill Division of the Haliimaile plantation. Thanks to his education and hard work, coupled with the fact that his dad had started the company, he progressed through a number of jobs at Haliimale plantation and the Kahului cannery, eventually becoming vice president and general manager in 1967.

To provide some background: In 1962, at the instigation of Alexander & Baldwin, Maui Pineapple Company merged with Baldwin Packers, Ltd., an older, money-losing pineapple operation in West Maui. Baldwin Packers' cannery (now the site of The Cannery shopping center in Lahaina) was closed to consolidate the fruit processing at Kahului cannery. One result of this merger was that A&B, with an interest in both companies, gained control of the newly formed company. In 1967, A&B decided to take over the direct management of the firm, which left Colin in the ranks of the unemployed. More significantly, at that time, the management of A&B felt there was no future in the pineapple industry, and also that they should concentrate on developing the Wailea area, which they owned completely, rather than risk their credit on a remote area at Honolua, of which they owed only a bit more than half. Not unreasonable perhaps—except to the Camerons.

What followed was a series of interesting maneuvers and negotiations, including a proxy fight that resulted in a board seat for Colin at A&B for one year. Aided by Bank of America president Rudy Peterson, an old friend of J. Walter Cameron, and with additional help from another friend, Ralph Phillips of Dean Witter, the Cameron family acquired control of Maui Pine from A&B and other minority shareholders. On December 6, 1969 the company went public and changed its name to Maui Land & Pineapple Company, Inc., thus reflecting the wave of interest in Hawaii landholding companies by mainland investors.

As often happens when one reflects upon past events, there exist chance events which may have vast implications upon the course of history. In this case, one week after the company went public, the bottom fell out of the new issues market. Had they delayed, the Camerons would have lost any chance of regaining control of Maui Land & Pineapple Company.

In the late 1960s, the pineapple industry was in a worldwide slump caused by low profit margins, high production costs and antiquated canneries. Undeterred, the Camerons had great faith in the pineapple industry and upon gaining control, they invested substantial amounts of money on modernizing the plant and estabilishing new training techniques in order to return pineapple to profitability. The company was fortunate to have Joseph W. Hartley, Jr., in charge of pineapple operations. He brought the operation to its present high standards as one of the most efficient pineapple canneries in the world. Joe Hartley continues to manage the direct the pineapple company as president.

Management also began the long process of developing the oceanfront Honolua lands into what is today the Kapalua resort. Kapalua was a new venture for the company and for Colin. While the plan for quality development has been successful at the resort, the process has been more complex and difficult than he could have envisioned requiring an investment of over $50 million of company funds over the first 10 years. The overall design and planning concept remain intact, but profitability did not occur until very recently, in 1986. The resort's remote location and the small company's limited resources added to the difficulty of developing a major destination resort without the backing of a deep-pocket partner. But direct control over the resort's 700 acres (as well as 23,000 agricultural acres), joined by the family's long-term and continuing interest in the project, ahs assured that the quality of the resort will not be compromised. Each project at Kapalua must fit into the long-term goal of creating both a first-class resort and a residential community.

The early beginnings at Kapalua provided Colin with a wealth of on-the-job training regarding building, marketing, and managing. Perseverance through difficult financial periods has paid off, and with a strong management team in place at Kapalua, Colin feels confident of continued success.

As well as enjoying the challenges of building Maui Land & Pineapple

Company into the country's largest private label pineapple and creating one of the finest resorts in the United States, Colin has been actively involved in community activities here in the islands and on the Mainland.

Six years after his return to Maui with his young family, he was asked to join the board of trustees of Maunalolu College, a small, independent, two-year college located in Makawao. In 1965, he became chairman of the board, coincident with the retirement of Dr. KC Leebrick as president and at approximately the time of the opening of Maui Community College. He was faced with finding a new president for the college, coping with the competition from the new *"low-cost"* community college, and raising funds in order to continue to operate. His answer was to recruit Jerry Speakman, Jr. as president; to add an upper division to the college; and to extensively recruit students from the mainland, the Pacific, and other neighbor islands. He almost made it—but in the end, the college was forced to accept a merger with United States International University of San Diego which closed the campus several years later, thus ending Maui's only four-year educational institution.

Another early, and in this case, more enduring connection was with Lahaina Restoration Foundation. Colin was a founding director and vice president starting in 1962. He served as president from 1982 to 1986 and still serves as a director. The foundation has provided historic guidance to what is predominantly a commercial area. Projects such as restoring the Baldwin House, the Seamen's Hospital, the Carthaginian whaling ship and the Wo Hing Temple, have offered visitors and residents the opportunity to see part of Lahaina as it was in the 1800s.

Politically, Colin and Margaret were very active in the Republican Party, he serving as chairman of the Maui GOP from 1957 to 1962, Margaret as president of the Maui League of Republican Women from 1954 to 1959 and vice president of the State League of Republican Women for some years after. During this time the couple travelled extensively throughout the county— these being the days of campaign rallies—making their way across the island from Hana to Ulupalakua, and across the channel to Molokai and Lanai. Although they didn't elect many Republicans to office in this predominantly Democratic state, they made many lasting friendships.

Colin was proud to be asked to join the board of the newly formed Maui Savings and Loan Association by its founder, Sam Hironaka. He served in this capacity until 1973, when it was acquired by the American Savings and Loan Association. He also served as a director of the Maui Philharmonic Society for four years, from 1974 to 1978. He is president of the Kapalua

Music Assembly, which he and Margaret founded. The assembly offers music classes for children and organizes the Kapalua Music Festival every summer.

At the request of former headmaster Roger Melrose, Colin chaired the Seabury Hall long-range planning committee in 1977 and 1978, which produced a plan still being followed today in its essentials.

In its fifteenth year of service, the J. Walter Cameron Center, founded by his father, has become one of Colin's major interests since his father's death in 1976. He is vice president of the center and chairman of its long rance planning committee.

After J. Walter's death, Colin also took up his father's role aat *The Maui News* as chief executive, taking the paper from three days a week to six, and getting the company into a new building in order to meet the needs of the growing staff. Although he still serves as president of the company, he is not the active publisher of the newspaper.

Colin's major business activities include serving as a director of the Bank of Hawaii and Hawaiian Airlines. He was a director of Hawaiian Electric Company for many years and is still on the board of its subsidiary, Maui Electric Company.

He also enjoys serving on the Board of Visitors of the Fletcher School of Law and Diplomacy, a graduate school affiliated with Tufts University of Medford, Massachussetts, and on the Visiting Committee for East Asian Studies of Harvard University.

Along with Hannibal Tavares and Donald Malcom, he is responsible for the creation of the Maui Economic Development Board (MEDB). Incorporated in 1981 as a nonprofit corporation, MEDB enjoys state, county, and private sector support and is dedicated to diversifying Maui's economy and promoting educational opportunities in order to provide new varieties of careers for our residents.

Other organizations with which he is involed are: the North Pacific Forum, the Japan Western United States Association, the Pacific Basin Economic Council, and the Honolulu Institute for Foreign Relations. With the aid of Donald Malcolm, he also plans to establish the Kapalua Pacific Center, dedicated to promoting increased understanding and communications among the Pacific nations.

Colin describes himself as "singularly non-athletic" insofar as coordinated competitive sports go, but he enjoys hiking through Haleakala Crater and he begins each morning whit a half-mile ocean swim. He still has a few "dusty" trophies from participation in state pistol tournaments through the aegis of the Maui Police Pistol Team. With two beautiful courses at Kapalua, golf director Gary Planos is doggedly teaching him to play "an only slightly embarrassing game of golf."

In 1978, the class of 1953 of the Harvard Business School celebrated its 25th anniversary. For his career profile, Colin eloquently summed up some thoughts and reflections about his life.

"If I were to briefly sum up how I felt about the last twenty-five years of my life, it would be a feeling of humble and bemused gratitude at my great good fortune.

"One—living on the island of Maui, in Hawaii, one of God's chosen places with its soft climate, its beauty, and its warm and wonderful peoples; small enough to know intimately, yet varied and exciting to live in.

"Two—being able to take a fine small company founded by my father, control over which had been lost to a larger corporation, and with luck, work, and the help of highly talented and dedicated associates, and the support of friendly bankers in difficult times, being able to wrest the company from the control of the larger firm (while its management wasn't looking, so to speak), expanding the original business of canned pineapples into a solidly profitable operation, and now creating a major top-of-the-line destination resort on some of our land.

'Three—as a result of this, I have not had five consecutive minutes of boredom in the last twenty-five years, while I have had enormous amounts of fun.

"Four—Maui is small enough so that efforts in cultural, political, and community affairs can be visible and hence have been emotionally rewarding.

"Five—and most important—I have enjoyed the love and support (reciprocated!) of a marvelous family, including four totally individual and wonderful children, and my wife Margaret, who combines a full, active life as a community worker with the role of mother. She also is the reason people invite us out; they put up with me so they can talk to her."

Sadly, on April 12, 1986, Margaret succumbed to cancer. While the loss of his wife and closest friend remains with him, Colin continues to work actively in the company and in community affairs, and is kept busy babysitting his grandchildren on the weekends. His greatest blessing is the loving support of his four children and their two spouses, all of whom live on Maui. He also is profoundly grateful for the many friends he has made in his lifetime on Maui. He continues with the knowledge that the thirty-five years Margaret and he spent together make him the luckiest man on earth.

NOTES

1. Maui Land and Pineapple Company, *Annual Report*, 1994: 4–6.
2. Harry Eagar, "Cameron's Vision Endures on Maui," *Building Industry*, September 1992, 65.
3. Maui Land and Pineapple Company, *Application for Special Management and Area Permit: Kapalua Bay Hotel and Shops*, January 25, 1976.
4. Maui Land and Pineapple Company, *Environmental Assessment: The Kapalua Village Hotel*, August 7, 1986.
5. Ibid.
6. Lucy Jokiel, "Colin Cameron's Toughest Decision," *Hawaii Business,* May 1989, 17.
7. Harry Eagar, "Cameron's Vision Endures on Maui," *Building Industry*, September 1992.65.
8. Linda Kephart, "Check-out time: It's goodbye Kapalua Bay Hotel, hello profitability for Maui Land & Pine," *Hawaii Business*, May 1985, 21.
9. Ibid.
10. Maui Land and Pineapple Company, *Annual Report,* 1990: 19.
11. *Alanui* is the Hawaiian term for "long trail."
12. Dana Naone Hall, interview by author, November 30, 1995, Law Offices of Isaac Hall, Wailuku.
13. Ibid.
14. Maui Planning Commission, Regular Meeting Minutes, December 19, 1986.
15. Colin Cameron, Speech given at special SMA hearing, February 20, 1987.
16. Maui Land and Pineapple Company, *Annual Report,* 1998.
17. Dana Naone Hall, interview by author, November 30, 1995, Law Offices of Isaac Hall, Wailuku.
18. Ibid.
19. Ibid.
20. Ibid.
21. Roger Fisher and William Ury, *Getting to Yes: Negotiating Agreement Without Giving In*, 2nd ed., (New York, N.Y.: Penguin Books, 1991), 99.
22. Carlsmith, Wichman, Case, Mukai and Ichiki, Motion in Opposition to Motions, February 13, 1987.
23. Dana Naone Hall, interview by author, November 30, 1995, Law Offices of Isaac Hall, Wailuku.
24. *Kupuna* is the Hawaiian term for "elder."
25. Ralson H. Nagata, State Parks Administrator, Honolulu, to Christopher L. Hart, Director, Maui County Planning Department, February 3, 1987.
26. Ralson H. Nagata, State Parks Administrator, Honolulu, to Christopher L. Hart, Director, Maui County Planning Department, February 3, 1987.

27. Dana Naone Hall, interview by author, November 30, 1995, Law Offices of Isaac Hall, Wailuku.

28. Manu Kahaialii, Testimony presented before the Maui Planning Commission regarding Kapalua Bay Resort Project, February 20, 1987.

29. Maui Planning Commission, Decision and Order, February 27, 1987.

30. Hoʻoponopono is a traditional Hawaiian way in which family conflicts were resolved. The process relied on the mediational interventions of trusted family elders.

31. Roger Fisher and William Ury, *Gettign to Yes: Negotiating Agreement Without Giving In,* 2nd ed., (New York, N.Y.: Penguin Books, 1991), 36.

32. Lucy Jokiel, "Colin Cameron's Toughest Decision," *Hawaii Business,* May 1989, 22.

33. Ibid.

34. Ibid.

35. Dana Naone Hall, interview by author, November 30, 1995, Law Offices Of Isaac Hall, Wailuku.

36. Lucy Jokiel, "Colin Cameron's Toughest Decision," *Hawaii Business,* May 1989, 22.

37. Andy Yamaguchi, "Waihee: Maui burial excavation must stop," *The Honolulu Advertiser*, December 24, 1988, A1.

38. Ibid.

39. Lucy Jokiel, "Colin Cameron's Toughest Decision," *Hawaii Business,* May 1989, 23.

40. Ibid.

41. Ibid.

42. Andy Yamaguchi, "Waihee: Maui burial excavation must stop." *The Honolulu Advertiser,* December 14, 1988, A1.

43. Lucy Jokiel, "Colin Cameron's Toughest Decision," *Hawaii Business*, May 1989, 23.

44. James K. Sebenius, "Negotiation Analysis: A Characterization and Review," *Management Science* 38 (January 1992): 21–24.

45. Samuel B. Bacharach and Edward J. Lawler, "Power Dependence and Power Paradoxes in Bargaining," *Negotiation Journal*, April 1986: 168–169

46. Lucy Jokiel, "Colin Cameron's Toughest Decision," *Hawaiian Business,* May 1989, 23.

47. Ibid., 24.

48. Howard Raiffa, "Preparing for Negotiations," Li and Fung Lecture, Chinese University of Hong Kong, November 1992, 8.

49. Lucy Jokiel, "Colin Cameron's Toughest Decision," *Hawaiian Business,* May 1989, 24.

Works Cited

Associated Press. "Group wants to block Maui resort after helping move Hawaiian graves." *The Honolulu Advertiser,* 22 December 1988.

Bacharach, Samuel B. and Edward J. Lawler. "Power Dependence and Power Paradoxes in Bargaining." *Negotiation Journal* (April 1986): 1167–174.

Burris, Jerry. "No cash promises made to Kapalua in land deal, Waihee says." *The Honolulu Advertiser,* 24 February 1989, A10.

Cameron, Colin. Speech given at Special SMA Hearing. 20 February 1987.

Conrow, Joan. "Permanent digging halt urged." *The Honolulu Advertiser,* 28 December 1988, A6.

Conrow, Joan, and Andy Yamaguchi. "Burial excavations halted until January 4." *The Honolulu Advertiser,* 24 December 1988, A1 and A4.

Eagar, Harry. "Cameron's Vision Endures on Maui." *Building Industry,* September 1992, 65.

Fisher, Roger and William Ury. *Getting to Yes: Negotiating Agreements Without Giving Inc.* 2nd ed. New York, NY: Penguin Books, 1991.

Glauberman, Stu. "Restudy of burial site disinterment due." *The Honolulu Advertiser,* 21 December 1988, A8.

Hall, Dana Naone, Spokesperson for Hui Alanui O Mākena. Interview by author, 30 November 1995, Wailuku. Law Offices of Isaac Hall, Wailuku.

Honolulu Advertiser Staff. "Burial grounds dig remaining on hold in hotel site dispute." *The Honolulu Advertiser,* 4 January 1989, A3.

———. "$6 million settlement OK'd in Maui burial site dispute." *The Honolulu Advertiser,* 27 May 1989.

Jokiel, Lucy. "Colin Cameron's Toughest Decision." *Hawai'i Business,* 1 May 1989, 17.

Kahaialii, Manu. Testimony presented before the Maui Planning Commission regarding Kapalua Bay Resort Project. 20 February 1987.

Kephart, Linda. "Check-out time: It's goodbye Kapalue Bay Hotel, hello profitability for Maui Land & Pine," *Hawai'i Business,* May 1985, 21.

Knowles, Richard M., Records Administrator for Kapalua Land Company. Interview by author, 16 November 1995, Kapalua. Kapalua Land Company Accounting Offices, Kapalua.

Maui Land and Pineapple Company, Incorporated. *Annual Report.* 1988.

———. *Annual Report.* 1989.

———. *Annual Report.* 1990.

———. *Annual Report.* 1992.

———. *Annual Report.* 1994.

———. Environmental Assessment: The Kapalua Village Hotel. 7 August 1986.

———. Application for Special Management Area Permit: Kapalua Bay Hotel and Bay Shops. 25 January 1976.

Maui News Staff. "Collision course: Historical values and hotel plans were no mysteries." *The Maui News,* 4 January 1989, A1, A3, and A5.

Maui Planning Commission. Regular Meeting Minutes. 19 December 1986.

————. Regular Meeting Minutes. 2 February 1987.

————. Regular Meeting Minutes. 1 September 1987.

————. Decision and Order on Motions to reconsider, to reopen the docket and take further evidence, to vacate order for lack of adequate notice, to intervene, to require environmental assessment and environmental impact statements, and to waive rules. 27 February 1987.

Nagata, Ralston H., State Parks Administrator, Honolulu, to Christopher L. Hart, Director Maui County Planning Department. 3 February 1987.

————. 19 February 1987.

Raiffa, Howard. "Preparing for Negotiations." Li and Fung Lecture, Chinese University of Hong Kong, November 1992.

Sebenius, James K. "Negotiation Analysis: A Characterization and Review." *Management Science* 38 (January 1992): 18-38.

Tanji, Edwin. "Protest erupts at Maui burial site excavation." *The Sunday Star-Bulletin and Advertiser,* 11 December 1988, A3 and A7.

————. "Burial site a historical treasure." *The Sunday Star-Bulletin and Advertiser,* 11 December 1988, A20.

————. "OHA, hui: Stall building of hotel on burial ground." *The Honolulu Advertiser,* 17 December 1988, A-8.

————. "Honokahua burial probe is expanded." *The Honolulu Advertiser,* 6 January 1989, A20.

————. "Honokahua burial site pact hinted: Tavares sees a workable solution." *The Honolulu Advertiser,* 18 February 1989.

————. "Kapalua agrees to move hotel away from burial site." *The Honolulu Advertiser,* 22 February 1989, A3.

———— and Stu Glauberman. "Cameron suggests state buy easement to save burial site." *The Honolulu Advertiser,* 5 February 1989, A3.

————. "Kapalua Land preparing compensation request for Honokahua site." *The Honolulu Advertiser,* 15 March 1989, A5.

————. "Kapalua Land open on-site treatment." *The Honolulu Advertiset,* 18 March 1989, A2.

————. "Hawaiian burial accord could cost state $6 million." *The Honolulu Advertiser,* 19 April 1989, A1 and A3.

————. "Hawaiian remains laid back to rest: Final rites for 1,000 Maui reburials." *The Honolulu Advertiser,* 7 May 1990, A3.

Ury, William. *Getting Past No: Negotiating with Difficult People.* New York, NY: Bantam Books, 1991.

Waite, David. "Plan approved for Honokahua remains reburial." *The Sunday Star-Bulletin and Advertiser,* 3 September 1989, A7.

Yamaguchi, Andy. "Waihee: Maui burial excavation must stop." *The Honolulu Advertiser,* 24 December 1988, A1.

HONOKAHUA NANI Ē[1]

Returning to Who We Are

Edward Halealoha Ayau

INTRODUCTION

Even in these difficult times when economic interests exert a seemingly all-powerful hand in what happens to our islands, it is still possible to claim places where our culture can revive and the spirits of our ancestors and their iwi can rest undisturbed. Honokahua, a place of endings, was the beginning of my efforts to protect burial sites—a lifelong task to help make firm the foundation from which we can continue to grow and thrive as a people.[2]

The contemporary movement in Hawai'i to care for and protect iwi kūpuna (ancestral Hawaiian skeletal remains) and moepū (funerary possessions) began as an awakening laced with powerlessness, disconnection, reconnection, frustration, and sheer determination. The ability to care for and protect family burial sites had always been instinctual and a significant element of the identity of a Hawaiian 'ohana (family). However, in a short period of time, powerful social, political, religious, and physical forces, brought on by foreigner intervention in the affairs of the Kingdom of Hawai'i, effectively stripped Nā 'Ōiwi (Hawaiians) of their ancestral home lands, sovereign authority over those lands and resources, and life itself, reducing the native population from nearly a million at the time of contact in 1778, to approximately thirty thousand by the time of the overthrow in 1893.[3]

Lost in the morass of this social and governmental upheaval was the kuleana (responsibility, duty, privilege) to care for and protect family burial sites. With Honokahua, the disconnection from the profound responsibility to the ancestral foundation of the 'ohana, and by extension the lāhui (nation), lay exposed for all to see. An ʻōlelo noʻeau (proverb, wise saying) provided the traditional belief,

Mai kaulaʻi i nā iwi i ka lā
Don't expose the bones to the sun.

Protecting bones from disturbance and exposure was critical. However, the exhumation of the iwi kūpuna and moepū of approximately 1,100 ancestral Hawaiians from two burial areas in the upper and lower sand dunes at Kapalua Bay, known as Honokahua, not only ran contrary to traditional beliefs and practices, it also epitomized all that was wrong with the historic preservation process at that time. These disturbing events took place without prior notice to, and informed consent from, lineal descents, without any meaningful discussion within the Hawaiian community, and with little regard for the sensitivities of the living cultural and lineal descendants. They exposed the failure of the historic preservation process to protect Hawaiian burial sites. In addition, they revealed that a significant kuleana was missing from the Hawaiian cultural conscience: how to culturally care for iwi kūpuna and moepū that had become exposed and how to healthily process the anxiety and anguish of burial disturbance.

The proposed Kapalua development project was considered by the Maui County Planning Commission at a time when little attention was focused on Hawaiian concerns. It was as if the needs of Nā ʻŌiwi had become invisible to government agencies, developers, and archaeologists. Being disenfranchised in such a powerful manner led to harmful impacts on the Hawaiian psyche. However, the power of Honokahua was that these impacts helped form the catalyst for significant change. This author did not take part in opposing what took place at Honokahua vis-à-vis the Kapalua development that would become the Ritz-Carlton Hotel in the late 1980s into the early 1990s. My efforts with regard to Honokahua were peripheral[4], and with regard to islands-wide burial site protection, would come a few years later.

This chapter seeks to explore what occurred at Honokahua, primarily from the perspective of a key participant. It provides observations of the profound impacts it had on living and deceased Hawaiians, and on the historic preservation review process relating to unmarked Hawaiian burial sites. The mana (spiritual energy) created by Honokahua by such leaders as Dana Nāone Hall, Rev. Charles Kauluwehi Maxwell, and Edward and Pualani Kanahele would change the cultural, legal and administrative landscapes regarding burial sites. This change occurred at a time when issues of Native American Indian burial protection and repatriation, which included Native Hawaiians and Alaska Natives, were being debated nationally. The results were two significant pieces of federal repatriation laws characterized as human rights legislation to rectify past mistreatment of ancestral remains, their possessions, and sacred objects and patrimony. Honokahua also gave birth to an organization who would work to repatriate and rebury iwi kūpuna and moepū for twenty-five years. Finally, a federal criminal case involving iwi from Maui is shared to highlight another impact of Honokahua in the area of law improving enforcement. What happened at Honokahua can be summed up in the Hawaiian words hōʻala hou, which is to awaken awareness, as these ancestors woke up living Hawaiians to their duties and responsibilities in the interdependent relationship between the living and the deceased.

> A he ʻāina nani ʻo Honokahua   This beautiful land of Honokahua
> Ka hono kaulana aʻo Piʻilani   The famous bay of Maui's King Piʻilani
> Me nā puʻu one kū i ka mālie   With its peaceful sand hills
> Hāliʻi mau ana nā iwi kūpuna   That covers the bones of our ancestors[5]

A Chance Occurrence

On December 19, 1986, Dana Nāone Hall and Isaac Hall were attending the Maui County Planning Commission meeting on behalf of Hui Alanui o Mākena, an organization working to protect public access to shorelines as an integral part of Hawaiian identity. While there, they learned for the first time about a planned project by Maui Land and Pineapple Company, through its subsidiary Kapalua Land Company, to build a luxury hotel on the shores of Kapalua Bay. The commission was considering whether to grant a Special Management Area (SMA) permit to develop in this shoreline area. Of particular concern to the Halls was the presence of a section of the Piʻilani trail and a burial site at this shoreline property, which they had just become aware of. Despite a request to defer any action on the SMA permit until Hui Alanui o Mākena had the opportunity to review and comment on the application, the planning commission granted the permit.

The Halls obtained a copy of the archaeological report which provided information regarding a section of the Piʻilani trail and the Honokahua burial site indicating that the burials were identified by archaeologists in the 1960s and the burial site was placed on the Hawaiʻi Register of Historic Places.

However, due to legal concerns raised by the Hawai'i Department of the Attorney General regarding lack of notice to and approval by the landowner, several historic sites, including the Honokahua burial site, were removed from the register in the 1970s. Frustratingly, while the legal rights of landowners were being recognized, the rights and responsibilities of the deceased and their descendants were not. In January 1987, members of Hui Alanui o Mākena visited the Honokahua burial site. Dana Nāone Hall describes their experience and concerns about the project plans.

> The shoreline dune consisted of two connected sand formations—an upper dune and a lower dune. Fragmented human skeletal remains were visible on the dune surface…We left Honokahua with the feeling that something more needed to be done. A review of the hotel development plans revealed that the entire dune (and, consequently all of the burials in it—an unknown number at that time) would be removed. An underground basement and parking garage were planned for the lower dune, and the new lobby of the hotel would displace the stepping-stone trail on the upper dune.[6]

Thereafter, Hui Alanui o Mākena informed the community about the situation, sought the support of the Office of Hawaiian Affairs, and submitted a motion for reconsideration of the planning commission's approval of the SMA permit.

On February 20, 1987, the Maui Planning Commission sealed the fate of the ancestors buried at Honokahua by denying the motion for reconsideration, despite testimony advocating for the preservation in place of the Honokahua burial site and the section of the Pi'ilani trail by every speaker, with the exception of Colin Cameron, the president of Kapalua Land Company, and his attorney. In its decision, the planning commission also sealed the fate of Hui Alanui o Mākena, inviting the organization, along with the Hawai'i Historic Preservation Officer, Kapalua Land Company, and the Office of Hawaiian Affairs to develop so-called sensitive disinterment and reinterment plans for the ancestral skeletal remains and funerary possessions at the Honokahua burial site. Dana Nāone Hall eloquently describes the hearing in a most powerful way.

> Sorrowful as the commission's adverse decision was—the mood following the meeting was black and thunderous—I felt, inexplicably, that we had

not been defeated, that Hawaiian people had spoken up to protect the graves of their ancestors and that somehow, someday, there would be a cataclysmic shift. I had no reason to feel this way, but perhaps in stepping forward and speaking up we had reconnected to our ancestors in a fundamental way.[7]

Hall further laments.

> The hui was faced with a daunting dilemma. How could it participate in devising the conditions under which the very burials it had sought to protect were dug up? The thrust of the testimony had been that there was nothing inherently sensitive about disinterment... For the Hui, it was not so simple, and as the crisis of conscience deepened, the kūpuna buried in the Honokahua sand dune made their presence known.[8]

One can imagine the kaumaha (heaviness) experienced by Hui Alanui o Mākena members during this time of this deepening "crisis of conscience." I would describe what Hui Alanui o Mākena was experiencing as a spiritual situation in which there is a need to connect to kūpuna (ancestors) for inspiration, insight, and understanding in order to help lift the kaumaha and understand the path forward. In our training, the pule (prayer) that would have been applicable to this situation is Pule Ikaika (Prayer for Strength), which aptly provides.

> E ke Akua mau loa kiʻekiʻe a me nā kūpuna o mākou
> E aloha mai ʻoukou i nā mea i kaumaha ʻia
> E kala wale mai ʻoukou i ko mākou hewa
> A me ko mākou haumia
> A me ko mākou ʻai kū
> A me ko mākou ʻaiā
> A me ko mākou waha heʻe
> A me ko mākou hoʻohiki ʻino ʻana iā ʻoukou
> E nā mai ko ʻoukou inaina me ko mākou haʻahaʻa
> E maliu mai ʻoukou
> E hoʻōla iā mākou i nā mea Hawaiʻi kūpono
> E hoʻāla iā mākou i ka naʻau pono no kēia hana
> E hoʻohui iā mākou i hoʻokahi manaʻo
> ʻO ko ʻoukou manaʻo ka mea pololei

Alaila nō, e holo mua mākou i ka ikaika i ka haʻahaʻa i ka manaʻo
   huikauʻole
A me ka hoʻomaopopo o kēia hana nui
Eia no mākou ka ʻoukou keiki moʻopuna kekahi
A noho mai noho mai noho mai
A pēlā no ʻāmama ua noa

To the God of the highest and also to our ancestors
Be kind to us who are burdened
Pardon us for our mistakes
And our imperfections
And our ceremonial faults
And our weaknesses of the heart
And our speech impediments
And our non-fulfillment of vows
Let your anger be appeased by our humility this day
Look with favor upon us
Grant life to us in the true Hawaiian sense
Awaken within us the true depth of this work
Allow us to become one in mind
Your thoughts are the correct ones
And only then will we go forward in strength, in humility,
   with unprecedented ideals
And with the understanding of this important function
We are here your children, your descendants
Abide with us, so be it[9]
Thus, it is finish, it is free.

According to Hall, Hui Alanui o Mākena was able to:

> Put a definitive end to the dilemma about whether to participate in
> developing procedures for the disinterment plan. The kūpuna had shown
> themselves and we could not ignore what was about to happen to them. If
> anything, we had a duty to be there to comfort them and to bear witness
> to the coming acts of desecration.[10]

Without formal training in the care of iwi kūpuna, two members of Hui
Alanui o Mākena, Ron Makaula Dela Cruz and Leslie Kuloloio, were moved

to conduct a ceremony. It was Dela Cruz who sensed a strong need to prepare a hoʻokupu (offering) of mea ʻai (food) and kapa (bark cloth) which he had never done before. The two men sat with the kūpuna at the dunes and ate with them while natural weather signs surrounded and inspired. A connection to the kūpuna of Honokahua was established that included clarity of thought on how to proceed.

The kuleana for Hui Alanui o Mākena was now clear—they must participate and watch over the kūpuna and must ensure they are returned to the sands of Honokahua. The level of courage required to reach such a conclusion given the heaviness of the situation warrants acknowledgement. It is also important to recognize that instincts generated in our naʻau (small intestines, which Hawaiians acknowledge as the seat of thought, intellect and emotion), which may have lain dormant for generations, are still present and functional within the Hawaiian conscience and activated when ceremonial protocols are performed to establish ʻike pāpālua (avenues of communication) with the kūpuna. This was a pivotal event.

Hui Alanui o Mākena would spend the next several months negotiating with Paul H. Rosendahl, Inc. (PHRI), the archaeological firm hired by Kapalua Land Company, to fashion procedures for the removal, storage, examination, and reburial of the iwi kūpuna and moepū, which were memorialized in a signed memorandum of agreement (MOA) amongst the four parties. The perspective of Hui Alanui o Mākena on this challenging process was as follows.

> Our primary position, from which we never wavered, was that the burial site should be protected and preserved, not dug up. Lacking the power to impose our point of view on the other parties, we turned our attention to limiting the amount of disturbance that would occur to the iwi kūpuna, especially with regard to osteological examinations, and to assure that any moepū, grave goods, found with specific individuals would be reburied together with those same individuals. We had no example to go by. Instead, we had to think deeply and feel our way around problems, guided by the overriding desire to reduce whatever possible additional harm to the kūpuna. It later turned out that the resolutions of many of the thorny issues we puzzled over (before arriving at a way to handle them) constituted the precursor thinking necessary to—and later incorporated in—Hawaiʻi's burial law, Chapter 6E-32. But that was several years away.[11]

Disinterment by PHRI began in August of 1987 and involved a handful of archaeologists. Strict adherence to the terms of the MOA was advocated by Hui Alanui o Mākena to ensure that the least intrusive methods of handling of the iwi were used, that moepū found with an individual be kept with the individual for reburial purposes, and that storage of each individual was documented accurately. In a year's time, several hundred kūpuna had been disinterred with still work ongoing. The methodic removal and storage process was both time-consuming and expensive, but as the months passed on, the pace of removal quickened.

Kapalua Land Company raised concerns that the project would not be able to meet the requirement to initiate construction within the two-year window following the grant of the SMA permit. Kapalua Land Company proposed a plan to accelerate disinterment from the lower dune and to begin construction in the lower dune while removal continued in the upper dune. A barrier would be erected to separate the two areas. In addition, the archaeological crew was significantly expanded and excavations accelerated. Hui Alanui o Mākena vehemently opposed Kapalua Land Company's plan, reiterating its consistent opposition to the disinterment and stating that if the developer was unable to comply with the terms of the MOA, disinterment should be halted in its entirety. To promote opposition to the proposed plan, Dana Nāone Hall solicited the support of the Office of Hawaiian Affairs (OHA), one of the signatories to the MOA. The strategy was that if two of the signatories were opposed to amending the process, it would place pressure on the State Historic Preservation Officer, a third signatory, to oppose the plan, and if not, it would at least create a stalemate. The OHA trustees agreed to oppose the Kapalua Land Company's proposed plan.

Awareness of the situation at Honokahua increased in the community. Edward Kanahele, husband of Pualani Kanaka'ole Kanahele, wrote a letter to the editor bringing attention to the dire situation at Honokahua and media coverage swelled placing Honokahua at the forefront of the thoughts and conscience of many throughout Hawai'i. Dana Nāone Hall describes this situation as follows.

> Disturbing and displacing Native Hawaiian iwi was not new. What differentiated Honokahua was a drawn-out excavation process that occurred over many months, not a quick unearthing and scattering witnessed by a few. It provided the time necessary for people to comprehend the magnitude of what was happening and, most importantly, to reflect on the

spiritual and moral dimensions of such actions. Once the reality of Honokahua pierced the public conscience, the digging had to stop.

Community members throughout the islands were outraged by the
news coming out of Honokahua, with the disinterments numbering 791 individuals by mid-October 1988, and a minimum of sixty individuals identified
from the scattered bone material collected at the site. What followed was an
outpouring of concern, anguish, disbelief, and sheer determination to halt
further excavations. Concerned Hawaiians and their supporters opposed the
disinterments and demanded a halt to the excavations. In mid-October, a
protest was held opposing the excavations. On December 11, a protest was
held at Honokahua, and some placed blame on Hui Alanui o Mākena and
the Office of Hawaiian Affairs, while others recognized that the responsibility
lay with the county planning commission for granting the SMA permit for
the development without meaningful consultation with the Hawaiian community. There simply was no legal authority to protect unmarked burial sites.
Emotions were running high. On December 20, Governor John Waiheʻe
appointed a two-person task force to review whether Honokahua should be
used as a resort location.[12] Starting on December 22, 1988, a twenty-four-hour
vigil was held at the state capitol to protest the excavation at Honokahua. The
vigil then moved to the grounds of ʻIolani Palace.

Immediately following the vigil, Governor Waiheʻe met with concerned
Hawaiian activists, calling the matter a moral issue, and stating that the digging must stop. The task force he established was tasked with resolving the
dispute. The governor was joined by Maui Mayor Hannibal Tavares, who
also supported an end to the excavations. The Kapalua Land Company stated
that although it had all of its permits, and therefore the legal right to proceed,
it would briefly halt the excavations in recognition of a cooling off period,
and to attempt to work out a solution. Maui Land and Pineapple Company
President Colin Cameron stated publicly that he was "very sensitive to the
Hawaiians' concerns, since [he] was born there."[13] Cameron further stated
that it was not practical to consider an alternate site for the hotel. However,
Harold Masumoto, state planning director and task force member, maintained that relocation of the hotel was the only real option. Cameron went
on to state that disinterment efforts would resume if state and county officials
did not offer a solution soon.[14]

As it turns out, the excavations did not resume and Kapalua Land Company agreed to change its plans. In the ensuing months, a resolution was

reached whereby the State of Hawai'i purchased a preservation and conservation easement from Kapalua Land Company for the 13.6-acre property for $5 million dollars and paid $500,000 for the reburial of the iwi kūpuna and moepū of an estimated 1,100 ancestral Hawaiians back to their original place of interment. The hotel was moved inland to allow for the protection of the Honokahua burial site in perpetuity. An estimated one thousand additional ancestral graves were left in place, undisturbed. The four parties to the MOA signed the Honokahua Burial Site Agreement, which replaced most of the MOA and effectively concluded all remaining legalities.

In the months that followed, the next monumental challenge for Hui Alanui o Mākena would be to ceremonially reinter the 1,100 iwi kūpuna and their moepū back into their original burial sites in the upper and lower dunes. Making this task even more daunting was the lack of any known protocol for doing so. As they had done from the beginning, the group would follow their na'au instincts, pooling their knowledge of mortuary practices and continuing to connect to the kūpuna for inspiration and guidance. A group was formed and led by noted kapa maker Pua Van Dorpe to prepare the kapa to wrap the iwi kūpuna and moepū for reinterment. The wrapping of the iwi took place in two phases, based on their place of origin.

A reburial of all the individuals, artifacts and manuports[15] from the lower dune were reinterred in one phase back in the lower dune, and a second phase involved the reinterment of the iwi, artifacts and manuports collected from the upper dune back to that dune feature.[16]

In the end, Hui Alanui o Mākena was able to protect in place approximately half of the iwi kūpuna and moepū buried at Honokahua, and rebury the other half where their families had originally interred them. The circle was now complete. Hall describes the situation as follows.

During negotiations regarding the Honokahua Site, Colin Cameron stated that what he and his partners sought in the resolution of the issue was to be made whole again. I might add that our cultural desire as Hawaiians paralleled that economic desire, and by the end of April of this year [1990], the site was made whole again with the reinterment of the iwi.[17]

The momentum created by the powerful events at Honokahua carried over into the legislative realm.

Photo of Honokahua burial site during excavations. (Photo by Ken Miller, *Honolulu Star-Bulletin*, Tues. Jan. 3, 1989.) Courtesy of the Hawai'i State Archives.

Photo of Honokahua burial site during excavations (from the collection of Dana Nāone Hall, Hui Alanui o Mākena)

Photo of gathering at Honokahua to acknowledge that the burials and moepū had all been reinterred and the site would be protected in perpetuity based on a conservation easement with the State of Hawai'i. Hawaiians from across the islands offered ho'okupu to the iwi kūpuna on May 6, 1990. The State Legislature had just passed the new burial law (from the collection of Dana Nāone Hall, Hui Alanui o Makena). Courtesy of Masako Cordray.

ACT 306 (SESSION 1990)

While the Honokahua issue was being resolved, a bill was introduced during the 1989 legislative session to amend Hawaii Revised Statutes Chapter 6E, the state historic preservation law, to establish greater protection for unmarked burial sites over fifty years old. The intent was to create a legally binding process that would prevent a situation similar to Honokahua from happening again. However, the lawmakers did not approve legislation that session. Nonetheless, Chairman William Patty of the State of Hawai'i Department of Land and Natural Resources (DLNR), who also served as the Hawai'i State Historic Preservation Officer, announced that DLNR would administratively establish five island burial councils to assist the state in its decision-making regarding unmarked burial sites over fifty years old. Interim councils were established for the islands of Hawai'i, Maui/Lāna'i, Moloka'i, O'ahu, and Kaua'i/Ni'ihau in an advisory capacity to assist the newly established Hawai'i

State Historic Preservation Division. The councils were comprised of Hawaiian community and large landowner representatives, with the majority of members being of Hawaiian ancestry. This was a significant development in the march toward legal empowerment of Hawaiians to speak on behalf of their ancestors in matters involving the proper treatment of unmarked burial sites over fifty years old.

In the summer of 1989, efforts were undertaken to consult with Hawaiian stakeholders and large landowner/developer representatives to work out issues of contention contained in the previous failed legislation. It was no secret that developers opposed the bill, and unless their concerns were addressed, or at least flushed out to determine whether resolution could be achieved, the fate of the next legislation would be no different. Having just graduated from law school at the University of Colorado, and having just taken the Hawaiʻi Bar Exam, this author had just joined the Native Hawaiian Legal Corporation.

My caseload included the representation of a Hawaiian named Kalāhoʻohie Mossman, on whose behalf amendments to the historic preservation law would be undertaken. Work on redrafting the legislation also included Dr Don Hibbard, administrator of the State Historic Preservation Division, and Dr. Davianna McGregor, a professor from the University of Hawaiʻi at Mānoa. A critical issue was the identification of the state agency that would house the program which would administer the island burial councils and support the work on Hawaiian burial sites. At that time, there was a lack of faith in the ability and commitment of the Office of Hawaiian Affairs to do so. As a result, the revised legislation named DLNR as the appropriate agency through its State Historic Preservation Division.[18]

Following numerous consultation and strategy meetings, advocacy efforts, testimonies before state house and senate committees, and a conversation with then speaker of the Hawaiʻi House Representative Henry Peters (who was also a Bishop Estate Trustee), the legislature passed Act 306,[19] amending the state historic preservation law to:

- establish permanent island burial councils made up of regional area and large landowner/developer representatives;[20]
- authorize the councils to determine the treatment of previously identified native Hawaiian burial sites over fifty years old;[21]
- establish criteria to determine whether to preserve in place or relocate native Hawaiian burial sites;[22]

- delineate a process for the treatment of inadvertently discovered human skeletal remains;[23]
- increase penalties for burial site violations;[24]
- require the promulgation of administrative rules to implement the new law;[25] and
- exempt department records relating to the location and description of burial sites from the requirements of HRS section 92F-12.[26]

In September 1990, this author left the practice of law at the Native Hawaiian Legal Corporation to become the first coordinator of the newly established Burial Sites Program at the State Historic Preservation Division. While in this capacity, I administered the island burial councils, educated state and local agencies about the new burial law, and helped promulgate Hawai'i Administrative Rules Chapter 13-300 in 1996, entitled, Rules of Practice and Procedure Relating to Burial Sites and Human Remains, to implement the 1990 amendments to HRS Chapter 6E.[27]

The momentum of Honokahua led to the enactment of a promising new state law that sought to place responsibility for determining treatment of Hawaiian burial sites with the Hawaiian community while seeking to balance the interests of large property owners and developers. Dana Nāone Hall acknowledges this nexus.

> This significant piece of legislation is the direct result of what occurred at Honokahua with the uncovering of the site and its second and final sealing, emphasizing one interpretation of the name Kapalua as twice covered. I share in the deep satisfaction of the many people who helped to bring about the particular resolution at Honokahua and the more generalized and far-reaching protection that is afforded all prehistoric burial sites through the new legislation.

AT THE NATIONAL LEVEL

While the complexities of Honokahua were unfolding in the islands, at the national level a debate was raging over the treatment of Native American skeletal remains and funerary objects held by museums, federal agencies, and other federally funded institutions. Federal legislation S. 978 was pending at the time that would establish a process for repatriation of Native American human remains from the Smithsonian Institute. US Senator Daniel Inouye, chairman of the US Senate Committee on Indian Affairs, assigned staffers Lurline McGregor and this author to pose the question to the Hawaiian community as to which organization should be named in the legislation to conduct repatriation. On October 2, 1989, a burials symposium was held at the state capitol and this specific question was posed. The response was to name the group Mālama I Nā Kūpuna O Hawaiʻi Nei, which was established by Edward and Pualani Kanahele in response to the events at Honokahua.

On November 28, 1989, President George Bush signed S. 978 into law,[28] which established "a living memorial to Native Americans and their traditions which shall be known as the National Museum of the American Indian."[29] The law further requires the secretary of the Smithsonian Institute to inventory and identify all Native American human remains and funerary objects in its collections and if by a preponderance of the evidence the human remains are identified as being Native Hawaiian, the secretary is required to "enter into an agreement with appropriate Native Hawaiian organizations with expertise in Native Hawaiian affairs (which may include the Office of Hawaiian Affairs and Mālama I Nā Kūpuna o Hawaiʻi Nei) to provide for the return of such human remains and funerary objects."[30]

On May 14, 1990, Hui Mālama I Nā Kūpuna O Hawaiʻi Nei (Hui Mālama) discovered that a partial inventory of the Hawaiian remains was completed on December 1, 1989. Thereafter, Hui Mālama completed the inventory and arranged for repatriation. On July 18, 1990, thirteen Hui Mālama members entered the Smithsonian Museum of Natural History and ceremonially prepared eighty iwi kūpuna for repatriation. However, the group was forced to leave behind the skulls of 132 kūpuna from the island of Kauaʻi which were to await repatriation by community members. While Native Hawaiians were the first to repatriate under the new law, its authority was limited to the Smithsonian Institute. Many federal agencies and institutions across the United States have in their possession the remains and funerary objects of thousands of Native Americans, including Native Hawaiians. A more comprehensive law was needed to be inclusive of these institutions and to expand the scope of what items qualify for repatriation.

On November 16, 1990, the Native American Graves Protection and Repatriation Act (NAGPRA), Pub. L. 101-601, 25 USC 3001 et seq., 104 Stat. 3048, was enacted. NAGPRA requires federal agencies and institutions that receive federal funding to return Native American, which includes Native Hawaiian, cultural items such as human skeletal remains, funerary objects, sacred objects and cultural patrimony to lineal descendants, culturally affiliated Indian tribes, Alaska Native Corporations, and Native Hawaiian organizations. NAGPRA is widely seen as human rights law, as property law and as administrative law. Both the Office of Hawaiian Affairs and Hui Mālama are specifically named in NAGPRA as having standing to submit claims for repatriation. Since 1990, Hui Mālama has conducted over 100 repatriation cases based upon the authority of NAGPRA, which is discussed in the next section. In addition, the first dispute of a museum decision to refuse to repatriate pursuant to NAGPRA was filed by Hui Mālama against the University of California Phoebe Apperson Hearst Museum. The NAGPRA Review Committee recommended repatriation of one skull and the examination of the second to confirm its cultural affiliation. That skull was confirmed to be Native Hawaiian and repatriated.

NAGPRA also establishes procedures for the inadvertent discovery or planned excavation of Native American cultural items on federal or tribal lands, which for Hawaiians is defined as Hawaiian Home Lands. Furthermore, NAGPRA makes it a criminal offense to traffic in Native American human remains without right of possession, or in Native American cultural items obtained in violation of the Act. Penalties for a first offense may reach twelve months imprisonment and a $100,000 fine.[31]

Hui Mālama I Nā Kūpuna O Hawai'i Nei

Born from the mana of Honokahua was a Native Hawaiian organization named Hui Mālama I Nā Kūpuna O Hawai'i Nei, as discussed above. The group was trained in contemporary cultural and spiritual practices regarding the care of iwi kūpuna and moepū, which were grounded in traditional knowledge, values, and practices. The organization was intended to be an interim response to the problems created by the desecration of ancestral Hawaiian burials by the Kapalua Land Company.

Native Hawaiian identity is defined in a multitude of ways. The following discussion focuses on traditional values, thoughts, practices, and wise sayings that have helped shape an important part of this identity—specifically, the fundamental responsibility to care for and protect iwi kūpuna and moepū.[32] The term Kanaka 'Ōiwi is a traditional way of identifying ourselves as indigenous people. While kanaka is a generic term for *people*, the word 'ōiwi metaphorically means *native*, but literally translates as, *of the bone*. The word ʻōiwi defines us as the indigenous people of Hawaiʻi and also demonstrates that Hawaiian identity is a function of the bones of our ancestors. This is based on the belief that iwi contain mana (spiritual essence), even after death. Thus, who we are includes those ancestors who came before us.

Likewise, our homeland is referred to as kulāiwi, which literally translates as *bone plain* and which means *native land*, indicating a connection between the land and the people. Our homeland is defined as the place in which the bones of our ancestors and eventually ourselves and our descendants, are buried. Kulāiwi indicates an inter-relationship between ʻōiwi and ka ʻāina (the land). Note again the presence of the root word iwi as it relates to ʻōiwi, another expression of Hawaiian identity. In addition, the word kanu means both, *to bury/a burial,* and *to plant/a planting.* The first kanu in the moʻolelo (oral traditions) of our people was the burial of Hāloanaka, the still-born child of Wākea and Hoʻohōkūkalani. From that spot grew the first kalo (taro), our staple food. Their next son was also named Hāloa and it is from him that Kanaka ʻŌiwi descend. This moʻolelo establishes the interconnection between the gods, the land, and the people. The burial of iwi results in physical growth of plants and the spiritual growth of mana. The descendants feed off the foods of the land and are nourished spiritually by the knowledge that the iwi kūpuna are well cared for and in their rightful place. The people of old understood well the importance of protecting and caring for iwi kūpuna. Each family identified those who carried the kuleana (responsibility) of ensuring that all iwi received kanu pono (a proper burial). This meant that the iwi were buried with ceremony and treasured possessions needed in the spiritual world were hoʻomoepū ʻia (laid to rest) with the iwi. Secrecy was important. The iwi and moepū were hidden, for those who sought a person's mana would seek the bones to appropriate their spiritual power. The tranquility of a person's spirit depends on the level of protection provided to his or her iwi.

Conducting proper burials was especially important for Kanaka ʻŌiwi because of the belief that ancestors became ʻaumākua (guardians) of living descendants and that these ʻaumākua must be cared for in order to maintain the pono (balance and unity) of the family. The kuleana to care for iwi kūpuna was the same as the responsibility to maintain harmony between the living, the dead, and the land. At the level of the aliʻi nui (ruling chief), the ability to maintain the tranquility of the kingdom was dependent upon the degree to which the aliʻi cared for the akua (gods) and ʻaumākua. This was evidenced in part by the state of gravesites throughout the islands. When there was peace in the kingdom, the people were buried properly; when there were treacherous rulers, the bones were dug up.

Ola nā iwi is a traditional saying that translates to *the bones live*. It is said of an elder who is well cared for by his or her family and also of the family members who provide such care. This ʻōlelo noʻeau serves to remind us that our kūpuna (ancestors) reside within our own iwi. Thus, we are the sum of all ancestral family members who collectively gave us life. This relationship gives rise to a profound duty to care for and protect the bones of our kūpuna. The care of the iwi kūpuna is a kuleana (duty, responsibility, privilege) more than anything else. The relationship between the ancestors and the living is best described as interdependent, whereby each cares for and protects the other. Families maintain this particular kuleana by assuring that the ancestors are kanu pono, or properly buried and protected. This responsibility also recognizes that the physical and spiritual health of the family is a function of the well-being of the ancestors.

One important way to maintain the kuleana to care for the iwi is to prevent their exposure, as explained by the saying, Mai kaulaʻi i nā iwi i ka lā, which means *don't expose the bones to the sun*. One reason to prevent exposure of iwi is that the ʻuhane (spirit) associated with the iwi resides in a world known as pō, or darkness. Thus, the proper place for iwi is to be placed in the ʻāina so mana from the iwi can nourish the land physically and spiritually. From this ʻōlelo noʻeau we understand that the responsibility to care for the iwi includes protection from disturbances that would result in exposure. Another ʻōlelo noʻeau provides that the placement of items with the iwi establishes an inseparable bond between both, whereby the items are forever considered moepū, or the possession of the dead. Mai lawe wale i nā mea i hoʻomoepū ʻia, which translates to, *don't wantonly take things placed with the dead*, makes clear that the prohibition against disturbing iwi extends to moepū.[33] These values demonstrate the profound respect and aloha held for the ancestors which form another basis for the kuleana to care for their bones. By protecting the iwi and burial sites, the ancestors' connection to their place of burial is assured. Maintaining the kuleana to care for the iwi and moepū is a profound expression of our cultural identity as Kanaka ʻŌiwi. It is hoped that the time has come for all iwi kūpuna that have been removed from ancestral burial sites to be kanu pono (properly buried). By reburying the iwi, the ancestral foundation is strengthened, the interdependence between the past and present continues, and the land is reinfused with mana necessary to sustain the ancestors, the living, and the generations to come.

ʻAuamo i ke Kuleana (Carry the Responsibility)

The achievements I am about to share are the result of the application of knowledge and instincts gained from ancestry, education, and Hawaiian cultural training in discipline, courage, and focus to help restore the ancestral foundation. Our work involved the identification, negotiation, and repatriation of over six thousand ancestral Hawaiian remains from museums, government agencies, and private individuals in the United States (a total of 118 cases). In some of the cases, we partnered with Native Hawaiian organizations, including the Office of Hawaiian Affairs and the island burial councils.

Notable institutions in the United States included the Smithsonian Museum of Natural History, American Museum of Natural History, Field Museum of Natural History, University of Pennsylvania Museum of Archaeology, Bernice Pauahi Bishop Museum, University of California Phoebe Apperson Hearst Museum, Peabody & Essex Museum, Harvard University Peabody Museum of Archaeology, Yale University Peabody Museum of Natural History, Dartmouth College Hood Museum of Art, US Navy, US Army, US Air Force, and the US Fish and Wildlife Service. In addition, thirteen international repatriation cases were conducted from such institutions as the University of Zurich (Switzerland), South Australian Museum, Royal Ontario Museum (Canada), University of Edinburgh (Scotland), Statens Historiska Museet and the Karolinska Institutet (Sweden), Maidstone Museum, Hunterian Museum, Royal College of Surgeons of England, Natural History Museum, Science Museum/Wellcome Trust, Oxford Museum of Natural History (England), and the Museum für Volkerkunde Dresden (Germany). The complete list of repatriations is on file with the author.

Strategic Approaches

Over the past twenty-nine years, we have empowered ourselves by inviting and involving our ancestors to guide us. We have been trained to utilize and trust our ancestral instincts. In death, our ancestors yearn to be a part of the family again. We used them in this way and believe they want us to because, by doing so, by uttering their name, by asking for their help and guidance, by placing them in the position of supporting the family once again—they live on. Strategically, we advocated legal principles, including free prior and informed consent.[34] We maintain that absent consent, acquisition is de facto theft, and theft cannot form the basis for the legitimate acquisition and continued possession of ancestral human remains and funerary possessions. Theft is theft. Strategically, we also sought to create favorable *battlefield* conditions, if you will. We must be careful in asserting legal rights, as in our experience we have seen museums respond by asserting their perceived legal rights that resulted in drawn out legal disputes. Instead, we asserted that our claim is based primarily on our kuleana, or cultural duty, as living descendants, and that we were the only party to this dispute that held these duties to the ancestral remains. Whereas museums seek to take from the ancestors, we seek to give back to them their place in our family. We asserted that our position is humane and that of the museums is not. We further asserted that there is no room at the family table for the museum's asserted rights to continue the taking, which at its very best, only reifies the ill impacts of colonialism. In these expressions of humanity, the fact that we seek to restore our family, says something about us. The fact that museums seek to maintain separation says something about them.

In addition, we learned to protect ourselves from the psychological harm inherent in the revelation that our ancestors were stolen, repeatedly, and shipped off to foreign places without knowledge or consent. Each time we learned of a repeated heinous act of burial site desecration, we were subjected to an incredible level of harm. Our protection came in the form of pule, the traditional prayers taught to us, and knowing who we are as Kanaka ʻŌiwi. Armed with such understanding, we were able to shield ourselves from these ill effects. In making this statement I don't mean to imply that we were not get negatively impacted. We were. However, we learned to positively process this negativity so that it did not consume us in anger and weaken our ability to focus on the goal of returning the ancestor's home.

We were trained to understand that negativity demands a seat at the table, and that we must make room for it. By acknowledging the negative and putting it in its place, we achieve a balanced perspective and establish the confidence to proceed and be successful. Strategically, our principle tools in these repatriation disputes are our humanity, our aloha, and our values of ʻohana (family) that are especially respectful of kūpuna. By respecting our ancestors through repatriation and reburial, we demonstrate profound respect for ourselves and provide a powerful lesson to our keiki (children) to love themselves, to help them know that they are never alone and to help protect their minds from the extremely harmful thoughts that can lead to suicide, and to understand and appreciate their place in the remarkable lineage that is our Hawaiian people.

We were trained to initiate a repatriation case by envisioning the result, which of course is reburial. Next, we would embrace that vision with all our heart and soul, which in Hawaiian means we would internalize it in our naʻau and prevent any doubt from entering our minds. We would then work backward with the confidence that we would prevail because we already know the outcome. This approach proved effective over the twenty-nine years of our repatriation and reburial work. We would project confidence and clarity of thought through our advocacy work. In the tradition of the royal twins Kamanawa and Kameʻeiamoku, I would offer the museum either peace or battle. It did not matter which option they chose, as the outcome would be the same. In international repatriation cases involving the Natural History Museum in London (which lasted 23 years) and the Staatliches Museum fur Volkerkunde in Dresden (26 years), both of which were highly contentious, the ancestors were repatriated. Perseverance is key, as the outcome does not come with a timeline. It is not whether they will come home, it's when.

Our national repatriation work involved implementation of the Native American Graves Protection and Repatriation Act and the National Museum of the American Indian Act. There is no equivalent legal authority in the international arena, unless a particular foreign country has a law that supports, or at least provides, for repatriation, like the 2004 Human Tissues Act in England. Most museums comply in good faith. There is no international prohibition on the assertion of aloha, of ʻohana, and of mālama iwi kūpuna. These are universal values that apply in all jurisdictions and form the foundation of Hawaiian law and the basis for our claims of responsibility for iwi and moepū.

Since 2007, with passage of the United Nations Declaration of the Rights of Indigenous Peoples, we asserted these declarations in certain international repatriation cases, principally as the context to effectively frame the dispute vis-à-vis the museum and our organization as claimant. With the declaration as the proper context, we then asserted our Hawaiian values as the controlling principles in the absence of statutory law or other legal authority. We assert a family's inherent ability and right to remain together because the treatment of the dead and their possessions are principally family matters. Museums would consistently assert the need for scientific study to glean information from human remains to justify maintaining possession. We responded by asserting that while science is an important undertaking, it is not an absolute right and cannot overcome the values and principles of ʻohana (family).

Through my repatriation experiences I came to coin the term, *intellec-*

tual savagery. An intellectual savage is one who utilizes his or her intellect to deny others their humanity. Strategically, we use this tool to overcome the museum argument for continued possession of human remains and funerary possessions for scientific purposes, while simultaneously ignoring our family values, which are an important source of our laws.

On January 23, 2015, at the direction of our kumu, I formally dissolved Hui Mālama I Nā Kūpuna O Hawai'i Nei. The organization was never intended to be permanent but rather an interim response while the awareness of this important kuleana was restored to the na'au of the Hawaiian people. This goal has certainly been achieved. Because cases are still pending especially in the international arena, my efforts to conduct repatriation have now shifted to support the Office of Hawaiian Affairs, which under the leadership of Ka Pouhana Dr. Kamana'opono Crabbe, has significantly increased efforts on several pending cases.

The Case of the Ebay Sale of an Iwi Po'o from Kā'anapali

On September 8, 2004, a man from Los Angeles, California was charged with violating the Archaeological Resources Protection Act (ARPA) after he sold the skull of an ancestral Native Hawaiian on the internet. Jerry David Hasson was named in the one-count criminal complaint that alleged he had offered the skull for sale on Ebay.com. He claimed that it was a two-hundred-year-old warrior who died on Maui in the 1790s.[35] On his Ebay.com page, which included a picture of the iwi po'o (which is highly offensive because of the exposure of the iwi), Hasson posted the following statements in February 2004.

> I personally discovered this human skull [pictured], along with the entire skeletal remains, in the summer of 1969 on the Kaanapali Beach on Maui. At that time, the site was being excavated for the development of the Whaler's Village and when a field of battle artifacts and human remains were uncovered, construction was halted while an historical investigation was conducted by the Lahaina Historical Society and the Bishop Museum. From the battle artifacts and skeletal remains uncovered, it was determined that this location was one of King Kamehameha's bloody battle sites in his war to unite the Hawaiian Islands in the 1790's and that the remains uncovered were of Hawaiian warriors who fought for or against King Kamehameha. Guards were posted at the excavation site to keep out the curious. Being a teenager, I along with some friends (including Fra-

sier Heston, the son of Charlton Heston) decided to sneak over late one
night and see what we could find. While digging in the sand, we began
to uncover an entire skeleton and, of course, I decided to keep the skull.[36]

Hasson put the skull up for auction with bidding starting at $1,000 and with
an immediate purchase price of $12,500.

> For the last thirty-five years, I've kept this 200-year-old Hawaiian Warrior
> as a souvenir of my youth but now it's time to give him up to the highest
> bidder. Included with this brave warrior's skull comes a notarized Certif-
> icate of Authenticity.[37]

Shortly after the offer to sell was posted on Ebay, Manu Boyd and Anne
Keʻala Kelly of the Office of Hawaiian Affairs notified the author about the
posting. On behalf of Hui Mālama, I contacted Hasson by email, and then
by telephone, to warn him that selling the skull was a violation of federal law.
I recall him telling me something to the effect that the skull was his property. I responded that actually it's the remains of a person. I further advised
Hasson to immediately terminate the sale and to return the iwi poʻo (skull)
to our organization for ceremonial reburial. Soon after that conversation, I
was contacted by telephone by John H. Fryar, a special agent from the US
Department of the Interior, Bureau of Indian Affairs, Office of Law Enforcement Services, who was monitoring Hasson's Ebay site. He had seen my email
warning Hasson that the sale of the skull could violate ARPA. Special agent
Fryar contacted Hasson and, posing as a buyer, negotiated the purchase of
the skull.

> Hasson told the undercover agent that there might be a problem with the
> selling of the skull because it was an antiquity. Hasson then proposed that
> he would present the skull as a gift to the agent if he purchased another
> one of Hasson's auction items. On February 12, the agent sent Hasson a
> cashier's check in the amount of $2,500 for the purchase of a collector's
> edition of a comic book fanzine. On February 18, the agent received the
> skull from Hasson via Federal Express at his office in New Mexico.[38]

Thereafter, an expert from the University of Hawaiʻi Department of Anthropology examined the skull and identified it as an adult female, approximately
fifty years old at the time of death, and of Polynesian ancestry who lived in

precontact Hawai'i prior to 1778. Hasson was facing the maximum punishment of five years in prison and a fine of up to $250,000.

As part of the its case, the U.S. Attorney's Office obtained a declaration from Rev. Charles Kauluwehi Maxwell, Sr., aged sixty-six, who at that time was a senior board member of Hui Mālama, to corroborate certain elements of Hasson's Ebay posting, specifically with regard to the circumstances under which he obtained the skull (such as being with Frasier Heston, son of actor Charlton Heston) and the location and timing of the discovery (during the development of Whaler's Village at Kā'anapali Beach). Maxwell attested to the following:

7. The motion picture movie, *The Hawaiians* was filmed on locations on the Island of Maui in 1969 including Mā'alaea and Lāhaina.
8. I had a small part in the movie, *The Hawaiians* as a keystone cop and met Charlton Heston during filming. I even have a picture with him. At that time (1969), I was 34 years old and working as a policeman for Maui County.
9. The actors in the movie, including Charlton Heston and Geraldine Chapman, stayed at the Sheraton Maui Hotel located at Black Rock in Kā'anapali. I know this because I went to the Sheraton with them after filming.
10. At that time (1969), there was construction work going on next to the Sheraton Maui Hotel. This was for the Whaler's Village Shopping Center, situated approximately 300 yards away from the hotel in the direction of Lāhaina.
11. The property where the Whaler's Village Shopping Center was built upon is a remnant sand dune.
12. Traditionally, it was a common practice for Native Hawaiians to bury their deceased family members in sand dunes. Here on Maui, hundreds of iwi kūpuna (ancestral bones) and moepū (funerary possessions) originally buried in sand dunes have been disturbed by construction activities.[39]

In Special Agent Fryar's affidavit, he states the following.

6. On February 4, 2004, I received information that a 200-year old skull of a Native Hawaiian (the skull) was being offered for sale on an Ebay Internet auction site. The auction was reported by Anne Keala Kelly,

a Native Hawaiian and resident of Hawaii, who provided information relating to Ebay auction number 3271708941, with the heading
200 YEAR OLD HAWAIIAN HUMAN SKULL. Ms. Kelly stated
that while the auction of the skull had been closed, it was still available to be viewed on the Ebay auction site.

7. I later received (from the Bishop Museum located in Honolulu,
Hawaii) a copy of an email message dated February 3, 2004, that
had been sent to the person offering the skull for sale on Ebay (later
identified as JERRY DAVID HASSON) from Edward Halealoha
Ayau, who is a member of a Native Hawaiian organization known
as Hui Malama I Na Kupuna O Hawaiʻi Nei. The purpose of this
organization is to provide guidance and expertise in decisions dealing
with Native Hawaiian cultural issues, particularly burial issues. In his
message to HASSON, Edward Ayau advised the following:

a. The sale of the skull would be a violation of Title 18 USC 1170,
   and that Native Hawaiians are considered Native Americans under
   NAGPRA.
b. The sale of the skull might also violate the federal Archaeological Resources Protection Act (ARPA), Title 16 USC 470, et seq.,
   which prohibits the interstate or foreign commerce in archaeological resources that may have been unlawfully removed in violation
   of any state or local laws.
c. HASSON should therefore terminate the sale of the skull and return
   it to the Native Hawaiian organization for ceremonial reburial.
d. "Your (HASSON's) theft and now attempted sale of our ancestor's
   remains offends us deeply."
e. "Our goal is to provide proper care and treatment for all of our
   ancestors. Be respectful and do the right thing."[40]

Defendant Hasson signed a plea agreement in which he plead guilty
to "trafficking in interstate commerce of an archaeological resource, namely
the skull of a Native Hawaiian, in violation of 16 USC §470ee(c)."[41] Defendant Hasson also agreed to pay full restitution to the victims of the offense,
including Hui Mālama for costs to be incurred in repatriating the skull back
to Hawaiʻi. Based on information provided in part by Hui Mālama, US
District Court Judge Howard Matz convicted and sentenced Hasson to a
$13,000 fine, six hundred hours of community service to be served helping

the elderly of his community, and a written public apology to be printed in the Honolulu Advertiser and Ka Wai Ola (the OHA newsletter). Additionally, an Ebay bulletin board dedicated to archaeological memorabilia was created. Hui Mālama recommended jail time in addition to these terms, but the judge only imposed nonpenal sanctions. At that time, I stated that the judge decided to impose most of the sanctions Hui Mālama sought and that we hoped this story would be widely publicized to serve notice on those grave robbers who hoped to profit at the expense of our kūpuna and their burial possessions. In compliance with a term of the plea agreement, Hasson published the following statement,

Public Apology

I wish to publicly apologize for desecrating and attempting to sell the ancestral remains of Native Hawaiians. As a teenager, I removed these remains from a burial site located on the island of Maui, and then took them to the mainland. In 2004, I attempted to unlawfully sell the remains on the internet. I was caught when a member of Hui Malama I Na Kupuna O Hawaii Nei saw my offer on the internet and notified authorities. The remains were later recovered by an undercover agent with the Bureau of Indian Affairs. As a result of my actions, I was charged with a violation of the federal Archaeological Resources Protection Act. In 2005, I plead guilty to that charge and am now a convicted felon. The remains have been returned to the island of Maui. The State of Hawai'i's Department of Land and Natural Resources, State Historic Preservation Division is currently working with the Maui/Lanai Islands Burial Council, the Daughters and Sons of Hawaiian Warriors-Mamakakaua, and the Hui Malama I Na Kapuna [sic] O Hawaii Nei, to reinter the remains at an appropriate site on that island. My actions were wrong and insensitive to the culture and feelings of Native Hawaiians. I am truly sorry for my offending actions. I hope that others will learn from my experience and will be deterred from unlawfully disturbing, removing, or trafficking in the ancestral remains and cultural artifacts of Native Hawaiians. I also hope that you will accept my apology. Sincerely, Jerry David Hasson. (This statement was approved by the United States Attorney's Office, Central District of California).[42]

On November 1, 2005, in my capacity as Hui Mālama Executive Director and accompanied by Hawai'i State Historic Preservation Division

(SHPD) Administrator Melanie Chinen, we returned from New Mexico after successfully retrieving the iwi poʻo that had been stolen from Kāʻanapali forty years ago. In Albuquerque, we accepted the remains from special agent Fryer, who had conducted the successful undercover investigation of the case. With the prosecution completed, the Maui/Lānaʻi Islands Burial Council and the SHPD respectfully conducted reburial.

CONCLUSION

The anguish and enlightenment of Honokahua resulted in the reawakening of the Hawaiian conscience to the kuleana to care for the ancestral dead and their possessions. This instinct had laid dormant for years and we were being given a second chance. The mana generated by these events galvanized many Hawaiians to return to who we are and to once again carry this critical responsibility. Uncertainty was replaced by reconnection to the naʻau and to the kūpuna through ʻike papalua (avenues of communication).

> Na wai hoʻi ka ʻole o ke akamai, he alanui imaʻa i ka hele ʻia e o kākou mau mākua
>
> Who would not be wise on the path so long walked upon by our ancestors

New cultural practices were established to address the extensive problem of disinterment and removal. Born were contemporary reburial ceremonies based on traditional beliefs and values. In time, they will become tradition. Honoring the sanctity of the afterlife directly reflects upon the high level of Hawaiian humanity. Indeed, it was Sir William E. Gladstone who wrote the following.

> Show me the manner in which a nation or a community cares for its dead and I will measure with mathematical exactness the tender mercies of its people, their respect for the laws of the land, and their loyalty to high ideals.[43]

What began as a chance occurrence at a planning commission meeting turned into an epic journey of revelation and change. Many came away with a better understanding of our interdependent relationship with our ancestors. It was a good start. The words iwi kūpuna and moepū were reintroduced into the Hawaiian vocabulary, and disinterment and reinterment were introduced on the English side. We came to understand that burial treatment was not limited to iwi in the ground facing disinterment, and that there was an extensive history of theft of ancestral bones, funerary possessions, and sacred objects that started during the early years of contact with foreigners. This led to a concerted research effort to identify national and international institutions and individuals who held iwi kūpuna and moepū that had been removed without consent, and to undertake the arduous task of repatriation. This also led to a keen sense of the need to enforce our values of aloha and mālama as with the Ebay case. All of this mana and inspiration came from the ancestors of Honokahua and their sacrifice to reconnect us to an important aspect of our humanity. And for this we are grateful. Alas, enough praise. There is still so much work to do. Dana Nāone Hall pointed out the following.

> Years later, implementation of the burial law has weakened and the law is being distorted by interpretations that divest island burial councils of

Author at the Natural History Museum, London 2013. Courtesy of ʻŌiwi TV.

Hui Mālama members at Natural History Museum, London 2013. Courtesy of ʻŌiwi TV.

Iwi Kūpuna packed in crate for the journey home, Natural History Museum, London 2013. Courtesy of ʻŌiwi TV.

Natural History Museum
building, London 2013.
Courtesy of 'Ōiwi TV.

Repatriation ceremony with Hui Mālama at the Smithsonian, 1990. Courtesy of Hui
Mālama.

their proper jurisdiction, thereby denying burial sites and the places where they are found the protection they deserve. While the current situation is regrettable, it can be corrected. The iwi of our ancestors are planted in the land. We exist and flourish because they exist. Honokahua still calls, and we must answer that call today.[44]

The next generation of Hawaiians will need to take their rightful place in this lineage of responsibility, as there remains a significant need to improve the administration of the island burial councils by the Hawaiʻi State Historic Preservation Division. As Papa Mau Pialug, master navigator from Satawal Micronesia once stated, "If I have courage, it is because I believe in the knowledge of my ancestors." Hawaiians at Honokahua in the late 1980s, in particular Dana Nāone Hall, had the courage to believe in the knowledge of their kūpuna and follow their naʻau. The rest, as they say, is history. Ola nā iwi! The bones live!

Hui pū nei kākou no nā kūpuna	People of Maui, unite for our kūpuna
E mālama pono i ke one hānau	Protect our history, the place of my birth
E hui hou kākou a hāliʻaliʻa	May all unite in recalling
I ke one kaulana o Honokahua	Famous sands of Honokahua[45]

Notes

1. This chapter is named for the mele *Honokahua Nani Ē*, by Rev. Charles Kauluwehi Maxwell, Sr with Hawaiian lyrics by Malia Craver and music by Kenneth Makuakāne (January 4, 1987) because it poetically reflects the struggle and beauty, the anguish and awareness, and the frustration and determination that is Honokahua. It serves as a kāhea (calling) to Hawaiians to protect the burial places of their ancestors. Notably, Rev. Maxwell was also a founding board member of Hui Mālama I Nā Kūpuna O Hawaiʻi Nei (Group Caring for the Ancestors of Hawaiʻi) and helped mentor the author.

2. Dana Nāone Hall, Paʻa ke Kahua, Published in *I Ulu I Ka ʻĀina: Land*, ed. Jonathan K Osorio (Honolulu: University of Hawaii Press, 2014) at 39; and republished in *Life of the Land Articulations of a Native Writer*, Dana Nāone Hall (Honolulu: ʻAi Pōhaku Press, 2017) at 69 (hereinafter Hall).

3. David E Stannard, *Before the Horror: The Population of Hawaii on the Eve of Western Contact* (Honolulu: University of Hawaii Press, 1989).

4. In January 1989, while a third-year law student at the University of Colorado I was flown to Maui by Dr Emmett Aluli to attend makahiki ceremonies on

Kahoʻolawe and to help with legislation to protect Hawaiian burial sites following the exhumations at Honokahua. My first visit to the sand dune burial site featured exposed excavations which were psychologically and emotionally ʻeha (painful) and a pivotal point in my life because unbeknownst to me at the time it re-awakened within me the instinctual need to care for and protect iwi kūpuna and moepū.

5. *Honokahua Nani Ē* (January 4, 1987).

6. Hall at 70.

7. Hall at 71.

8. Hall at 72.

9. Pule Ikaika was a prayer reported by David Malo and adapted by our kumu to support us to prepare for the care of iwi kūpuna and their moepū. It is used in situations where kaumaha (heaviness) needs to be lifted by providing the necessary strength to do so.

10. Hall at 72.

11. Hall at 72-73.

12. Hawaii Tempest Over Burial Ground, Kendall J. Willis, A Special to the New York Times (January 4, 1989 at A00011).

13. Ibid.

14. Ibid.

15. In archaeology and anthropology, a manuport is a natural object which has been moved from its original context by human agency but otherwise remains unmodified. The word derives from the Latin words manus meaning *hand* and portare which means *to carry*. (https://en.wikipedia.org/ wiki/Manuport).

16. Email communication from Dana Nāone Hall (July 30, 2018).

17. Archaeological Conference Talk, Historic Hawaii Foundation, Wailea, 1990 as published in *Life of the Land Articulations of a Native Writer*, Dana Nāone Hall (Honolulu: ʻAi Pōhaku Press, 2017) at 91.

18. Today, this author believes that the time has come to amend the historic preservation law once more and to designate the Office of Hawaiian Affairs as the proper agency to administer the Burial Sites Program including administration of the island burial councils.

19. Governor Waiheʻe, who had intervened to halt the disinterments at Honokahua and authorized the State to purchase the development rights for the 13.6 acre parcel and by all accounts a hero of Honokahua, allowed Act 306 to pass into law without his signature.

20. HRS §6E-43.5(a)(b)(Sess.1990). Significantly, subsection (b) provides, The membership of each council shall include at least one representative from each geographic region of the island as well as representatives of development and larger property owner interests. Regional representatives shall be selected from the Hawaiian community on the basis of their understanding of the culture,

history, burial beliefs, customs, and practices of native Hawaiians. The councils shall have a minimum of nine and a maximum of fifteen members, and *have a ratio of not more than three to one and no less then two to one in favor of regional representatives.*(emphasis added). This language guaranteed that regional representatives from the Hawaiian community would always be in the majority on the councils.

21. HRS §6E-43.5(f)(1).
22. HRS §6E-43(b).
23. HRS §6E-43.6.
24. HRS §6E-11(b)(c)(d).
25. HRS §6E-43.5(c). In September 1990, this author left the practice of law at the Native Hawaiian Legal Corporation to become the first head of the newly established Burial Sites Program at the State Historic Preservation Division. While in this capacity, I helped promulgate Hawai'i Administrative Rules Chapter 13-300 in 1996 to implement the amendments to HRS Chapter 6E.
26. §6E-43.5(e).
27. For a more comprehensive review of the state burial law and its impacts, see *Ho'i Hou I Ka Iwikuamo'o A Legal Primer for the Protection of Iwi Kūpuna in Hawai'i Nei.* Natasha Baldauf and Malia Akutagawa, Ka Huli Ao Center for Excellence in Native Hawaiian Law, William S. Richardson School of Law, University of Hawai'i at Mānoa (2013) at 23–47.
28. S. 978 was introduced by Senator Daniel K. Inouye, Chairman of the Senate Select Committee on Indian Affairs.
29. 20 USC § 80q-1, P.L. 101–185 (1989).
30. 20 USC § 80q-11(a)(2).
31. Natasha Baldauf and Malia Akutagawa, Ka Huli Ao Center for Excellence in Native Hawaiian Law, William S. Richardson School of Law, University of Hawai'i at Mānoa (2013) at 52–102.
32. The sources for this information are numerous and include Edward L. H. Kanahele and Pualani Kanaka'ole Kanahele (through direct training and education); our kūpuna; Edward L. H. Kanahele 1989, Hawaiian Burial Beliefs, a paper; Samuel M. Kamakau. 1870. Ka Mo'olelo Hawai'i. Ke Au Okoa VI (25):1; David Malo. 1987. Ka Mo'olelo Hawai'i (Hawaiian Antiquities) edited by Malcolm Naea Chun. Originally published 1858. Honolulu: The Folk Press, Kapi'olani Community College; and Mary Kawena Pukui. 1983. 'Ōlelo No'eau: Hawaiian Proverbs and Poetical Sayings. No. 71. Honolulu: Bishop Museum Press.
33. For a broader discussion of moepū in the specific context of the so-called Forbes Cave in Kawaihae, Hawai'i, see, *Honour thy ancestor's possessions*, Edward Halealoha Ayau, as published in Conservation, Identity and Ownership in Indigenous Archaeology, Edited by Bill Sillar and Cressida Fforde (Public Archaeology Volume 4 at 193–197).

34. See, United Nations Declaration of the Rights of Indigenous Peoples, Article 12 which provides, Indigenous Peoples have the right to . . . repatriation of their human remains. Article 11 section 2 provides the standard of taking without free, prior and informed consent or in violation of their laws, traditions and customs.

35. News Release, *Orange County Resident Charged with Selling 200-Year Old Skull of Native Hawaiian on Ebay*, (Debra W. Yang, United States Attorney, Central District of California) September 8, 2004 at page 1.

36. A copy of the text from the Ebay page was made and is on file with the author.

37. Ibid.

38. Ibid at 2.

39. Declaration of Rev. Charles Kauluwehi Maxwell, Sr, Pukalani, Maui, Hawaiʻi February 12, 2004.

40. Affidavit of John Fryar, Special Agent, Bureau of Indian Affairs September 2004 at 3–4.

41. Plea Agreement for Defendant Jerry David Hasson, *United States of America v. Jerry David Hasson*, at 1–2.

42. A copy of the published notice is on file with the author.

43. William Ewart Gladstone was a British liberal politician (29 December 1809–19 May 1898). In a sixty-year career he served as Prime Minister four times and penned many famous quotes.

44. Hall at 76.

45. *Honokahua Nani Ē.*

About the Contributors

E. Halealoha Ayau, Esq. is the former Executive Director of Hui Mālama I Nā Kūpuna O Hawai'i Nei and served as the first director of the State Burial Sites Program in the Department of Land and Natural Resources, where he drafted and helped to promulgate Hawai'i Administrative Rules Chapter 13-300 for Human Remains and Burial Sites, and led successful efforts to enact laws to establish the island burial councils. Raised on Hawaiian homestead on Molokai, he attended Kamehameha Schools, the University of Redlands (BA, 1987) and the University of Colorado (JD, 1989). He currently works for the Department of Hawaiian Home Lands.

Lance D. Collins is an attorney in private practice on the island of Maui. He also holds a Ph.D. in Political Science from the University of Hawai'i at Mānoa. He was the compiler and indexer of the 17 volume Proceedings of the Charter Commissions of the County of Maui (1966–2012). His research interests focus on the Philippines, American colonialism in the Pacific, and legal history.

Tomone "Karen" Hanada has resided on Maui since 1988 and has seen a lot of change occur on the island during the past 30 years. She is interested in principled negotiation and conflict resolution processes that improve relationships and outcomes for all stakeholders. Tomone earned her BA and MBA degrees from the University of Hawai'i at Mānoa and works as a State of Hawai'i public servant.

Ikaika Hussey has a Master's degree in Political Science from the University of Hawai'i at Mānoa and is presently earning his graduate diploma in Economics from the London School of Economics. He is a co-editor of *A Nation Rising: Hawaiian Movements for Life, Land and Sovereignty* published by Duke University Press, 2014 and publishes *Summit Magazine*.

SYDNEY IAUKEA is from the island of Maui. She is the author of *The Queen and I: A Story of Dispossessions and Reconnections in Hawai'i* and *Keka'a: The Making and Saving of North Beach West Maui*. Sydney has a PhD in Political Science is she is currently lecturing at Leeward Community College and the University of Hawai'i at Mānoa.

BIANCA KAI ISAKI, Ph.D., Esq. has published on the intersections between settler colonialism, natural resource exploitation, conservation efforts, and houselessness in Hawai'i. Through her legal research corporation, she works on environmental and Hawaiian land rights issues. She also serves on the board of KAHEA: The Hawaiian-Environmental Alliance and teaches women's studies at the University of Hawai'i.

DIANE K. LETOTO was a long time lecturer at the University of Hawai'i and founder of the Phoenix Dance Chamber Chinese Dance School of Honolulu. She earned her Ph.D. from the University of Hawai'i and holds a Master's Degree in both American Studies and Dance. Her dissertation was entitled "Silenced Practices: A Politics of Dancescapes." She has given a number of presentations at academic conferences such as: "Reading the Dance as Text: Heartbeat Hawai'i;" (2010), "Multiculturalism and performing Cultural Identity: Entanglement with the Indigenous" (2010), "Looking Forward/ Looking Backward: the "authentic" hula and Chinese dance in Hawai'i", "Sandalwood Sojourns: Constructing Cultural Identity Through Dance" (2005) and "Mapping Economic Structure, Tourism and Culture via Tihati Productions, Ltd." (2003).

Originally from Canada, BRIAN RICHARDSON is a graduate of the Political Science and Philosophy Departments at the University of Hawai'i at Mānoa. His fields of research include 18th century European exploration in the Pacific, European political philosophy, and information systems in higher education. He has written a book on the voyages of Captain Cook, *Longitude and Empire: How Captain Cook's Voyages Changed the World*.

INDEX

Matin, Sharyn, 91
Matties, Zoe, 69
Maui Economic Development Association, 33–34
Maui Land and Pineapple Company, 110–111,
    119–121, **122–124**, 131, 136, 167, 189–191,
    193–204. *See also* Kapalua Land Company;
    land development
Maui Minyo Dance Group, **22**
Maui Minyo Kai, **19–20**, 25n49
Maui Plan (1958), 33–34
Maui Taiko, 15
mauka; defined, 23n8; gentlemen's estates in, 51
Maxwell, Charles Kauluwehi, Sr., 261, 268n1
mediation, 200–204, 235n30
memorandum of agreement (MOA), 197,
    209–214, 245
Midkiff, Frank, 159
migration, bon dancing, 10–12
Mitchell, W.J.T., 72
MOA. *See* memorandum of agreement
Mortgage Act (1874), 156
mortgages, 180–183
Moten, Fred, 63, 78
Murayama, Milton, 155

Nandy, Ashis, 65
Napili Bay land use, 166
National Defense Housing Act (1940), 163
National Museum of the American Indian Act,
    258
National Pollutant Discharge Elimination System
    permit, 105–108
Native American Graves Protection and Repatria-
    tion Act (1990), 252–253, 258
Native Hawaiians; and agricultural dispossession,
    66–70; burial culture of, 252–259, 264–
    268, **265–267**; burial site cultural signifi-
    cance, 190–191, **192**; demographics during
    plantation period, 238; fighting fake agri-
    cultural development, 57–58; fishing rights
    in Honolua Bay, 128–129; and Honokahua
    burial site, 188–189, 240–241; housing for,
    160–164; Hui Alanui O Mākena, 190–191,
    192; and 1958 plan, 34; and 1968 plan,
    45; regional burial councils of, 249–251,
    269n19, 269n20; and settler futurity,
    76–78; and settler sexual culture, 75–76;
    theft and sale of bones from, 259–264

1953 Territory of Hawaii Public Works (report),
    32

Oʻahu tourism development, 37–38
O-bon; dates of, 1, 23n7; defined, 22n1; Dharma
    message in, 26n72; at Shingon Mission,
    1–3; Toro Nagashi and, 7. *See also* bon
    dance
Odaishiko, 6
Office of Hawaiian Affairs, 195–197, 245, 259,
    269n18
Okuma, Cheryl, 93, 96, 100, 104
Organic Act (1900), 160

Paltin, Tamara, 125, 128
Paul H. Rosendahl, Inc., 244–245
Picture Bride (film), 7–8
picture brides, 6
pidgin language, 5–6
Piʻilani trail, 240–241
Pioneer Mill Company, 30–31, 144n33
plantation period; housing availability during,
    156–160; housing segregation during,
    155–156; Maui Land and Pineapple Com-
    pany predecessors, 119–121; Native Hawai-
    ian demographics, 238; Native Hawaiian
    housing in, 160–164; regional planning
    emergence from, 33–48; sugar plantations,
    4–7, 30–32. *See also* gentlemen's estates
plantation workers; historic background of, 4–6;
    Japanese and Chinese demographics, 6
Pokemon Ondo, 16
pollution, Honolua Bay, 138, 142
Puʻu Kului, 136–138, **138–141**

quiet title cases, 119–120, 144n27

regional planning (West Maui); 1958 plan, 33–34;
    1966 plan, 35–36; 1968 plan, 39–47; tour-
    ism and, 36–39
repatriation (Native Hawaiian), 252–268, **265–267**
Rifkin, Mark, 75–76
Roehrig, Nathan, 61
Rose, Louis, 149
Rosendahl, Paul, 197

S. 978 (federal legislation), 251–252
Sakura Ondo, 13